THEY MUST GO

THEY MUST GO

BY RABBI MEIR KAHANE

Grosset & Dunlap
A Filmways Company
Publishers   New York

Copyright © 1981 by Meir Kahane

Contents

Preface

Ramle city. A motley mix of some 40,000 Middle Eastern residents, all but 5,000 of whom are Jews from Arab lands. It is not a pretty city, and the main street is a garish potpourri of fast-food shops with loud music blaring from loudspeakers. Off toward the edge of the city, where it meets its sister town of Lydda, stands the Ramle prison. It is the maximum security prison in Israel, and its grim gray walls with barbed-wire coils at the top are capped by sentry boxes set every fifty yards. In this prison, with its more than 700 murderers, rapists, robbers, and Arab terrorists, I wrote this book.

It was on the evening of May 13, 1980 that they came for me: four plainclothesmen with a piece of paper, an unprecedented Administrative Detention Order mandating my imprisonment for six months without trial or charges. And so Ramle Prison, the prison I had driven past so many times, the one vaguely suggesting a Hollywood movie prison out of the thirties and forties, became my home.

My particular "home" was a tiny cell, some six by nine feet in size, in Wing Nine. My immediate neighbor to my left was a veteran Yemeni Jewish criminal named Adani, who was serving the last part of a fifteen-year sentence for armed robbery. On my right was a Bedouin Arab, imprisoned for the rape and murder of a Jewish girl in the Negev area of the country. The possibility of his having been apprehended would have been slim if not for the fact that he added greed to his original sin. Having buried the body in a well, he applied for the reward by contacting the police to say that he had "discovered" it. Incredibly, his life

1

sentence had been reduced, and he was preparing to go home after having served a mere eighteen years.

There were some seventy prisoners in the wing, fifty-eight of them Jewish. Of those, the overwhelming majority were Jews from Eastern or Arab lands, Sephardim. Perhaps more than any thing else, this is the accusing finger that points at the Israeli Establishment, for what the Muslims could not do during more than 1,000 years of domination of the Jews in their lands, the Jewish Establishment of Israel accomplished in less than 25: the spiritual destruction of hundreds of thousands of Sephardic Jews who came to the Holy Land with their religion, Zionism, and basic Jewish values. Less than three decades later, they were deep into crime, violence, drugs, prostitution, and pell-mell emigration from the country. In my wing alone there were four Yemeni Jewish murderers. I doubt that there had been a total of four Jewish murders in the 2,000 years of exile in Yemen. . . .

The greatest enemy of modern man is boredom. In prison, it can drive men mad. And so I instituted a stiff, disciplined daily regimen of study and writing that would keep me busy from early morning (4:30 A.M.) until lights-out (midnight). This schedule included regular study not only of Bible, Talmud, and Law but also of other writings of various kinds. I have, for example, been creating a biblical commentary for the past ten years, and, ironically, never did I have so much time—and peace and quiet—to work on it as in prisons. It is a labor of love, and I spent many hours on it, daily, while in Ramle.

That in itself gives more than a passing clue to the attitude of the prison guards and officials toward me. It goes without saying that the Jewish prisoners treated me with respect and admiration. Not only did I represent, in the eyes of these Jews from Arab lands, opposition to the Establishment they so hated, but they had a genuine gut feeling that the Arab poses a terrible threat to Jews within Israel. No Ashkenazic Jew from Europe can really appreciate this, for he has not lived with an Arab majority. He has not tasted the bitter dregs of Jewish minority status under Muslim rule.

Even more significant, the average *guard* was overwhelmingly sympathetic to me. It was clear to all that I was not an ordinary criminal and that I had been imprisoned for my ideas—ideas that so many of those guards, as well as Jews throughout the country, privately espoused. Therefore, I was allowed as many books as I wished, things that I could not have done without while writing my commentaries.

And that is the key to the writing of this book. It would have been impossible to write the manuscript, with all its facts, dates, incidents, quotes, and names, had the prison officials not allowed me to bring in all my private papers and newspaper clippings. It is thanks to them that this book was written, a fact they knew about and to which they conveniently closed their official eyes.

Cell 23 in Wing Nine of Ramle Prison was, thus, the scene of many hours each day, many days a week, more than two continuous months of writing. I had no typewriter, and so each page had to be handwritten. Moreover, never knowing when the authorities might change their attitude and confiscate the work, I smuggled out each chapter as it was finished and thus never had the opportunity to look back at what I had written. Nevertheless, I gained strength through the encouragement of the other prisoners. On the door of my cell I had placed a large Hebrew sign that read: "How good it is to be a good Jew." Every time a prisoner passed, he would shout the message out to me and smile. Indeed. "How good it is to be a *good* Jew."

Meir Kahane

Introduction: Arabs and Jews— Only Separation

"The State of Israel . . . will ensure *complete equality of social and political rights to all its inhabitants* irrespective of religion, race or sex. . . .

"We appeal . . . to the Arab inhabitants of the State of Israel to preserve peace and participate in the upbuilding of the state *on the basis of full and equal citizenship.*" (Declaration of Independence, State of Israel, 5 Iyar 5708 [May 14, 1948])

"Today, I am in the minority. *The state is democratic.* Who says that in the year 2000 we Arabs will still be the minority: Today I accept the fact that this is a Jewish state with an Arab minority. *But when we are the majority, I will not accept the fact of a Jewish state with an Arab majority.*" (Na'ama Saud, teacher from the Israeli Arab village of Araba, May 28, 1976)

"Let the leaders of the Zionist movement . . . find their nation some uninhabited country. (Arab writer Issat Darwazeh in the Haifa Arabic newspaper *Al-Karmel,* 1921)

"And the L-rd said unto Abram . . . Lift up now thine eyes and look from the place where thou art, northward and southward and eastward and westward. For all the land which thou seest, to thee will I give it and to thy seed forever." (Genesis 13:14–15)

"We do not recognize the right which you call "historic" of the Jewish people to this land—this is our fundamental principle. . . . In this land only the Palestinian Arab people have historic right." (Mahmud Muhareb, chairman of the Arab Student Committee, Hebrew University in Jerusalem 1978)

"And if you will not drive out the inhabitants of the land from before you, then those that you let remain of them shall be thorns in your eyes and thistles in your sides and shall torment you in the land wherein you dwell." (Numbers 33:55)

5

Some years ago I was arrested by the Israeli police and charged with "incitement to revolution." The grounds? I had reached the conclusion that it was impossible to find a solution for the Arab-Jewish confrontation in the Land of Israel (both the State of Israel and the lands liberated in 1967); that the Jewish state was inevitably headed toward a situation like that in Northern Ireland; that the only possible way to avoid or to mitigate it was the emigration of Arabs. Consequently, I had sent letters to several thousand Arabs offering them an opportunity (funds and visas) to emigrate voluntarily. The fact that many Arabs replied positively and that a major Arab village in the Galilee, Gush Halev, offered to move all its inhabitants to Canada in return for a village there did not prevent the worried Israeli government from arresting me.

Four long years and one important war later, a scandal broke in Israel. It was revealed that Yisrael Koenig, a high official in the Ministry of the Interior who is in charge of the northern region of Israel, had drafted a secret memorandum in which he warned of the increasing danger of Arab growth (which would make Arabs in the Galilee a majority by 1978) as well as of increasing Arab national militancy. His solution included several measures that he hoped would lead to Arab emigration.

The pity is that vital years have passed since my original proposal, wasted years that saw the Yom Kippur War produce a major psychological change in Arab thinking. In the aftermath of that war and its political consequences, vast numbers of Arabs, who in 1972 were depressed and convinced that Israeli sovereignty could not be destroyed, are today just as convinced that time is on their side, that it will not be long before the Zionist state collapses. Then they—the Arabs—will hold sway over all that will be "Palestine." The necessary corollary is, of course, that hundreds of thousands who were potential voluntary émigrés nine years ago are now determined to stay and await the day of Arab victory. *But they must go.*

It is in order to convince the Jew of this that I have written this book.

The problem with so many people who proclaim the virtues of coexistence between the Jewish majority of the Jewish state and its Arab minority is that they hold the Arab, as well as his intelligence, and his national pride, in contempt.

There is an ultimately insoluble contradiction between a Jewish state of Israel that is the fulfillment of the 2,000-year-old Jewish-Zionist dream and a state in which Arabs and Jews possess equal rights—including the right of the Arabs democratically and peacefully to put an end to the Jewish state. Those who refuse to give the Arab that right but tell him he is equal think he is a fool. He is not.

The reality of the situation is, therefore, clear. The Jews and Arabs of the Land of Israel ultimately cannot coexist in a Jewish-Zionist state. A time bomb in the Holy Land ticks away relentlessly.

A Jewish state means Jewish orientation and ties. It means Jewish culture and a Jewish spirit in the Jewish body politic. But above all, a Jewish state means Jewish sovereignty and control of its destiny. That can be accomplished only by a permanent Jewish majority and a small, insignificant, and placid Arab minority. But the Arabs believe that the Jews are thieves who stole their land. The Arabs feel no ties to or emotions for a state that breathes "Jewishness." And they grow, quantitatively and qualitatively. They will surely make violent demands for more power, including "autonomy" in various parts of the land. Eventually, the very majorityship of Jews will be threatened by the Arab birthrate. The result will be bloody conflict.

If we hope to avoid this terrible result, there is only one path for us to take: the immediate transfer of Arabs from Eretz Yisrael, the Land of Israel, to their own lands. For Arabs and Jews of Eretz Yisrael there is only one answer: separation, Jews in their land, Arabs in theirs. Separation. Only separation.

I know only too well what the reaction of the vast majority of people will be to my words. Indeed, it is being completed even as I sit in Ramle Prison. My real crime is my ideas concerning the awful danger that exists to the State of Israel because of the very presence of its large and growing number of Arab citizens. My real threat to the very confused and frightened government is that my ideas are quietly shared by hundreds of thousands of Jews in Israel who, in anger and frustration, now move to support me and give me the power to make my ideas a force in the land.

My ideas are not only suppressed by the government but

twisted, defamed, and subjected to emotional and hysterical diatribes by people who are too frightened to consider them intelligently or to debate them intellectually. It is far easier to shout "Fascist!" or "Racist!" than to think. It is ironic, though I suppose inevitable, that those whose "Jewishness" is irrelevant to them and who lack scholarly knowledge of "Jewish values" should shout at me, "Un-Jewish!"

If one wants to know what *Jewish* values are, the place to search for them is not in Karl Marx or Edmund Burke or Thomas Jefferson. *Jewish* values are found in *Jewish* sources, most of which are vast wildernesses unexplored by the hysterical critics who have suddenly discovered "Jewish" morality.

I love the Jewish people and the Jewish state, and it is because of this that I preach the words I do. I am committed to Judaism and real Jewish values, and every word in this book—disagreeable as it may be to most—is *Judaism*.

It is a human failing to be unwilling to think about, let alone acknowledge, uncomfortable realities. Painful decisions are delayed and painful problems avoided. That which is unbearably difficult to contemplate is put out of mind, denied, and we think that to look away will make the problem go away. It is a human delusion that we Jews—so eager to find peace and tranquility after centuries of suffering—have developed to the finest of arts.

But the Arab problem will not go away, because the very existence of the Jewish state creates it.

And precisely because the reality is so painful and so clearly threatening to the very foundation of the Zionist-Jewish state, Jews make haste to delude themselves with patent nonsense and cosmetic camouflage. The Arab-Jewish problem in the State of Israel threatens the very philosophy and most deeply held beliefs of Jews. It lays bare the glaring foolishness and misconceptions upon which political Zionism is based. *Worst of all,* for the secular, Western-oriented Jew, it clearly and inexorably forces him to choose between Western liberal democracy and a *Jewish* state.

I do not wish to lose the Jewish state through either war or peace. I do not wish to see Arabs or Jews killed in the Land of Israel, but many, many will die, I fear. And if it happens, it will not be because we will have done what I call for, but rather because we will *not* have done it. And so, let there not be hysteria or vituperation or blind refusal to listen, but rather patience to read these pages and honesty in evaluating them. Finally, let each and every Jew ask himself or herself this question: Am I prepared—given peace and an Arab population growth that will make the Arab minority a majority—to allow that majority—democratically—to change the name of the state to "Palestine"; to abolish the Law of Return, which gives every *Jew* automatic entry and citizenship (and which was the key in Zionist leaders' minds to keeping a Jewish majority); and to end—peacefully and democratically—the Jewish state?

The problem is that no Jewish leader in Israel or the Exile has the courage to ask the question or to teach it to the Jewish people. We avoid it even as we raise our money for the "Jewish" state, make our vacation plans for three weeks in the "Jewish" state, and sing the *"Hatikva"* at bar mitzvahs. The problem is that no one thinks about the question. *The problem is that so few think.* Dear Jew, do think. It may save the lives of millions. Even your own.

Dedicated with awe and love to my late father,
Rabbi Yechezkel Shraga, son of Rabbi Nachman HaKohen,
of blessed memory, who returned his soul to His Maker
  8 Adar 5738

CHAPTER 1

Togetherness in Israel

"It is a sin for a man to delude his neighbor; it is a crime to delude himself."
The Rabbi of Kotsk

In 1973, to commemorate the twenty-fifth anniversary of the State of Israel, the government issued a pamphlet titled *Arabs in Israel.* The introduction to the pamphlet reads as follows:

The Israeli Arabs

Since the creation of the State of Israel its minority population has grown from 150,000 to 400,000. During the 25 years of statehood remarkable accomplishments in many fields have been achieved by this minority.

The principle of equal rights for the Arabs of Israel, pro-claimed in the Declaration of Independence, has indeed been re-alized. The minorities enjoy religious freedom, full voting rights and the right of founding political organizations, both nationally and locally.

The educational system has developed considerably. The number of students and pupils has grown from 10,000 on the eve of the foundation of the State, to 125,000 today. 10,000 students attend secondary schools, and more than 1,000 study at institutes of higher learning.

The Arab village has changed its face since the creation of the State. In the framework of two five-year plans basic services were established: roads, water, electricity, schools, health centers and other institutions of public interest. The completion of these services marked the beginning of the industrialization of the Arab village. Factories and workshops, which also employ Arab women, were opened; modern, mechanized agricultural systems were introduced, which enable a more efficient and intensive exploitation and thus a higher yield. 45,000 (11,250 acres) dunams are now being irrigated by artificial means, as

11

compared to 8,000 (2,000 acres) dunams before the introduction of the new systems.

The socio-economic development of this section of the
population greatly advances its integration into all fields of
life of the State of Israel.

An idyllic description of Jewish-Arab togetherness in Israel.
It is three years later, March 30, 1976. Nine A.M. The
Galilee, northern Israel, home of 300,000 Israeli Arabs. The village of Sakhnin, a model of social and economic progress since
1948. It has good roads, electricity, water, schools, appliances,
television sets in every home. It has "greatly advanced its integration into all fields of life of the State of Israel."

More than 1,000 equal citizens of Israel—Arabs—are in the
street facing a small number of police and soldiers. It is "Land
Day," and the crowd grows larger by the minute. *"Falastin,
Falastin!"* ("Palestine, Palestine!"), the mob roars. Other
chants and shouts are heard: "The Galilee is Arab!" "We will
free the Galilee with blood and spirit!" Rocks are suddenly
thrown in the direction of the soldiers and police. The small
group of security men stare in disbelief and growing ner-
vousness. A fiery Molotov cocktail smashes against a wall a few
yards away. More and heavier stones, flaming torches, lighted
cans of gasoline, and by now the soldiers are surrounded by a
growing circle of hate-filled faces. "Our villages do not belong to
Israel," shouts a young Arab. "We belong to the State of
Palestine!"

The Israeli papers report what happened:

"The dams burst. *'We are all Fatah,'* men and women
shouted in chorus, even as they threw stones and other objects at
the police. The police fired warning shots into the air which only
increased the agitation. The rioters began to move toward the
police and soldiers, threatening to trample them. Not even the
pointing of the rifles at them stopped the mob. 'They're
overrunning us,' the police shouted into their radios" (*Maariv*,
March 31, 1976).

"The mob wandered through the main street, raining
stones, torches, and firebombs on the military and police vehicles. Some of the excited youth wanted to set up roadblocks.
Others moved closer to the security forces—with clear intent to
burn the vehicles. In face of the dangerous situation the soldiers

fired into the air, but it seemed as if no one in that crowd of burning passions paid any attention.

"The mob of demonstrators noticed the Israeli force beginning to withdraw. The large crowd began close pursuit of the Israeli forces. Running hysterically, they threw stones and roared: 'Charge them—*Eleyhom!'* Thousands moved toward the soldiers, and at that critical moment, the commander of the force gave orders to fire . . ." (*Yediot Aharonot*, March 31, 1976).

An Israeli journalist who attempted to get past a roadblock in the village was attacked by Arabs shouting: "Get out of here! This is Palestine!" He later reported: "It was terrible there. I do not remember such chaos since 1948. Every Jew was a candidate for murder. I saw them with the lust for murder burning in their eyes. Slogans such as *'Eleyhom'* and *'Itbach Al-Yahud'* ["slaughter the Jews"] are moderate in view of what I heard. From all sides came cries for the liquidation of Israel, to destroy all the Jews, for a *jihad* ["holy war"]. It is difficult to believe that such a scene could take place in the State of Israel, 1976."

The journalist added: "Such hatred of the state and the Jews is difficult to comprehend. What happened there was not mere rioting or chaos. *It was a revolt. The Arab revolt of 1976 . . . It was a revolt in the full sense of the word.*" (*Maariv*, March 31, 1976).

The revolt spread to villages and towns, throughout the Galilee and the "Triangle," the two main centers of Arab population in Israel. In Sakhnin, Araba, Deir Hanna, Beth Netora, Tira, Tayba, Kalansuwa, Kfar Kana, Nazareth, and dozens of other places, violence and rioting occurred. For the first time in Israel's existence, its Arab citizens had called a political general strike. When quiet was finally restored, six Arabs were dead and more than thirty-five Israeli soldiers and police injured. In the words of *Maariv* correspondent Yosef Valter, returning from the Arab village of Umm al-Fahm: "It was not pleasant for a Jew to wander there. . . ."

The pamphlet issued by the Israeli government in 1973 attempted to give the impression that the Arabs of Israel feel themselves part of the state and that the years since 1948, years that have brought them social and economic benefits, have also made them loyal to Israel, have made them see their destiny and that of the Jewish state as mutual.

It is a devoutly desired illusion that every Israeli leader and official spreads. It is a persistent delusion that grows louder and more frantic, the more obvious its patent falsehood. Together with oranges and diamonds, it ranks as one of Israel's major exports, this myth of the loyal, loving Arab of Israel. It is shouted forth—to the accompaniment of loud and happy American Jewish applause—at breakfasts, brunches, lunches, teas, dinners, suppers, and other stomach frameworks for fund-raising. The soothing legend of "our good Arabs who are equal and free and who appreciate and love Israel" is fed, along with liver, chicken, and stuffed derma, to the Hadassah's portly and younger suburban matrons, Long Island Jewish Centers, UJA and Israel Bond donors, and the ever-aging and ever-fewer "Zionists" who compose the ranks of the Zionist Organization of America. It is adopted by Reform and Conservative rabbis whose ignorance of the Israeli scene complements similar lack of knowledge of Judaism. It ranks among the hoariest of the legends and myths of world Jewry. *To look at reality and to think otherwise is simply too unbearably painful.*

And yet, even the *Jerusalem Post* was forced to see what was before its very eyes. In an article titled "Shattered Illusions" (April 2, 1976), the *Post*'s Yosef Goell wrote: "Part of the Israeli Arab community hates Israel with barely veiled, intense hatred." True. And one could also add: The greatest part of the Israeli Arab community is hostile to and alienated from the state and would dearly love to exchange it for a "Palestine."

What happened? What occurred to "change" the Israeli Arabs? What has caused an eruption of sheer hatred against the State of Israel by its own Arab citizens? After the Land Day revolt, almost everyone asked those questions. Gallons of ink and reams of paper and countless words, words, and more words were produced in an effort to understand. One could almost hear the shattering of the urgently held illusions of nearly three decades. Pity. For had people only *wished* to see, the signs were there, and had been there for many years, clear and obvious. *The Arab revolt of 1976 and all the future greater and bloodier ones are immutable and inevitable.*

There is hatred and hostility on the part of the vast majority of Israeli Arabs for the state in which they live. And it is neither a recent development nor a limited phenomenon of Land Day,

1976. It takes many forms—words, attitudes, violence. All form a picture of a large and growing minority that poses a threat to the very existence of the Jewish state—a time bomb ticking away. Consider:

• The majority of the chairmen of Arab local councils in Israel—the recognized spokesmen of Israel's Arabs and the touted "moderate" body—on January 20, 1979, approved a resolution "welcoming the struggle of their brethren in the West Bank and Gaza Strip against the occupation, annexation, and colonialist settlements and expressed their solidarity with the struggle of the Palestinian people under the leadership of the PLO to establish its independent state."

• In the Jerusalem neighborhood of East Talpiot on November 26, 1979, kindergarten teacher Yael Aviv was playing in a small park with the children in her care. Suddenly six Arabs appeared, who began throwing stones at the terrified children and shouting: "Jews, go home!" A group of young girls across the street burst into hysterics and it took an hour to calm them. Said the teacher: "I will not take the children there anymore. That is enough for me." Said Sara Graetz, a resident and a survivor of the Holocaust: "I would have never believed that this could occur in an independent Jewish state." As this was happening, the family of Binyamin Sachar was recovering from an attack on their automobile as they drove through the Arab village of Bet Tzafafa, at Jerusalem's southern edge. Stones smashed the windows of the car and a shaken Sachar said: "I never thought that here in Jerusalem I would have to worry about attacks."

• The head of Israel's northern command, General Avigdor Ben-Gal, told an interviewer in the army magazine *Bamachane* (September 1979) that numerous Jewish settlements in the Galilee had turned to him with requests for protection from local Arabs. The Jews claimed that "they feel themselves isolated and asked for Israeli forces to protect them." Numerous incidents of Arab attacks on persons and property were listed. *Ben-Gal approved the paving of parallel roads to Jewish settlements so that the Jewish settlers would not have to pass through Arab villages at night.*

• "Lately I hear, even from the most moderate of Arabs, open statements such as: 'Get ready. Soon you will have to move out of your house. We will get your house and the houses of all

the Jews of the Galilee. It is ours! All the Galilee is ours.'" The
speaker is Micha Goldman, thirty, the young chairman of the
Jewish settlements in the Galilee, in an interview for *Maariv*
(August 17, 1979). He continued: "I meet a great deal with
Arab leaders in the Galilee. What I hear from them now is in-
comparably more serious and extreme than anything said just
two and three years ago. Not only extremists but those who were
considered 'moderates' speak today about the nonrecognition of
Israel, and about their demand for 'Arab autonomy' in the
Galilee, à la Sadat. The extremists go further and talk of a
Palestinian state of which the Galilee would be part. Even one
who just passes through the Galilee sees frightening man-
ifestations. For example, you drive behind an Arab automobile
and they put their hands out and signal 'We will slaughter you'
or 'Get out.'

"The real change came after Camp David . . . which was
seen by the Arabs as a far-reaching sign of Israeli weakness. . . .
Today, there is no doubt among the Galilee Arabs that a Palestinian state will arise, and they tie their own future to it."

• On July 2, 1979, no fewer than eighty buses and trucks
brought 6,000 Israeli Arabs to the Knesset in Jerusalem. There,
in front of the symbol of the Jewish state, the mob of Israeli
citizens roared: "The Galilee is Arab—Jews out!" "With blood
and soul we will free you, mountains of Galilee!"

• Jewish women on buses heavily traveled by Arabs are subject to pawing and sexual advances. The same is true in the
marketplace of the Old City of Jerusalem. Following the Land
Day riots of March 1976, *Maariv* reporter Dalia Mazori described her visit to the Jewish town of Upper Nazareth. She
quotes a young Jewish girl: "'Young Arabs suddenly began to
rub against me, a thing that never happened in Nazareth,' said
a pretty young Israeli. According to her, when she protested,
they responded with loud curses. . . . Many of the Jewish wom-
en said they would not go down to Nazareth to purchase anymore, preferring the higher prices to the degrading treatment
they have recently been accorded. 'The main thing is to avoid
the looks of hate,' one said.

"In discussing whether the question was 'land expropriation,' all agreed that the expressions of hatred were a sign of
something much deeper and serious, much more worrisome."

• In the very heart of Israel, the area of Emek Yizrael, south of the Galilee, sits the "Triangle." There, along the main road from Hadera to Afula and the surrounding area, are concentrated no fewer than 50,000 Israeli Arabs. In the Wadi Ara area, surrounded by this huge Arab population, sits one lone Jewish settlement, Mei Ami. Its nearest neighbor is the largest Arab village of them all, Umm al-Fahm, one of the most openly anti-Israel centers. (On January 20, 1980, a bloody attack was made on a visiting Jewish soccer team. Cries of "Down with Zionism" and "Khomeini" were shouted, and police had to use tear gas and fire into the air to rescue the Jews, as hundreds of Israeli Arabs tried to break down the door to the locker room. Said a police official: "This is more than the usual soccer riot. . . .")

In the summer of 1979, arsonists set three consecutive fires that burned down 110 dunams (2,705 acres) of Jewish National Fund trees owned by Mei Ami. Police traced the tracks of the arsonists to one of the nearby Arab villages. The bitter Jewish settlers accuse the Arabs of Umm al-Fahm of the destruction of a tractor and claim that millions of dollars in damage have resulted from Arab activities.

The secretary of the settlement, Oren Mitki, complains of shots fired at night at Mei Ami. Police know that hundreds of stolen automatic weapons have reached Arab villages in Israel. All the Jewish settlements in the area are plagued by Arabs who steal anything that is not nailed down. One member of Kibbutz Ayal told *Maariv* reporter Amos Levav, "We will open a new industry—attack dogs. We cannot take it anymore."

• The village of Ma'ilya was always known as a "moderate" Arab village, being the subject of various Israeli myths. It was Christian, educated, and had prospered greatly under Jewish rule. Ergo—it was surely moderate. On the morning of July 9, 1979, hundreds of the "moderate" inhabitants charged a Jewish National Fund tractor, bloodying two of its drivers (who had to be hospitalized), while one woman shouted: "Sons of dogs! Your day will yet come!" The tractor, under court order, was attempting to pave a road as part of the project to establish a Jewish outpost on state land near Ma'ilya. The Arabs swore not to allow the outpost to go up and at a meeting held earlier, for the first time, called the police and the state "the enemy."

• On January 5, 1980, sixty Bedouins attacked Israeli

troops who were attempting to remove Bedouin trespassers from state land. Said one soldier: "'I saw one Bedouin attack a soldier with an ax . . . others took out knives. One Bedouin scout serving with the army loaded his rifle and threatened to shoot us'" (*Yediot Aharonot*, January 6, 1980).

•   The following was the headline of a page-one story in *Maariv* (June 19, 1979): "The Plague of Weapons Thefts from the Army and Their Sale to Arabs Worsens." The story said: "Recently an Israeli Arab, resident of Araba, was arrested. In his possession were seven 'Uzis' [automatic weapons] and two pistols." The question is: What purpose do the Arabs have in mind for these weapons and how many of them are in their possession today?

•   With little fanfare, Israeli Arabs have taken part in terrorist actions against Israel and have joined the ranks of the PLO as active agents. The following is a small but representative list that tells part of the story of Israeli Arab ties to terrorism:

1. In July 1980 five Arabs from the Israeli village of Makr were arrested. They were charged with operating a Fatah (PLO) cell in their village and of having planted bombs in crowded Jewish areas on five separate occasions. The police chief of the Galilee, David Franco, told a press conference on July 20 that the fact that the five were Israeli citizens was cause for serious concern. The residents of the village of Makr, some four miles from Acre, live in brand-new apartments built for them by the government.

2. Headline in *Maariv*, October 29, 1979: "PLO Allocates Funds to Organize Young Arabs in Israel."

3. "A young 24-year old Arab has been arrested for cooperating with Iraqi intelligence. . . . The arrest surprised many in the old city of Acre, where he lives" (*Yediot Aharonot*, February 21, 1979).

4. Headline: "Mantsour Kardush, Leader of El Ard (Anti-Israeli Group), Suspected of Connection with Terrorist Group" (*Yediot Aharonot*, February 18, 1979).

5. Headline: "Israeli Arab Arrested in Connection with Attacks as PLO Agent" (*Yediot Aharonot*, March 5, 1978).

6. "A secret wireless radio station capable of long-range transmissions has been discovered in the home of an Arab of the village of Kalansuwa in the Triangle, Salah Gzawi, 25. . . . In

Gzawi's home were also found two pistols and an 'Uzi' . . ." (*Maariv*, February 22, 1976).

7. "Haifa: The police yesterday arrested five young Arabs in connection with the delayed-action hand grenades discovered in local cinemas. . . . Three of the men are residents of the West Bank and the other two from the Acre area" (*Jerusalem Post*, July 18, 1973).

8. Headline: "Ten Arabs Arrested in Galilee; Suspected of Organizing Sabotage" (*Maariv*, June 21, 1973).

9. "Six young Arabs, residents of Lydda, suspected of membership in the Popular Front for the Liberation of Palestine, planned to carry out in the next few days a series of attacks throughout the country. This was revealed by investigation of the suspects arrested October 30" (*Maariv*, November 19, 1972).

10. "Terror Cell Bared in Galilee Village

"The security authorities have uncovered a six-man sabotage cell in Nahf, Western Galilee. . . . The investigation established that the group was preparing to ambush army cars on Galilee roads and to carry out sabotage acts in the industrial plants of Carmiel . . ." (*Jerusalem Post*, October 10, 1971).

11. And from Eliyahu Amikam, columnist for *Yediot Aharonot* (July 12, 1974): "Ziad J'bali, commander of the band of murderers that carried out the operation in Ma'alot [where more than twenty schoolchildren were killed], was born in Tayba, Israel. Ahmed Abad Alal, the 'hero' of the Nahariya murders, spent the 23 years of his life in Acre, where he was born. . . . 200 Israeli Arabs recently left the country. The papers wrote that 'apparently' they will join the terrorist groups. Two Hebrew U. graduates, attorney Sabry Jareis and Jazi Daniel, are now numbered among the ideologicians of the 'Palestine Liberation Movement.'"

A random sample; there are many more. Of course, the professional apologists will point out how many Arabs did *not* participate in anti-state activities. The Nazis might have also "proved" the "loyalty" of Belgians, Frenchmen, and Dutchmen by the low number of active underground people in these countries. Of course, few people have the courage to participate in dangerous activities. The question is: How many Arabs *privately* sympathize with and support the minority? The answer is: Many, very many.

For years the signs have been there, the signs of an Israeli

Arab population rapidly growing—in quantity, in quality, and in boldness. The alienation from and hatred of the Jewish state is so palpable as to be clear to all but those who will not see. And every so often voices are raised—voices of warning.

Eli Reches is director of Tel Aviv University's Shiloah Institute for Middle Eastern Studies. On February 23, 1978, he spoke at a "day of study" of the Arab-Israeli question and issued the following warning: "Too little attention is being paid to the growing radicalization of Israeli Arabs, with the elite strata becoming increasingly ultranationalist." He added that even ostensible "moderates," like the Committee of Local Council Chairmen, have swung close to "extremist" lines. Reches is what is termed an "Arabist"—to wit, an official expert on Arab affairs. Israel, of course, abounds in such experts, all of whom raise fascinating questions, issue solemn warnings, *and have not the slightest solution to offer.*

Worse, the majority of Israelis, including those in government, simply refuse to think seriously about the awesome problem. Like all governments that face excruciating questions, the Israeli government simply pushes the Arab problem out of sight and mind, hoping that it will somehow go away or that if the dam finally does burst, it will be after the present government has gone.

But the hate and the danger grow and will not go away.

A Hasidic Jew, Meir Yuskuvitz, went to the Western Wall to pray on the night of September 15, 1979. It was the eve of the Jewish Days of Penitence. His automobile broke down in the heart of the all-Arab area, and his son-in-law went for help. When he returned, he found Yuskuvitz shot dead. Terrorists took credit for the murder.

Not a week goes by that Jews are not beaten and women molested in the Old City of Jerusalem. Arab boldness grows in relation to the police response that they simply "cannot handle the situation." The pity, of course, is that more than half of the Old City police are Arab. . . .

But Arab boldness and brazenness are hardly limited to Jerusalem. When the settlers of Mei Ami complained to the local police about attacks by Arabs of the Triangle, Aaron Dolov of *Maariv* wrote (August 17, 1979): "To the great surprise of the settlers, they heard from the officers that 'we cannot cope with the problems. . . . The Arabs of the Triangle hide their weapons in places that are difficult to uncover.'" Those weapons will someday be used against Jews.

Hate? On May Day, 1976, at a huge Arab rally in Nazareth to celebrate brotherhood and solidarity, Samiah Al Kassen, an Israeli Arab poet, delighted the crowd by reading one of his works. The full text appeared on May 7 in the Arab-language newspaper *Al-Atihad*. It reads, in part:

> *O Joshua, son of Nun*
> *Listen!*
> *You stopped the sun on the walls of Jericho*
> *Did you satisfy the desire of your murderous God?*
>
> *You will murder in the day and inherit the murdered*
> *All the oceans in the world cannot clean your hands . . .*
>
> *Who has the deed to the land, to history?*
> *Who has the deed?*
> *You have the weapons, the army, the clubs*
> *You have the flag, the newspapers, the embassies*
> *True, true: but in my pocket, I will preserve the deed:*
>
> *As long as there are stones on this land*
> *as long as there are empty bottles*
> *we will throw them on your tanks.*

Poetry is the marching tune of national rebellion. Israeli Arabs honor their poets especially when they write of the destruction of the Zionist state. In February 1977 the PLO's press attaché at the UN, Rashed Hussein, died in a New York City hotel fire. He had been born in the Israeli Arab village of Musmus, and on February 8 the Israeli government allowed his body to be buried there. Thousands of Arab citizens of Israel streamed through a muddy, winding path to hear Arab Knesset member Tewfik Zayad declare: "We shall never give in until the goal that Rashed Hussein and his friends [*sic*] advocated, fought for, and struggled for is fulfilled."

Hussein's "friends" are the PLO. We all know what they have "advocated, fought for, and struggled for." When an Israeli Arab, a Knesset member (and mayor of Nazareth), pledges to see that these are "fulfilled," what does that say about the Arabs of Israel?

Too many simply do not understand that the Arab-Israeli

question is not limited to one side of the "Green Line," the pre–
June 1967 border. Of course, Judea and Samaria (the West
Bank) are claimed by the "Palestinians." But it is not only their
cities and towns—Hebron, Bethlehem, Shechem, Jericho—that
are in question. Nasir Ad-Din an-Nashashibi's book, *Return
Ticket,* expresses the total aim: "Do you not remember Jaffa and
its delightful shore, Haifa and its lofty mountain, Beth Shean
and the fields of crops and fruit, Nazareth and the Christian
bells, Acre and the fortress, the streets of Jerusalem, my dear
Jerusalem, Tiberias and its peaceful shore with the golden
waves . . .?"

Every one of the places mentioned is inside the State of Israel. *They* are what Nashashibi wishes to see under Arab rule.
They are what every Israeli Arab—*in different ways*—would like to
see under Arab rule. Do not underestimate the intensity of the
desire or the hatred. The passionate hatred that an Israeli saw
in the eyes of Israeli Arabs in Sakhnin on Land Day is reflected
in Nashashibi's book: "I shall see the hatred in the eyes of my
son and your sons. I shall see how they take revenge. . . . I want
them to wash away the disaster of 1948 with the blood of those
who prevent them from entering their land. Their homeland is
dear to them, but revenge is dearer. We will enter their lairs in
Tel Aviv. We will smash Tel Aviv with axes, guns, hands, fingernails and teeth. . . . We shall sing the hymns of the triumphed,
avenging return. . . ."

At a conference of the Galilee council held in Acre on December 26, 1979, delegates were told that at least four Arab villages in the Galilee now get substantial PLO funding in addition
to Israeli government support. One name given was that of the
village of Dir-Al-Asad, which was sent $20,000 from a Scandina-
vian address. The money was used to defeat the council head
and give victory to an "extremist."

On August 10, 1979, thirty-six Knesset members took part
in a tour of the Golan Heights. Their guide was the head of the
northern military command, General Ben-Gal. At Kibbutz Ein
Zivan he told the thirty-six legislators: "First priority, today,
must be given to the Jewish settlement in the Galilee, because of
the growing strength of the Arab residents there. Their hatred of
Israel is growing. *They are becoming a cancer in our body . . . . They
are waiting for the moment to hit us.*"

No matter that Defense Minister Ezer Weizman, engrossed

in his love affair with the Arab on the Nile, criticized Ben-Gal, declaring that "the Arabs of the Galilee are citizens of Israel and no one has the right to question their loyalty." No matter that on top of that nonsequitur he ordered the general to "correct" the statement. No matter. Ben-Gal knew exactly what he was saying, because he understood the full dimension of the situation. When a general in the Israeli Defense Forces calls Israeli Arabs "a cancer," one is again confronted by the thousands of stunned Jews who ask: "What happened? The Arabs of Israel were always quiet, loyal citizens enjoying progress and equal rights. What caused them to change? *What happened?*"

The answer is: *Nothing.* Nothing basic, nothing fundamental, has changed at all. The hatred was always there. The alienation was never absent. Objective, historical reasons prevented the reality from emerging during the first twenty years of the State of Israel, but those have passed. *And the real reason* Jews are so shocked today is that Israel never wanted to see the reality. The government and the people built elaborate illusions and self-delusions. We believed what we *wanted* to believe. But truth will out, and with a vengeance. The illusions are shattered, the delusions battered, and there is left only one last chance to face bitter reality.

CHAPTER 2

Coexisting with the "Palestinians"

There never was anything but bitter Arab hostility, resentment, and hatred of the Jewish stranger who wanted "his"—the Arab's—land. Nothing the Zionist did contributed to this hate, except one thing: he existed.

In 1921, in 1929, and in 1936–38 there were no Jewish "occupation" troops patrolling "the West Bank." There was no such thing as "occupied Arab lands of 1967." All the reasons for bloodshed, violence, war, and hatred that today's Arabs and confused Jews point to as being at "the heart" of the Arab-Jewish problem did not exist then. Hebron and Shechem and Tulkarm and Ramallah and Bethlehem and Jericho were not under Jewish military occupation, and there was no need for world organizations and national governments to issue resolutions calling for withdrawal from and return of the "occupied territories to their rightful owners." *In fact, there was not even a Jewish state in existence,* and by all logic the "Palestinians" should have coexisted peacefully and in friendship with the Jews.

They did not. And it is important to recall the reality of the Palestinians' "coexisting" with their Jewish cousins *before* the "Zionist aggression of 1967," for it appears to me more than necessary to teach the past to a foolish generation that insists on repeating it. It is essential to rid ourselves of the illusion that if only Israel would be more "flexible" and "reasonable" and "compromising," peace can be attained. It is vital that we cease babbling about the "obstacles to peace" that are the Jewish settlements of Kiryat Arba or Kedumim or Tekoa. It is of para-

25

mount importance to realize that the Arab-Israeli conflict did not begin in 1967 or in the Sinai campaign of 1956 or when the state came into being in 1948. The conflict began many decades earlier, *and it is not an Arab-Israeli one.* It is an *Arab-Jewish* conflict. Jewish blood was shed in the land of Israel by Arabs long before 1967, or 1947 or 1927. And the issue then was indeed one of "settlements," but the conflict raged about the new Zionist settlements of Tel Aviv and Petah Tikva and Rehovot and Hadera and those in West Jerusalem. The "hate affair" between Arabs and Jews began before there was such a thing as Jewish settlements in Judea-Samaria and will continue even if by some madness the Jews of Israel should agree to give up the liberated lands.

All kinds of foolish people today speak of the need to recognize the "Palestinians." I agree. Come let us recognize them for what they are. Meet them and know them, just as the Jews of the Land of Israel knew them, thirty-five and forty-five and fifty-five years ago, long before the "Israeli aggression of 1967."

The Pogroms of 1921

On 23 Nisan in the year 5681 (May 1, 1921), Arab mobs began to gather in Jaffa. That city, unlike Jerusalem and others, was considered a model of Jewish-Arab coexistence. (It is remarkable how many Jewish illusions have risen and fallen during the past eighty years of struggle with the Arabs.) The Jews and Arabs of Jaffa had extensive commercial relations, and the Sephardic Jews, who had lived there for generations, were almost indistinguishable from the Arabs in their general daily deportment. Nevertheless, the mobs began to gather. The heavy sticks and metal bars they carried left no doubt as to their intentions. For days the Arabic paper *Falastin* had been agitating against Zionism with particular venom. Now, in the mixed Jewish-Arab neighborhoods of Nve Shalom and Menashiya, the mob began to attack Jews in the streets with stones and heavy metal rods, but their major targets were the Jewish stores and homes—with their property and women.

The Jews attempted to defend themselves, and since the mob did not have guns, the police could have easily driven them off. But the police were Arabs—*first and foremost Arabs.* Most protected the Arab rioters, while others removed their badges and joined them, shooting at the Jews. In the first attack, thirteen Jews were killed, and the looting and pillaging spread to other areas of the city. Gradually, the mob focused on the center of Zionism in the city, Bet Ha'Olim (Immigrant House).

In their simple naiveté and belief that Arabs and Jews could coexist in peace, the Zionists had acquired a large, two-story building in the all-Arab Ajemi section of Jaffa. At the time there were about one hundred new immigrants in the building that was the symbol of Jewish immigration. So great was the confidence of the Jews in their ability to live in peace with their neighbors that they had no weapons of any kind. After all, this was not Czarist Russia. This was the Land of Israel, the land to which the Jews had come to escape pogroms.

Around 1:00 P.M. the mob began to gather. Pioneers standing in the street were stoned and beaten. One Arab attempted to throw a primitive homemade bomb, but it blew up in his hands and he was killed. This only infuriated the mob, which began to approach the building. The Jews ripped iron posts from the gate and blocked the entrance to the front and side yards. They beat off the Arabs' first attack, and several Arabs were carried away by their comrades. It appeared that despite the huge mob, the Jews would be able to defend themselves.

At 2:00 P.M., the watchmen on the roof reported that several policemen were approaching. A general sigh of relief arose, until the police—Arabs—arrived. They suddenly began shooting at the Jews, and two grenades were thrown into the courtyard, killing and wounding several of them. According to *The Book of the Haganah*, the attack was led by the head of the prison, Hana Burdkush, a member of a "respectable" Christian Arab family. The police burst into the yard, shouting to the mob: "What are you waiting for? Kill them all!"

Their spirits broken, most of the Jews attempted to flee. The males who were not fortunate enough to escape were brutally murdered. Several women pleaded with a policeman to save them. He took them into an alley, stripped them of their valuables, and tried to rape one of them. When silence descended on the building, thirteen were dead and twenty-six-wounded, and for the rest of the day, Arabs looted Jewish stores and houses. Except for the language, the clothing, and the palm trees, it might very well have been Kishinev.

In the early-morning hours of May 2, six Jewish bodies were found in the Abu Kabir section between Jaffa and Tel Aviv. They included the famous writer Y. C. Brenner, and the news horrified the Jewish community. The six had been beaten to death, their bodies stripped and mutilated.

The reaction of the Jews was instructive. Zionist leaders Nahum Sokolow, Pinchas Ruttenburg, Meir Dizengoff, and others met and decided to seek conciliation. The Jaffa Arab "notables" agreed to accept the offer of peace from the victims, but at the meeting held in the Jaffa municipality, and to the loud applause of the Arabs, Omar Al-Bittar, the mayor, declared that he could not speak for the "Arab nation" and each person would have to use his individual initiative to calm passions. Nothing daunted, the Tel Aviv Jewish town council announced that "the sheikhs have promised us that they will persuade the inhabitants to be calm." Those who had lived in European exile in which their safety and security depended on the whim of the Gentile felt right at home in the Exile of Ishmael.

The results of the Jaffa massacre were 43 Jews murdered, 134 wounded, and untold property damage. It was now 27 Nisan, May 5. Petah Tikva's turn.

The news of the Jaffa pogrom encouraged the Arabs of the villages near the large settlement of Petah Tikva to cast covetous eyes on that thriving Jewish colony. By May 3 all the Arab workers had left, a sure sign of impending attack. The two small colonies of Ein Hai and Kfar Saba had heard of frenzied meetings in the nearby Arab villages of Kalkilya, Tira, and Miski, where plans had been formulated for destruction of the Jewish settlements. The Jews hastily evacuated the two colonies, and after being attacked and having part of their cattle plundered by the Bedouins of Abu-Kishk, they arrived, fearfully, in Petah Tikva.

On the evening of 26 Nisan (May 4), watchmen saw the flames of Kfar Saba and Ein Hai, which had been torched by their Arab neighbors. Scouts reported that hundreds of Arabs from all the villages in the area were now on their way to attack Petah Tikva. A group of riders under the leadership of veteran Avraham Shapira rode out to meet the attackers and found them leading away 700 of the settlement's cattle. Under a hail of bullets the Jews had to flee. The Jews in the settlement awaited the

Arab attack with sinking hearts. They had only forty guns, and the Arabs had large quantities of weapons and ammunition.

The attack began. Desperately the defenders held on within a fixed radius. The Arabs attacked, looted, and burned houses outside the defense perimeter. Four Jews were dead, and the colony was on the verge of collapse and slaughter when British troops arrived to save them.

Only courage and miracles saved the large settlement of Hadera and Rehovot from slaughter. The book *History of the Haganah* (Israel Defense Ministry) describes the attack on Rehovot by Arabs of Ramle: "Thousands of men, women and children came like locusts upon this settlement, with the usual battle-cries: *'Eleyhom'* ["Charge them"] and *'Itbach Al-Yahud'* ["Slaughter the Jews"]. They approached the settlement looting everything in their path and burning huts in the orchards."

Coexistence in the month of May 1921, forty-six years before the Israeli "occupation" that is the real obstacle to peace in the Middle East. . . .

November 2, 1921, marked the fourth anniversary of the Balfour Declaration that had promised the Jews an enigmatic "national home." The Arab press, leaders in the drive for an end to Zionism, called for a day of mourning, a work stoppage, and demonstrations to protest the declaration, which they coined "the death sentence passed on the Palestinian people."

In Jerusalem, 5,000 Jews were packed into the Jewish quarter, most of them totally unfamiliar with self-defense. The day of the general strike saw thousands of frenzied Arabs attacking those Jews, mostly Sephardic, who lived in the Muslim quarter. The Sephardim remained there in the mistaken belief that the Arabs were opposed only to the recent European, or Ashkenazic, immigrants. They were wrong. To the credit of the Arabs, they did not discriminate against Jews on the basis of communal background. They killed all—equally.

Among the Jews killed in the first assault was a sexton in the Yeshiva Torat Chaim and nineteen-year-old Yitzhak Mesner, who was stabbed to death while escorting a group of women and children to safety.

At 11:30 hundreds of screaming Arabs, headed by Sheikh Vad Al-Halili, attempted to smash into the Jewish quarter. They were driven back after a sharp struggle in which the sheikh

was killed. Five dead Jews and forty injured ones were brought
to the hospital, the victims of Arab demands for an end, not to
Jewish "occupation," but the Jewish existence in the land per
se.

The Pogroms of 1929

On Yom Kippur in the year 5689 (1928), the Arabs of Eretz
Yisrael discovered the Wailing (Western) Wall. More precisely,
they discovered that the one remnant of the Holy Temple of the
Jews was really a Muslim holy place. For hundreds of years,
Jews had come freely to the symbol of their exile and suffering,
to shed bitter tears and to plead with the Almighty to redeem
them from the four corners of the earth. But on Yom Kippur,
5689, a British policeman barged into the midst of the wor-
shipers to forcibly remove the partition that separated the men
and women, and thus he put into motion the forces of pogrom.

For years the British had claimed that they would keep the
"status quo" for religious sites in Jerusalem. The Wall had no
standing as a Muslim religious site at all, but the Muslims did
not wish to see it granted Jewish religious status. The British
viewed the partition between the sexes at the Yom Kippur services as an attempt to convert the Wall into a "synagogue."

The incident gave birth to Jewish indignation and to an
Arab myth. The Mufti of Jerusalem at the time, the supreme
Muslim leader, carved a historic niche for himself as a treach-
erous and murderous individual (he later spent the years of
World War II in Berlin calling upon Muslims to join in a holy
war on behalf of Adolf Hitler). His name was Haj Amin Al-
Husseini (a member of a Jerusalem family of "notables"), and
in 1929, in his position as Muslim theologian, he decreed that
the Wall was in reality a Muslim holy place. The reason? When
Muhammad allegedly went up to heaven from Jerusalem on his
wondrous horse, Al-Burak, he chose a spot near the Wall to
tether it. This wondrous tale of a wondrous horse had, of course,
not prevented Muslims, for centuries, from wondrously riding
through the area on horses and donkeys who left their un-
mistakably wondrous presence behind, on the ground. But no
matter. A political-religious legend was born, and for almost a
year the Arabs incited, lied, and heated the atmosphere that led
to the deadly pogroms of 1929.

In many towns, "committees for the defense of the Burak," were formed. On November 1, 1928, the Mufti convened a "religious" conference, which demanded that Jews be prevented from bringing religious items to the Wall. The Mufti added his pious wish that the British enforce this "in order that the Muslims themselves not be forced to enact measures to defend at all costs this Muslim holy place."

For months the Muslims resorted to various measures to harass the Jews at the Wall. New houses began to be built that interfered with and disturbed the prayers. A new "religious ritual" known as *Ziker* was introduced. It involved loud chanting, singing, and dancing with a background of drums and cymbals —to be performed exactly at Jewish prayer time. On 25 Tammuz (August 2, 1929) Jews were attacked and badly beaten at the Wall.

Jewish horror was hardly helped through the stupid comment by the socialist writer Moshe Beilinson, who called for Jewish "moderation" and calm, saying: "The value of the Wall is great but let us not forget: Of central importance to the revival of the nation are other values of immigration, work, land." Thus spoke a socialist Jewish spokesman and a not-too-clever one at that. The Mufti could only smile.

On Friday, 10 Av (August 16), thousands of Muslims, leaving prayers at the Al-Aksa mosque, marched past the wall, shouting: "*Allah Akhbar!*" ("G-d is great!"); "*Din Muhamad Kari Basif!*" ("The Law of Muhammad with the Sword"); and "Down with Zionism!" A bitter diatribe against the Jews was delivered, and Jewish prayer books were burned. The following day, the Sabbath, Arabs stabbed to death a young Jew, Avraham Mizrachi. Tension grew steadily.

The Mufti and other Arab leaders hastened to take advantage of the situation. Letters, reputedly signed by the Mufti (after the pogroms he claimed they had been forged), called on all Muslims to come to Jerusalem the following Friday to prevent the Jews from "seizing Al-Aksa." Thousands of Arabs began streaming into Jerusalem with long sticks that had sharp nails protruding from them. Above all, the cry rang out throughout every Arab village and town: "*Il Dula M'ana!*"—"The government is with us!"

And, indeed, it was. The British imperial, colonial government was represented by a new high commissioner named Chancellor, who—because of his recent arrival—allowed most of the decisions to be made by his chief aide, Harry Luke, a bitter anti-Zionist. Luke was the son of an assimilated Jewish family from Hungary named Lukach. The father had emigrated to England and in one fell swoop acquired a new country, religion, and name. The Hungarian Jew Lukach was now the British Protestant Luke. And having converted, Luke now acquired a gentile characteristic: he became anti-Semitic. No better friend in court did the Arabs have than Luke, whose policy of noninterference with the Mufti and Arab mobs led to the murder of scores of Jews.

Jerusalem

The pogrom in Jerusalem began on the Muslim holy day, Friday 17 Av (August 23). Thousands of Arabs streamed into the city carrying iron bars, sticks, and knives. In the courtyard inciters from Jerusalem and the two nearby villages of Lifta and Kalandia heated the atmosphere, and at 12:30 P.M. the mob burst forth, heading in two directions: toward the Jaffa and Damascus gates. At Jaffa gate, Jews who inadvertently passed by were attacked. Despite the presence of police, the two Ruttenberg brothers were beaten and stabbed to death. On Jaffa Road, Jewish stores were smashed by some sixty Arabs from Lifta and a Jewish newsman murdered. In the small Georgian quarter, home of poor Jewish families, four Jews including a woman and child were slaughtered and the humble homes looted. An attempt to smash into the Mea Sh'arim quarter was thwarted.

The worst attacks were on the outlying Jewish neighborhoods in the new, Jewish, part of the city. The neighborhood of Romema, through the Diskin Orphan Home, Givat Shaul, Montefiore, Bet Hakerem, Yefe Nof, and Bayit V'Gan, were targets of a large attack led by Arabs from the villages of Dir Yassin, Ein Kerem, and Lifta. Dir Yassin Arabs were the leaders and organizers of the attack, and the village became world-famous in 1948 when it received its just reward for the many Jews slaughtered by its citizens.

It was only an incredibly valiant defense by the Jews that prevented a massacre of major proportions. With few men and weapons, the defenders succeeded in throwing back thousands of Arabs. The situation in the outlying neighborhood of Bayit V'Gan was especially critical. All the women and children were evacuated and the defenders concentrated in homes near the woods. All the other homes were looted by Arabs from Ein Kerem, Malha, and Walaja. Three Jews—a student, David Vilnai; a guard, Mordechai Ben-Menashe; and a policeman, Gudel Yudelevitz—were killed.

The fighting continued for days. Saturday night, August 24, the first seventeen Jewish victims were taken from Hadassah Hospital to be buried. The British had provided only three policemen, who were weary and nervous. The burial ceremony was hurried as it came under attack from Arabs in Talpiot.

The next day, Arabs from Bet Tzefafa, Tzur Bahir, and other villages overran, looted, and burned to the ground the settlement of Ramat Rahel on the southern border of Jerusalem. Never had there been such a lengthy and widespread pogrom in Jerusalem. Coexistence was not working, despite the absence of a "legitimate grievance" known as "the occupied territories."

Just outside Jerusalem, astride the road to Tel Aviv, sat the small Jewish settlement of Motza. For decades its residents thought that they had enjoyed the best of relationships with the neighboring Arab village of Kolonia. On Saturday night, August 24, as the Jews of Jerusalem were being buried, thirty villagers from Kolonia, longtime acquaintances, "visited" the home of the Maklaf family (the house was the last one in the settlement). They slaughtered everyone, including eighty-five-year-old Rabbi Zalman Shach, a guest for the Sabbath. The women were first raped and then murdered, and the house was burned down.

The small settlement of Hartuv was wiped off the face of the earth. Friday night, August 23, as the men huddled together in one house (the women and children had been evacuated), a mob of Arabs from the nearby villages of Dir Aban, Eshtaol, and Tzar'a attacked. They looted everything in the spacious farm of Y. L. Goldberg. Cows, horses, wheat, furniture—everything was plundered by the crazed mob. At midnight, two British armored cars arrived to rescue the men from a massacre. The settlement was left for the mob, who literally razed it to the ground.

Destruction was also the fate of Migdal Eder, between Bethlehem and Hebron, as well as Kfar Uria near Hartuv. The settlement of Be'er Tuvya was composed of some 120 people. Most of them, terrified and near panic, were together in the large stable of Devora Korovkov. Arabs from the surrounding areas began their attacks. From the nearby settlement of Gedera came a reply to the Jews' desperate request for help: "We cannot help you. We have not enough men or ammunition for ourselves."

Perhaps more than anything else, the following statement by one of the Be'er Tuvya settlers tells the chilling reality of the "Palestinians" and what any ultimate victory of theirs would mean for the Jews. In the words of D. Yizraeli: "Several of the women asked the doctor to give them poison so that they not fall into the hands of the Arabs. He refused. But he said that all would defend the women and children until their last drop of blood. And if there was no other way, they would use their guns to save the honor of their women."

In the attack that followed, with the Arabs burning houses on all sides, it was, ironically, the doctor, Haim Yizraeli, who was the first to be killed, shot down in his white coat as he stood near the gate. Just hours earlier he had gone out to bind up the leg of an Arab who had attacked the settlement and been wounded. Herzl Rosen was slaughtered next, and Moshe Cohen, who had refused to leave his farm, pointing to the decades of good relations with his Arab neighbors, was stabbed numerous times and with his last remaining strength managed to reach shelter.

The arrival of British troops saved the rest of the settlers. But they were evacuated to "safety," and when they returned, the entire settlement had been burned to the ground. Literally, nothing was left.

Safad

High in the beautiful Galilean hills stood the city of the Kabbalists, Safad. Its 3,000 Jews had lived for generations with the Arabs. All spoke Arabic, and the Sephardic Jews were hardly distinguishable in their dress. As the days of pogroms receded, it appeared that Safad would be spared the horror.

But on 23 Av (August 29), at 5:30 P.M., a mob of Arabs burst into the Jewish quarter, led by Fuad Hajazi, a young clerk of the local government health office. The first place attacked was the Klinger gasoline storage house. As flames and smoke leaped into the air, the mob entered homes of the Jews they had known for years, stabbing, beating, raping, looting. The wind carried the flames onward; ironically, this saved many Jewish lives as the mob rushed to save their own homes. But eighteen Jews were dead and more than eighty others injured. Almost all the victims were elderly or women, many of whom had pleaded with their slaughterers to remember the favors they had done them over the years.

The same evening, the small Jewish settlement in Ein Zeitim was decimated. Three Jews were murdered, the rest fled to Safad, and their homes went up in flames. In the northeast part of the Galilee, the settlement of Yesud Ha'Ma'ale was destroyed by its "good neighbors" from the Arab village of Tlail.

In essence there was not a Jewish community of any consequence that was not attacked. Scores of Jews were slaughtered, and damage was estimated in the millions of English pounds. It was a shattering blow to the young Jewish community which had caught a glimpse of the reality of the "Palestinian." But nowhere was the full extent of "Palestinian" horror manifested more clearly than in the ancient city of Hebron.

Hebron

Long before the name "Palestinian" was invented, the Hebrew people, children of Abraham, Isaac, and Jacob, lived in Hebron. There Abraham purchased the Cave of Machpela, and there the Patriarchs and Matriarchs of the nation were buried. Hebron was the city given unto Caleb, the son of Jephune, for his faith in G-d. There David ruled as king for seven years before going to Jerusalem, and there Jews and Judaism were entwined for 3,500 years.

There, in 1929, occurred a massacre that took more Jewish lives than Kishinev.

It was a hot Friday morning, 17 Av in the year 5689 (August 23, 1929). Again, there was no Jewish state, no Jewish "occupation forces," no "occupied territories," to give the Arabs reasons to cry out against Zionism. In Hebron there lived some 500 Jews, mostly Sephardic, many with roots going back hundreds of years. Just a few weeks earlier the city had been visited by the Rebbe of Lubavitch. Rabbi Moshe Mordechai Epstein,

head of Yeshivat Slobodka, had moved the entire yeshiva to
Hebron just four years earlier, breathing new spiritual life into
the ancient town. Such synagogues as Avraham Avinu, the synagogue named after Reb Yehuda Bibas, and two Chabad synagogues were there. The Chabad yeshiva, Toras Emes, was
founded there. Jews lived and worked and prayed and studied—
and then—their Arab neighbors rose up to massacre, in cold
blood, sixty-seven of them. Scores of others were wounded; all
the rest fled, leaving their property behind. That was twenty
years before Dir Yassin.

Throughout the land there was growing tension as roving
bands of Arab gangsters, egged on by the Supreme Muslim
Council and the Mufti, agitated against the Jews. Incidents had
been reported in various places, but the Jews of Hebron were not
particularly worried. In the first place, they had lived in peace
for many, many years with their Arab neighbors. How was it
conceivable that those neighbors, for whom they had done so
much, would betray them? After all, despite various incidents
that had taken place in the past decade in Jerusalem, Jaffa,
Safad, and other places, there had never been trouble in
Hebron. Second, Arab dignitaries had repeatedly assured them
that no harm would come to them.

Just how sure the Jews of Hebron were that no problem
existed can be seen from the fact that Rabbi Avraham Yaakov
Orlinski, the Rabbi of Zichron Ya'akov, had arrived the previous day with his wife to celebrate the Sabbath with their
daughter and son-in-law, Eliezer Don Slonim. A delegation of
rabbis who met with the Arab governor of the town were informed that there was nothing to fear. He had more than enough
men to protect the Jews in case of any problem, and everyone
knew that the Hebron Arabs were opposed to the Supreme
Muslim Council. The Jews were reassured, but at a meeting of
several leaders (Messrs. Slonim, Melamed, Shneirson, Chaim
Bajayo, and others) it was planned to bring some of the Jews
who lived outside the main concentration of Jews into the center
of town. At about 1:00 P.M., after the Arabs had left the mosques,
a group of notables visited Slonim to boast of the quiet atmosphere in town and again guaranteed that nothing would
happen.

At approximately 2:30, an Arab courier arrived by motorcycle and told the Arabs gathered around him that he had just returned from Jerusalem, where "thousands of Muslims had been killed and their blood spilled like water." The Arabs, seeking blood, marched through the streets. Suddenly, elderly Rabbi Slonim appeared, headed for the office of the police chief. The Arabs leaped upon him and beat the aged rabbi unmercifully. Frightened Jews watched from their homes, as did the chief of police. A woman, Mrs. Sokolov, watching from her window, could not stand to see the sight and ran to the police chief. He curtly told her that it was none of her business, and "furthermore, it is the fault of the Jews anyhow." He advised her to lock herself in her home.

The mob then turned to the Grodzinski home. Y. L. Grodzinski, in testimony given later, stated: "When the riots began, there were people in our house. I saw a young Arab open the gate to our courtyard and tens of Arabs burst in. They surrounded the house and began banging on the doors. We hastily secured the doors as stones came smashing through the windows. When a shot was fired into the room, we went up to the second floor and called for help. Eliezer Don Slonim saw us and managed to get a group of police, who finally scattered the mob. We then all decided to move to the home of Slonim, since he had excellent relations with the Arabs and we felt sure that his house would not be attacked." How false this was will be seen later.

The bloodthirsty Arabs wanted Jews. They made their way to the Slobodka yeshiva. Because it was the eve of the Sabbath, most of the students were not there. Only the Yemeni *shammas* (sexton) and the perpetually diligent *masmid,* eternal learner of Torah, Shmuel Rosenholtz, were to be found. (Rosenholtz rarely left the study hall.) The mob, breathing fire, came charging into the courtyard. The *shammas* leaped into the well in time and covered himself; it saved his life. Not so Rosenholtz. Completely immersed in his Talmud, he did not even hear the mob come in. It was only when stones came flying into the hall, one smashing him in the head so that blood spurted over his Talmud, that he attempted to flee. But the mob was upon him and punctured his body with knife wounds, like a sieve.

The Hebron massacre has its first victim. The tragedy unfolds.

Evening now comes to Hebron, and the Sabbath will soon begin. The Arab mob that murdered Shmuel Rosenholtz in cold

blood has scattered and the streets are now silent. The police
arrive at the yeshiva and place the body of the martyr on a table,
appointing a policeman to watch over it. In every Jewish home
the Sabbath is greeted with trepidation and concern over what
will happen tomorrow. The son of Rabbi Moshe Mordechai
Epstein, head of the Slobodka-Hebron yeshiva, is called to the
office of the Hebron governor, an Arab, who is flanked by two
officers, one British and the other Arab. The governor tells the
son of the Rosh Yeshiva ("dean of the seminary") that he must
go to every Jewish house and warn the occupants not to walk
out. He says: "Let the Jews stay in their houses and I will be
responsible for their lives. . . ." The Jewish promise is given, and
the night passes in troubled silence, broken only by the sounds
of police on horses passing through the streets and various Jewish families leaving their homes for the "safety" of the house of
the respected Eliezer Don Slonim.

Early Sabbath morning, at five, the Jews are already up,
their leaders meeting to discuss what to do. It is suggested that
a telegram be hurriedly sent to Jerusalem to inform the
Haganah about the situation. But the telegraph office will not
open until eight and by that time it will already be impossible.
There is also a suggestion to send someone by automobile to
Jerusalem, but for some reason it is decided that an Arab should
be the driver, and no Arab can be found to do it. In the end the
Jews meet with an Arab police officer named Ibrahim Jarjura,
who tells them in the name of the police chief that "the Jews
must remain in their houses and only then can we take responsibility for their safety." The police chief, an Englishman named
Capireta, tells the Jewish leaders the same thing.

By 6:00 A.M., with Arabs now streaming into Hebron from
the surrounding countryside, E. D. Slonim and a yeshiva student, along with a police detail, go from Jewish house to house,
warning the Jews not to go out and not even to look out the
windows. Arab neighbors, meanwhile, gleefully tell their Jewish
"friends" that "today will be the slaughter." The streets are
now packed with Arabs, armed with guns, swords, and knives.
Cars speed through the streets with Arabs sitting on the roofs,
shouting slogans calling for death to the Jews. The atmosphere
is electric, and through it all walk the Arab and British police
officers, calmly. . . .

The Jewish leaders of the community meet at the home of

the Sephardic Rabbi Franco. Fear of a truly serious threat to their lives is now evident. It is clear that they must do something more than just sit and wait. It is decided to send a delegation to the British police chief to protest the forced penning of Jews in their homes instead of firmly letting the Arabs know that breaking the law will not be tolerated. A delegation is sent to the Britisher's office, and on the way they meet one of the heads of the Arab community, Isa Arafa. They tell him that if he can get the Hebron Arab leaders to announce publicly that they are responsible for the lives of the Jews, the Jews will continue their ties with the Arabs, including the continued bank credit that the Arabs need. If not, all commercial ties will be cut. The Arab agrees, but meanwhile he goes with them to see the British police chief. To everyone's amazement, the police chief refuses to see the delegation, shouting "What are you doing here? I told you a number of times that you must remain in your homes!"

The Arab listens, and now his tone changes. He tells Slonim: "If you will hand over the strangers in your midst, you will save your own lives." Slonim replies angrily: "We Jews are not like you Muslims. We are one people; there are no 'strangers' among us." In deep worry the Jews walk home, watching as thousands of Arabs shout and march through the streets, fully armed, while in their midst walk a few policemen carrying clubs.

Without the knowledge of the Jewish leaders, the slaughter has already begun. In one of the houses, farther away from the center, lives the Abushadid family. The father, Eliyahu, fifty-five, is a storekeeper, born in Hebron. He suddenly appears on the balcony of his home, screaming for help. No one hears or listens. The police are nowhere to be seen. Rocks begin flying into the house, smashing windows, and screams of terror are heard. Several women and children appear on the balcony. An Arab, his eyes filled with hate and lust, rushes at them, swinging a sword. He cuts and stabs again and again. Blood spurts over the balcony and drips into the street. Inside lie the bodies of Eliyahu Abushadid and his twenty-five-year-old son, Yitzchok, a simple tailor. Dead, too, are forty-five-year-old Yaakov Goslan, a smelter, also born in the city, and his eighteen-year-old son Moshe. The Arabs do not even look at the bodies; they are much too busy looting the house and throwing Jewish property over the balcony into the streets to the howling mob.

The mob now turns to the home of the revered scholar Rabbi Meir Kastel. The sixty-nine-year-old *Haham,* also born in Hebron, watches as the mob breaks down his door. He is murdered brutally. The mob loots his house and then burns it down over his body. On to the next . . .

Rabbeinu Hason, sixty-five, is one of the heads of the Sephardic rabbinate in Hebron. He is also a son of the city. He and his wife, Clara, fifty-nine, watch in terror as the mob burns down their door and then storms in. Both die a horrible death at the hands of the mob, which loots and then turns to Beit Hadassah . . .

Beit Hadassah. The building that in years to come will rouse the anger of the world and of too many Jews when "seized" by the Jewish "militants." Rabbi Meir Kahane will receive a sentence after "seizing" the building three times. Women from Kiryat Arba along with their children will "seize" it and be forced to remain for months without their husbands. It is a building in which the Israeli government will refuse to allow Jews to live. And six innocent Jews will be shot down in cold blood outside its doors. But it is also a building with a past that few know. . . .

In 1909 the cornerstone was laid in Hebron for a building that was to serve as both a medical clinic and synagogue for the Jews of the city. The pious and wealthy Baghdadian Jew (who later moved to Calcutta) Yosef Avraham Shalom gave the money both to build and to keep up this institution, which came to be known as Chesed L'Avraham. It was officially registered under the Ottoman Empire laws. The *Haham bashi,* chief rabbi of Hebron, Rabbi Suliman ben Eliyahu Mani, traveled to India to raise money from wealthy Iraqi Jews for the yeshiva. The Sason family was especially generous. Eventually the Hadassah organization took over the clinic. (This is the same Hadassah women's organization that decades later will condemn the "takeover" of the building by the women of Kiryat Arba.)

This institution, which did so much for both the Jews and the Arabs of Hebron and which in later years is to serve as the symbol of Jewish shame as Jewish governments bar Jews from returning to the scene of the massacres, is the next to feel the wrath of the crazed Arab mobs. . . .

The mob moves to the attack. Chesed L'Avraham is a place of worship and study as well as a medical clinic for Jews and Arabs alike. That matters little to the inflamed Arab mob. Among those who attack are many who have received free treatment in this same building. They climb through windows and smash down doors. Inside they savagely destroy everything they see. Medical equipment, medicine, drugs—everything is shattered in a hate-filled frenzy. And now flames leap toward the skies as the mob sets fire to the inside. The place is a raging inferno and the stones are blackened by the flames that lick at them. The synagogue is a scene of utter destruction, and the torn Torah Scrolls, desecrated by the Arab mob, now burn and become ashes. The building that served as a place of Jewish worship and study as well as a place of mercy and charity is gone. It does not matter to the howling Arabs that they will never again be able to heal their hurts and sicknesses as they did every day until now. Hatred perverts logic.

Next door to the Hadassah building lives Ben Zion Gershon, a crippled druggist whose kindness to the Arabs is legendary. We will never know how many Arabs he treated, most for free or for absurdly low fees. How many times did the Arabs thank him by blessing his name as they left? Today the mob shows the way it repays kindness. They burst into the apartment. Fingernails gouge out the crippled druggist's eyes, and he dies as knives pierce his body. His wife is assaulted, and both her arms are cut off (she dies later in the hospital in Jerusalem). The Arabs attempt to rape the daughter, but she struggles so successfully that they kill her in a horrible way.

The streets of Hebron are a nightmare of shouting Arabs. Screams are heard from dozens of houses—the screams of dying men, violated women, weeping children. And the pogrom continues.

On the road to Beersheba stands Beit Burland, where many yeshiva students from the Hebron yeshiva stay. The mob surrounds the house and breaks down both the front and back doors. The yeshiva student Arvaham Dov Shapira stands and fights bravely with a knife in his hand until he is dead. The young genius Zvi Heller is hit again and again, as he cries out: "I am only a boy!" The mob redoubles its efforts. The young student dies on the way to Jerusalem.

Yet another student, Moshe-Aron Ripps, begs his murderers a moment to say *Vidui,* the final confession. As he begins, they kill him. Two other students, Shmuel Izak Bernstein and Yeshachar Eliyahu Sandrow, are also victims. The latter, almost cut in two by the cruel mob, lingers and suffers for almost a day before dying.

No Jewish house is safe. On the road to Jerusalem the mob breaks into the home of the *shochet* (a ritual slaughterer), Yaakov Zev Reizman. The terrified Jew runs out the back door, but the mob catches him. He pleads with them and gives them all his money. For just a moment they leave him alone, but as he begins to run again, they chase him, catch him, and riddle his body with knife wounds. He dies in the gutter. His house is a scene of tragedy. On the floor lie his dead brother, another yeshiva genius, Moshe, and his mother-in-law, Frieda Haimson. The house is totally looted by the mob, which then leaves on its way to the next victims.

The next is the home of Eliezer Don Slonim. His house is a prestigious one. Slonim himself is one of the most important Jews in Hebron. As director of the Anglo-Palestine bank in the city, he is also the only Jew to sit on the Hebron town council. He has many "friends" among the Arabs. He knows all the notables and leaders of the town. They have promised him protection and assured him safety.

Because of this, Slonim tells as many Jews as possible to come to his home. "There we will be safe," is the consensus. Some seventy Jews are gathered. Wrapped in their prayer shawls, the men stand and pray the Sabbath service in fear and trepidation as they hear the howls of the mob and the screams of the victims outside. Many can see the terrible massacre in nearby Beit Burland. They can hear the mob pounding on the door of the adjoining house, that of Skolover. Suddenly, the windows of Slonim's house are smashed by a hundred rocks. The Jews scream. Men rush to bar the door. Outside, iron poles and beams are being brought up by the Arabs to smash down the doors. The house of Slonim will be no safer than all the rest.

Outside the house now stand hundreds of inflamed Arabs calling for Jewish blood. They charge up the narrow stone steps leading to the house. For fifteen minutes they pound on the door, then smash it with iron staves and batter it with poles.

Inside, the yeshiva students stand frantically against the doors, attempting to hold back the murderers. But suddenly there is a loud crash. A huge hole has been made in the front door! Shots ring out. Avraham Yanai, fifty-six, a poor Jew from Constantinople, falls, struck in the arm. A second shot catches twenty-seven-year-old Zalman Vilenski, secretary of Yeshiva Knesset Yisroel, in the face. He collapses in a pool of blood. Yet another bullet rips the stomach of Yisrael Mordechai Kaplan, a twenty-two-year-old yeshiva student from Vilkomir in Lithuania. Even as he falls, he continues to hold onto the door to try to keep the Arabs out. But only for a moment; he collapses and dies.

The yeshiva students show superhuman strength and bravery as they hold back the hordes. But under the assault of bullets they are forced to retreat with the rest into the inner rooms. The door to the roof bursts open and Arabs leap into the house. Two more yeshiva students now fall, twenty-six-year-old Dov Ber Lipin of Vitebsk and Alter Haim Shor, twenty-four, of Rozalia, Lithuania. Their bodies tumble out onto the steps, and the mob tramples them as it rushes inside. Eliezer Don Slonim, cool and strong to the end, fires his pistol at the mob, but a heavy metal pipe strikes him viciously in the head; he collapses.

Now there is no hope left, but the yeshiva students fight like lions. The sound of swords and knives slashing and cutting is mixed with the cries of women and children. Someone cries, "*Shma Yisrael* . . .!" Yisrael Lazarovski, a student from Letsch, Russia, is brutally stabbed and dies. He is only seventeen. Yisrael Hillel Kaplinski is older; he is twenty-one. Lying on the ground, felled by a bullet wound, he is attacked by a dozen Arabs who stab him repeatedly. A survivor recalls him shouting, "I am already dead and they still hit me!" And in a corner, in a pool of blood, wrapped in his prayer shawl, lies the Rabbi of Zichron Ya'akov, Rabbi Avraham Yaakov Orlinski, next to his dead wife, who had come to Hebron to spend a quiet Sabbath with their daughter and son-in-law, Eliezer Don Slonim.

Rabbi Tzvi Drobkin, sixty-seven, from Bobruysk, Russia, is known as "the *Iluy* ["genius"] of Shklov." The Arabs literally rip his belly in two and his insides pour out. He arrived just half a year earlier from bloody Russia, hoping to live a life of Torah and peace in the Holy Land.

And all the others, all the martyrs who died to sanctify G-d's name:

- Shlomo Yigal, twenty-four, from Slonim, Poland; Zev Berman, twenty-three, an American from Philadelphia; Yaakov Wechsler, just seventeen, son of a wealthy Jew from Chicago; and the son of the Rosh Yeshiva, Aharon David Epstein, also seventeen.
- Seventy-two-year-old Reb Aharon Leib Gotlovsky, from Herzeliyya, who had come to spend a happy Sabbath with his son-in-law, Bezalel Lazarovski. Both lie dead, along with Bezalel's five-year-old daughter, Dvora. She will lie in a Jerusalem hospital next to another five-year-old, little Aharon Slonim, son of Eliezer Don and his wife, Hana.
- Yaakov and Leah Grodzinski have been married just four months. He comes from Warsaw and runs a small hotel for yeshiva students. She is from Hungary, from the house of Turman. They die together.
- Here die, too, the noted principal of the Tel Nordau school in Tel Aviv, Eliezer Dovnikov, and his wife, Leah. They, too, came to spend a happy Sabbath in the city of the Patriarchs. And here too lies a simple, pious Persian Jew, twenty-seven-year-old Shimon Cohen.

In this one house, where they had gathered for safety, die twenty-four people; another thirteen are wounded, mostly gravely. Taking part in this awful slaughter are Arabs who just the day before did business and laughed together with Eliezer Don Slonim. They were his friends. . . .

The slaughter continues for half an hour. Every piece of property that can be moved is thrown out the door and windows. Pillows are cut, and the feathers fly through the air, some resting on the bodies of the dead, sticking to them, still wet with blood. The Arabs now leave, crying, "Let us go; there are no more Jews left to kill."

They are wrong. Miraculously, Jews have been saved— eleven of them are squeezed into a tiny bathroom that somehow the mob failed to notice. Still others lie under the bodies of the dead. They stagger out, fearfully, to look at the horrors the Arabs have left behind. There is a terrible quiet except for the moaning of the wounded and dying—and the sound of the mob, which has now moved on to its next victims.

One of the survivors, Y. L. Grodzinski, tells how he was saved: "As I ran into one of the rooms, I saw my mother standing at a window and crying, 'Help us!' A crowd of jeering, laughing Arabs stood and threw rocks at her. I seized her and pushed her behind a bookshelf that stood in the corner of the room. I then placed a young girl and a boy of twelve there. Finally I and another yeshiva student pushed ourselves into the narrow space. We could hardly breathe but lay there terrified as the Arabs burst into the room. The cries of the Jews who were being murdered were terrible. Every moment we expected the Arabs to find us and kill us, too. It was a miracle of G-d that, somehow, they did not. After an interminable time they left, and the only sounds we heard were those of the wounded and dying.

"I lifted myself up and tried to get out. It was very difficult because the shelves were very heavy and bodies blocked it. When I finally crawled out, my head swam and eyes darkened at the horrible sight. At my feet lay Eliezer Don Slonim, his wife, and young child, Aharon. They wallowed in their own blood. Next to them lay the bodies of Slonim's father-in-law, Rabbi Orlinski, and his wife. The rabbi lay in his *talis* ["prayer shawl"] and I thought how just a little while earlier I had heard him blessing us with the priestly blessing, 'and may He give you peace.' Now he, his wife, his daughter, son-in-law, and grandchild lay in a final peace.

"There were scores of other bodies, some dead, some wounded. The dead all had their skulls shattered and their intestines ripped out. The same picture was in the other rooms. There I saw my brother. I rushed to him. His head had been struck brutal blows with an ax. I threw water on him and he revived, but died of his wounds some hours later.

"Eliezer Dovnikov, the principal of the Tel Nordau school, in Tel Aviv, lay dead but there were no marks on his body. He had been strangled, his body lying next to that of his wife. The room was a scene of horror, and the vision of Bialik's *Ir HaHareiga* [City of slaughter; concerning the Kishinev pogrom] stood as a living ghost before me in all its horror.

"I went to the window and saw policemen passing. I called to them, asking them to send medical aid. Just at that moment, some Arabs passed by and saw me. They clenched their fists and waved them in my direction. I ran back to my hiding place, waiting to be rescued. . . ."

Meanwhile, the mob has moved on to new "adventures," the home of Moshe Goldschmidt, a Habad Hasid, thirty-one, from Yaktrinoslav, Russia. Some fifteen people are hiding in his house, and as the doors are broken down, they escape by jumping down into the adjoining yard. Moshe Goldschmidt, however, apparently counting on being able to appeal to the pity and mercy of the Arabs, remains behind. He falls to his knees and pleads with the Arabs, who only laugh at him and humiliate him before killing him in a brutal and indescribable manner.

In the Grodzinski home there are only three people. Moshe Grodzinski, fifty-four, of Warsaw, is the director of the yeshiva. He is killed with the first charge of the Arabs. Shragai Feivel Mitevsky, twenty-five, a yeshiva student from Lawdowa, Poland, is brutally wounded and dies a few days later in Jerusalem. The house is looted and wrecked. On to the worst of the horrors.

The mob is drunk on murder and brutality. Its cruelty is fed by atrocity. The scholar Reb Bezalel Smarik, from Zhitel in Lithuania, is seventy-three. The Arabs drag him outside and kill him obscenely on the doorstep of his home. Inside they murder three North American yeshiva students: Binyamin Halevi Horowitz, twenty, of New York; Tzvi Halevi Freuman, twenty-one, from Canada; and twenty-two-year-old Memphis-born David Scheinberg.

They now burst into the adjoining home of Shlomo Unger. The twenty-six-year-old Unger is a huge man, a mechanic, from Zgug, Poland. He looked like a Gentile and the mob pauses. One shouts at him: "Are you a Christian?" He can say yes and save his life. He looks with contempt at the mob of Arabs and says, "I am a Jew!" They leap on him with fury, his courage maddening them. They attack his wife; she loses her mind and dies a few days later. They leave two orphans, one two years old and the other two months. . . .

More, more! The baker Noah Imerman, from Slutzk and Slobodka, is killed as the Arabs thrust his head into the oven. Nahman Segal, thirty, of Skola, Poland, watches in horror as his Arab landlord opens the doors for the mob. He is holding his three-year-old child, Menachem. An Arab ax cuts through his hand, wounding the child fatally. Segal dies a few hours later. His wife has three fingers cut off, and a yeshiva student in the house loses his left hand. In the same house the great *masmid* ("eternal learner of Torah") of the yeshiva, Simcha Yitzhak Broida, twenty-eight, of Vilkomir, Lithuania, is dangled head down from the window and tortured to death. With him dies sixteen-year-old Brooklyn-born Chaim Krasner and a couple that have come to Hebron for a Sabbath visit, Asher Moshe and Chaya Gutman of Tel Aviv.

The Hebron yeshiva is looted and totally destroyed. All its records are ripped to shreds and the furniture destroyed in an orgy of madness. The home of the Rosh Yeshiva, Rabbi Epstein, is a major target of the murderers. They attack in a large force, throwing huge stones through the windows. The families inside are gripped by terror. The men desperately try to hold the doors against the mob, and the women cry out in panic. Across the street stands the home of the governor of Hebron. The cries of anguish move him to come out onto the balcony and order the police, who have been standing by the whole time, to chase the mob away. The mob is not impressed. Three times they return, and three times the governor calmly orders them to be dispersed. It is easily done, but not before sixty-eight-year-old Elimelech Zev Lichtenstein is murdered. The day before, when the first victim of the Arabs was killed in the yeshiva, Lichtenstein was in a side room. Today he has just been called up to the Torah, where he gave the traditional blessing of thanks, *Hagomel*, for having been saved. Now, fifteen minutes later, he is dead.

The day of horrors nears its end. Outside the small hotel, according to *The Book of Hebron* (edited by Oded Avisar, 1970), Eishel Avraham, Sheikh Talib, the Muslim religious leader of the town, walks up to the building in which dozens of Jews sit huddled in terror. He looks inside to see how many people he can count, then leaves. Some moments pass, and suddenly the sound of a large mob is heard. The Jews look out the windows to see hundreds of Arabs following the Sheikh. They stand around him, now, as he speaks to them: "You, Muslims! Inside are ten Americans whose parents are millionaires. Slaughter the Jews! Drink their blood! Today is the day of Islam! This is the day that the Prophet has commanded you! Allah and the prophets have commanded you to avenge the blood of your dead brethren in Jerusalem! Allah is great! Come with me and kill the Jews! Inside are beautiful Jewish women; take them!"

The mob attacks the home of the Cheichal family near the hotel. The yeshiva students, inside, fight wildly to hold the doors. At the very moment that they begin to splinter, the students see what they take to be a miracle: a British officer with five Arab policemen suddenly appears on horseback! The two Cheichal sons, Yisrael-Aryeh, twenty, and Eliyah Dov, seventeen, rush out past the surprised mob to the policemen. They plead with them to save the Jews inside. The policemen stare. The mob now angrily rushes at the two Jews who are standing and imploring the British officer to save their lives. They attack Yisrael-Aryeh. Bloodied, he turns like a madman on his attackers, smashing them with his fists, until he falls dead at the feet of his "rescuers."

The younger brother seizes the reins of the Britisher's horse and pleads for his life. As he does so the mob stabs him again and again, one Arab laughing and shouting, "Does it hurt, Jew?"

The two brothers die, but their deaths enable the other Jews, whose presence the Arab murderers have momentarily forgotten, to flee to safety.

And in the Jewish quarter, the Jewish ghetto, every house is looted, every synagogue destroyed. Reb Alter Platshy, the twenty-nine-year-old Sephardic sexton, is brutally murdered. He is a poverty-stricken plasterer, sole supporter of his six children and elderly widowed mother. Another pauper, elderly Yitzhak AbuHana, sixty-nine, dies a terrible death, and two other destitute Jews, Avraham Yani, fifty-nine, and his wife, Vida, both born in Constantinople, also fall victim to the killers.

The famous Sephardic synagogue, Avraham Avinu, built in the year 1501, is totally destroyed. The Arabs take the Torah Scrolls and with shouts of animal joy rip them to pieces and burn the shreds. This is the synagogue that will later be turned into a sheep pen. It is the synagogue that, after Israeli liberation of Hebron, will remain a sheep pen for years, with the Arab shepherd paying IL 60 a year for the "privilege" to the Israeli military government! It is the synagogue that the Israeli government will refuse for more than ten years to repair, out of fear of changing the "status quo," giving in only after Russian Jewish hero Professor Ben Zion Tavgar single-handedly drives out the sheep.

Only ghosts haunt the buildings today: the ghosts of Jews whose intestines were ripped out. The ghosts of Jews whose skulls were so viciously chopped that their brains poured out. The ghost of the elderly Jew who was castrated before being killed, of the young Jewish student whose body was found with a piece of flesh ripped from his throat, of the barber whose head was stuffed into a toilet, where he died. Of the woman who was hanged by her legs and whose hair was ripped from her head. Of the baker whose head was thrust into a lit oven. Of Rabbi Grodzinski, whose left eye was ripped out and whose skull was broken, even as the blood spattered the ceiling. Of the young woman teacher who was raped by thirteen Arabs before her parents' eyes. Of the young girl who was stripped naked and saved from rape only when she pleaded to be killed. The "merciful" Arabs agreed: they ripped open her belly before the eyes of her tiny sister, who hid under a bed. . . .

Hebron: where six more Jews die by Arab bullets in May 1980; nothing has changed. Hebron: where the impossibility of Arab-Jewish coexistence is written in blood.

1936–38

On the night of April 15, 1936, armed Arabs stopped several automobiles on the main road between Tulkarm and Shechem. They killed two Jews and injured two. It was the beginning of more than two years of terror, destruction, and murder of Jews. Four days later, Jaffa exploded in pogroms, with nine Jews murdered and fifty-seven injured the first day, and the Jewish neighborhoods bordering Tel Aviv set ablaze and looted. Five more Jews were slaughtered the next day: Yehuda Siman-Tov, Zelig Levinson, Shlomo Morrison, and two brothers, Tuvya and Yosef Prusak.

The massacres spread. A crowd of Jews leaving the Edison Cinema in Jerusalem were mowed down by Arab bullets. Left dead in their own blood were Dr. Shavchovsky, Alexander Polonsky, and Isaac Yolovsky. In another incident a bomb was thrown into a children's schoolyard. The murderous toll mounted as Jews were murdered near Kfar Saba, Yaknaam, Haifa, and Safad. In Safad, a gang of Arabs broke into the home of a poor scribe and killed him and his three small children in cold blood, despite the heartrending pleas of the mother. An incident that particularly shook the Jewish community was the murder of two Jewish nurses, Marta Fink and Nehama Tzedek, struck down by Arabs who threw a bomb from a train in the heart of Tel Aviv. The main thing was to kill Jews—none were spared.

Women, children, those who were "close" to the Arabs were killed. Lewish Billig, respected lecturer in Arabic literature at Hebrew University, who had devoted his life to Arabic studies and was a "good friend" of the Arabs, was murdered in his house in Jerusalem.

The first phase of the Arab riots and attacks, April–October 1936, ended with 82 Jews murdered and more than 400 wounded. Property damage was extensive: 200,000 trees were destroyed along with 16,500 dunams (4,125 acres) of crops. Damage ran into the millions of dollars.

Not until the end of 1938 did the murders end, in time for Hitler's Holocaust to begin. The Jewish community in Eretz Yisrael counted its dead: 517 men, women, and children. The cost in destruction to property was in the tens of millions. The Arabs had made it coldly clear that, for them, the very presence of Zionism in the form of Jews seeking their own homeland was unacceptable and would be met with death and destruction.

Nothing has changed, and nothing need surprise us. On July 23, 1937, the Arab Higher Committee, speaking for the Arabs of Eretz Yisrael, issued a statement of policy in regard to the Peel Commission's suggestion of the possibility of partitioning the country into Jewish and Arab states. The statement declared that "the Arabs of Palestine are the owners of the country. . . . The Jews on the other hand are a minority of intruders who before the war had no great standing in this country and whose political connections therewith had been severed for almost 2,000 years. . . .

"The Arabs have always repudiated the declaration given to Jews as an undertaking which Great Britain should never have assumed, and which, moreover, was against all natural principles, insofar as it aims at establishing an alien people in a country where no sort of justification exists for their settlement as a nation and at transferring to them the land which was at the time, and still is, inhabited by its historic owners, the Arabs."

That is what they said then, before there were "occupied territories" or Jewish settlements in them that constituted an "obstacle to peace." That was before there was an "occupation army" to defy a United Nations that was not even in existence. That is what the Arabs said, and those are the murders they committed—the death and destruction they effected—before there was even a Jewish state. All that they said then, they think today. All that they *did* then, they would do today if given the opportunity. Will we give it to them?

The first Jew to be killed in the rioting of 1936–38 was Yisrael Hazan, murdered near Tulkarm, in April 1936. Forty-three years later, in October 1979, an automobile carrying Tzvi Laufer, twenty-four, crashed into a truck in Tulkarm. He was killed instantly and the driver of the car severely injured. When soldiers arrived at the spot, they were horrified to find young Arabs from the nearby school happily dancing, singing, and clapping around the car containing the two dead Jews.

Nothing has changed, and if the Jew does not understand the real cause of the Arab-Jewish conflict, he will indeed, G-d forbid, give the Arab the opportunity for which he so longs: to liquidate the Jewish state.

CHAPTER 3

Of Declarations and Independence

On 5 Iyar, in the year 5708—May 14, 1948—David Ben-Gurion stood in Tel Aviv and read a historic document to a packed hall. It was the Declaration of the Establishment of the State of Israel, its Declaration of Independence. In it the State of Israel pledged that "It will ensure complete equality of social and political rights to all its inhabitants, irrespective of religion, race or sex." It also stated: "We appeal . . . to the Arab inhabitants of the State of Israel to preserve peace and participate in the upbuilding of the state on the basis of full and equal citizenship. . . ."

It would be pleasant to think that the Arab and Jew can share full and equal citizenship in a Jewish State of Israel. But it is infinitely more important just to *think,* clearly and honestly; for the *Jewish state* that was established by the Declaration of Independence makes that document a model of schizophrenia, correctly mirroring the ideologically confused people who wrote it. Consider the other parts of the declaration, its opening, major, and moving paragraphs.

"Eretz Yisrael was the birthplace *of the Jewish people.* . . . After being forcibly exiled from *their land* the people kept faith with it throughout their dispersion and never ceased to pray and hope for their return to it and for the restoration in it of *their political freedom.* . . .

"In the year 5657 [1897] . . . the First Zionist Congress convened and proclaimed the right *of the Jewish people* to national rebirth in *its own country.* . . .

53

"On the 29th November 1947, the United Nations General Assembly passed a resolution calling for the establishment of a *Jewish State* in Eretz Yisrael. This recognition by the United Nations of the right of *the Jewish People* to establish *their state* is irrevocable. This right is the natural right of *the Jewish people* to be masters of their own fate, like all other nations, in *their own sovereign state*.

"Accordingly we, members of the People's Council ... hereby declare the establishment of *a Jewish State* in Eretz Yisrael to be known as the State of Israel.

"The State of Israel will be open for *Jewish immigration* and for the Ingathering of the Exiles. . . ."

Note the innumerable clear statements of what Israel is meant to be. The land is "the birthplace of the Jewish people." The first words of the declaration of the state set the tone. It is the birthplace of the Jew—not the Arab—and it is the Jews who were "exiled from their land"; it is the Jews "who kept faith with it" and "never ceased to pray and hope for their return." Can we seriously expect the Arab to feel equal or to have a share in such a state? A declaration of independence that he is expected to see as his own begins by speaking of the land as the birthplace of the Jewish people. But he is not a Jew. The declaration speaks of an exile and a dream of return, but the Arab was not exiled, and if anything the dream of return of the Jew was the hope of making the Arab a minority. For the Arab who dreamed of Jews *not* returning, the Jewish dream is a nightmare!

When the Israeli Arab is told to rise for "his" national anthem, "*Hatikvah*" (the "hope"), and sing of "the Jewish soul yearning" and "the hope of 2,000 years," can he be expected to feel empathy? Indeed, Israel's resident self-hater, Uri Avnery, proposed in 1975 to change the anthem. His reason made eminently good sense—if you were an anti-Zionist: the song's motif of Jewish longing for Israel is not acceptable to Israel's Arabs. When the Israeli Arab looks upon the happy revelers on Israeli Independence Day, celebrating, in effect, the Arab defeat and the displacement of an Arab majority of Palestine by a Jewish majority of Israel, can he be seriously expected to join in? When, in the words of the Declaration of Independence, the Law of Return opens the gates "for Jewish immigration" and not Arab influx, for the cousins of the residents of Tel Aviv but not those of Nazareth, is it surprising that the Arab feels alienated from the state?

The concept "Jewish" is dinned into the Arab's angry head every day. Well, he is *not* Jewish, and what perverse madness prevents us from understanding his alienation and rage? Has it never occurred to anyone that the very existence of a Jewish state in the land where the Arab was once the majority makes him uncomfortable and that that is unacceptable to him?

The State of Israel came into being as the *Jewish* state, the sovereign homeland of the Jewish people. The State of Israel is the goal of *Zionism,* the movement of *Jewish* longing for a return to their homeland, a longing that began, not with Herzl in 1897, but with his great-great-ancestor, who wept as the Second Temple was destroyed in the year 70. The State of Israel is that homeland for which Jews pray three times daily, turning their faces, not toward Mecca or Rome, but toward Jerusalem. The State of Israel is the dream, vision, hope, tears, yearning of a Jewish people that suffered humiliation, exile, agony, poverty, robbery, rape, burning, drowning, gasing, pogroms, Crusades, Inquisitions, and Auschwitzes from its varied hosts throughout the world. The State of Israel is the Jewish conviction that "Never Again!" is a concept that can be realized only in a land where Jews control their own destiny, their own police and armed forces, their own guns to guarantee the kind of respect the *Zhid, Kike, Yahud,* and *Yevrei* never quite received from the mouths, fists, and boots of the majority culture where he resided in nervous insecurity. The State of Israel is the Jewish demand for a land in which Jews can preserve and create their own specific tradition and way of life free of the spiritual and social assimilation of foreign abrasive culture.

The State of Israel is the Jewish demand for what every other people sees as its natural right. The State of Israel is not a request, a plan, or a petition. It is not a favor sought while crouching like some pauper at the back door of the nobleman's mansion. The State of Israel is the Jewish demand and affirmation of *right* to the land. What the Arab state of Syria is to the Syrians, and the Polish state to the Poles and Burundi to Burundians and Muslim Pakistan to Muslim Pakistanis and Papua to Papuans, so is the Jewish state—*at least*—to the Jews.

There is nothing to be ashamed of. There is no need to grow

defensive about this. There is no place for apologies. The land is ours, the state is ours; let us be proud, let us be joyful, and, above all, let us be convinced. Israel: the *one* land that the Jewish people have the right—and the obligation—to demand. Israel: the sovereign Jewish state, owned and controlled by and for the Jewish people. This is Zionism; this is Judaism; this is *normalcy*.

But having said all this, let us know what this means for an Arab living in the state, and let us stop treating him with the contempt that we reserve for some backward idiot. If all that the Declaration of Independence says and implies is indeed true, the Arab is *not* equal.

The Arab of Israel can enjoy full religious and cultural freedoms, can say and write what he feels, can exercise political rights in the sense of voting for the party of his choice, just like a Jew. But to think that this makes the Arab of Israel feel that the state is his and that his national destiny there is the same as that of the Jews is to fail to understand the reality of being an Arab in what is de jure a Jewish state.

It is to fail to understand that not by bread alone does the Arab live, and that a man needs to dwell in and feel part of his own land, where the state represents his national and cultural aspirations, where the majority of the people—those who control the state—are *his* people. But when "his" state is one whose national roots, majority, language, religion, culture, holidays, and very destiny are different from his—what do we expect of the Arabs?

What do we think? That he is a fool who does not understand, or worse, a knave who can be bought with social and economic progress? How else can we explain the following Israeli "information"?

In 1975 the Israeli embassy in Washington issued a series of position papers and essays under the general heading "Background on Zionism." One was written by Professor Joseph Dan, of the Hebrew University of Jerusalem. In it, we (and the Arabs) find: "The Jewish people can continue to exist only if it has an independent state in its one and only homeland, the Land of Israel. There is nothing more to add to that basic definition of Zionism: *Jewish* independence in the Land of Israel."

Fair enough and certainly straightforward. Zionism is *Jewish* independence in a *Jewish* state in the land of the *Jews*. Now consider the second paper, issued by the government of Israel to explain Zionism and Israel. It is an excerpt of remarks by Chaim Herzog, former Israeli ambassador to the United Nations. After describing Zionism as the Jewish demand for "revived freedom and nationhood in its ancient homeland" and the Land of Israel as "the center of its national existence," Herzog stated that *"Arabs are free and equal citizens in our state."*

Free and equal in a state that is irrevocably *Jewish?* Does "free" mean free to work toward an *Arab* majority in Israel? Does "free" mean free to have many, many babies who in due time will be free to vote an Arab majority into the Knesset? Does "equal" mean equal rights for an Arab Knesset majority that could vote to change the name of the state to "Palestine" and abolish the Law of Return that today gives Jews and not Arabs automatic entry and citizenship? In a word, are the Arabs of the Jewish state for which Mr. Herzog's ancestors yearned for 2,000 years free and equal to go quietly, calmly, peacefully, democratically, to the polls and, by majority rule, vote an end to Zionism and that Jewish state?

And when yet another Israeli luminary, Michael Comay, former ambassador to Canada, writes to the *Jerusalem Post* (June 11, 1976), "I want an Israel which will remain both Jewish and democratic," what does he say to the equal *Arab* citizen of this Jewish democracy [*sic*] who asks him: If I have enough babies, do I have the right to want a Palestine that is both Arab and democratic . . .?

I do not feel sorry for the Arabs of Eretz Yisrael, no matter how much they feel that the land is theirs. I do not feel for them because I know that the land is *not* theirs, that it is *Jewish.* It is the one and only land that we have, whereas the Arab of Eretz Yisrael can find a home in any one of more than the twenty lands of his 100 million fellow Arabs. I feel no pain for one who robbed me of my land, no matter how loud his false claim to it. But as I feel neither pain nor guilt, I can understand this Arab and know the stupidity of the deception practiced on him. It is a deception that does not deceive; for the Arab of Eretz Yisrael may be a robber and murderer of Jews, but he is not a fool.

Indeed, when the "moderate" and the "dovish" Jewish leaders of Israel, those who gladden liberal hearts by calling for the return of the "occupied territories," do so because of "the need to retain a Jewish majority" and warn against "too many Arabs" (one recalls wryly Golda Meir's attack on me for "offending the sensibilities" of the Arabs, followed sometime later by the classic speech in which she spoke of the need to give up land because "I do not want to awaken each morning worrying about how many Arabs were born the previous night")—then think how "equal" the Arab of Israel feels.

The most outrageous offense against Arab sensibilities comes from all the liberals and leftists who grow livid with anger if certain people call for the transfer of Israeli Arabs from the country. But those who call for Arab transfer do so out of respect for the sincerity of the Arab belief that the land was stolen from him and out of knowledge that the Arab cannot feel love and empathy for a *Jewish* state. Because of this, they understand that there can never be peace or coexistence between Jew and Arab. This infuriates the "moralists." Yet it is these "moralists" who then proceed to warn against annexing land lest, G-d forbid, we import too many Arabs into our midst. What in the world does an Israeli Arab think when Israeli leaders, who swear that he is equal, proceed to say the following: "Do you want to have . . . a Jewish state in the whole of Eretz Yisrael? . . . Do you want to have democracy in that state? How then will it be a *Jewish* state? We want a Jewish state, even if it is not in the whole of the country" (David Ben-Gurion, Knesset debate, April 4, 1949).

Did Ben-Gurion ever think what the "equal" Arabs of the Jewish Israel who live in the state that is "not in the whole of the country" felt on hearing those words?

Or consider the thoughts of Abba Eban, whose ability to speak twelve languages had made him the darling of Jewish Centers and Hadassah groups in the Western world. He warns against annexing Judea-Samaria and the other liberated lands and asks: "Do we aspire to be a *Jewish* democracy [*sic*], or does our vision include a million Arab noncitizens held in an unwanted union with us forever?" (*Jerusalem Post*, April 23, 1976).

Even as the applause of the nonthinkers rises in a crescendo, the more perceptive may ask: A *Jewish* democracy? How in the world can the Israeli Arab think of that? Mr. Eban intones: "We cannot hold a million Arabs as noncitizens." In that case, asks the Israeli Arab, *why not make them citizens?* The answer that

Mr. Eban would give *would be that we do not want them because they are Arabs and not Jews.* But, of course, Mr. Eban detests the extremists who call for emigration of the Arabs. *They* are clearly racists.

And will Mr. Eban go to Nazareth tomorrow to repeat to his happy, equal Arabs of Israel the following words he once coined? "Israel's nationalism is more than a political movement. It is a faith, a religion, a culture, a civilization, a journey together of people across generations of martyrdom."

Dear Mr. Eban, do share those noble thoughts with Israel's Arabs. What tears of joy and empathy will flow in Nazareth square, or in Umm al-Fahm or Sakhnin or all the equal villages of equal Arab citizens who presumably commemorated the fast of Tisha B'Av with us for 2,500 years as they mourned the destruction of the Jewish Holy Temple "across generations of martyrdom."

The Arab of Israel sits in a land in which he was once the majority, which he controlled, *which was Arab, which was his.* The Jew came—from Russia, Poland, Morocco, and Brooklyn—and took it from him. *That is how the Arab sees it.* That is *his* reality. How do we expect him to feel and react, this man who feels robbed and bitter and alienated? That is the source of the problem, and it is insoluble.

The points I raise are so brutally plain and painful that people shrink from them. Better, for them, sugary delusions than bitter reality. And so, during all the years of the existence of Israel, and for all the decades of pre-Israel political Zionism, Zionist leaders eagerly, desperately, clung to a myth, which they fed, as an article of faith, to the Jewish masses. That myth proclaimed: The way to peaceful coexistence between Arab and Jew in the Land of Israel is to raise the standard of living and to create a new generation of educated Arabs—*the "head-and-stomach" policy of clever Israelis. . . .*

I say it again: All those who say this hold the Israeli Arab in nothing but contempt.

It should be obvious by now, as the result of scores of examples in other countries, that one does not buy the national aspirations of a people with indoor toilets. The Arabs of Israel, a minority who possess national aspirations, will not be bought off with material goods, electricity, or higher education. Indeed, it is clear that the more social, economic, and political progress is made and the more educated the Arabs become, the less satisfied they will be and the more extreme, nationalistic, and antagonistic to the Jewish state.

The question of higher living standards, more integration and opportunities, and greater education are not the ultimate issues for the Arabs. The Jewish-Arab conflict in Israel is not a social or economic or political one. It is much deeper than that; it has to do with the very definition and basis of the state. As long as Israel persists in defining itself de jure, officially, as the *Jewish* state, as long as it adheres to the Zionist and Judaistic credo of the land as belonging to the *Jewish* people, there will be hatred, conflict, blood, war.

But the leaders of Israel do not have the courage to say this. They persist in their ultimately catastrophic delusion that the solution to the Arab problem in Israel is greater progress toward social and economic equality, integration, and "goodwill."

And so, on June 19, 1976, the prime minister of Israel, Yitzhak Rabin, Defense Minister Shimon Peres, former Foreign Minister Abba Eban, a large gathering of Israeli top leadership, and hand-picked "loyal" Israeli Arabs met for a day-long symposium on the "Arab problem." It was less than three months after the Land Day Rebellion, and the shaken country had seen debates, articles, government meetings, studies, speeches, symposiums—all devoted to dissecting the "suddenly" angry Israeli Arab. The question on the lips of all worried Jews was: What makes Ahmed suddenly run wild? And, more important: How can we stop him?

Just a few years earlier, the frantic questions would not even have been raised. A fascinating example of the almost unbelievable Israeli delusion is to be found in an article written by Edwin Samuel in the May 1955 issue of the then prestigious *Commentary* magazine. Samuel, son of Viscount Herbert Samuel, the first British high commissioner for Palestine, wrote as an Israeli citizen and expert on Arab affairs. What did an Israeli expert write in those halcyon days when, like all good Arabs, the Israeli ones were seen, here and there, but seldom heard?

"With an overwhelming Jewish majority, it is extremely doubtful whether a separate Arab culture can be maintained. It seems more than probable—even if the Arab population reaches

250,000 [*sic*]—that it will become rapidly assimilated to the prevailing Jewish culture. . . . In Israel the Arab has little chance of maintaining his identity."

It seems incredible that Israelis once really believed that.

By 1967 it was clear that the Arab was not going to fade away, but he was still not a "problem" to the average Israeli. Nor, for that matter, was he a problem to the "nonaverage" one, the intellectual who always has so much to say on subjects whether they are within his field of expertise or not. Not only was the myth of the quiescent Arab still prevalent, but Israelis were certain that Ishmael was content.

A few months after the Six-Day War, *Midstream* magazine, a house organ for the Jewish Agency in New York, carried a symposium on "Prospects for Peace." Among the participants was Professor Ephraim Urbach, Talmudic researcher and arch-dove, once nominated by the National Religious Party to be its candidate for president of Israel. His comments prove that a candidate for the presidency of Israel can be just as obtuse as mere mortals. Said Urbach: "I am referring to the question of the Arabs in Israel—an area where we have already done a great deal. . . . What we have managed to accomplish for the Arab minority in terms of human rights and social, cultural, and economic conditions—what we have done has never been done before in the world. This has been a human and cultural enterprise of the first magnitude. Without any desire to assimilate this minority we have given it economic, social, and cultural conditions enabling it to prosper, conditions which the Arabs in neighboring lands still do not enjoy. . . . But for some reason this great human enterprise has been played down.

"Ultimately one has to admit that the Arabs in Israel have to a degree become reconciled to their situation."

Professor Urbach notwithstanding, the Arabs began to show disturbing evidence of nonreconciliation. By 1971 there was a troublesome rise in the number of Israeli Arabs who were found to be participating in terrorist groups and in terrorist activities. (Until the Six-Day War there had not been a single recorded instance of an Israeli Arab joining a terrorist group.) After a booby-trapped hand grenade exploded in Tel Aviv and the perpetrators were traced to the Israeli Arab village of Tira, Israelis grew upset. "Not to worry," said Shmuel Toledano.

Toledano was the expert's expert on Arabs, having served since 1966 as adviser to the prime minister on Arab affairs (he remained in that capacity until 1977). His job was to chart Arab policy. The following is from a brief biography (1974): "This period (from 1966) is considered to be a period of liberalization. . . . During this period, military rule [for Arab areas] as well as closed areas have been abolished. Free and untrammeled movements have been given to all Arab citizens. Land restrictions have been set aside. Large sums of money have been invested in the development of Arab and Druze villages. The Arabs of Israel have reached an impressive standard of living. . . ."

Toledano was the man who for more than a decade became the symbol of Israel's "goodwill, head-and-stomach" policy toward the Arabs. Under him the state exuded untold amounts of goodwill, devoted itself to feeding Arab stomachs and educating Arab heads, and raised high the magic banner of integration. Yet, to everyone's dismay, the fuller the stomach and head, the fatter the pocket, and the greater the Israeli goodwill, the more "difficult" the once quiet and "reconciled" Arabs became.

Not to worry, repeated Toledano. "If we will treat the Arabs fairly we will keep them from the frustrations that occasionally lead to extremism" (*Yediot Aharanot*, December 3, 1971).

And as Arab frustration led, despite everything else, to more discontent and "radicalization," Toledano wrote: "They [the young Arabs] are a perplexed national minority struggling to find their way in a very complicated situation. Sometimes, when the tension as to where he belongs is overwhelming, the young Arab feels he is torn in two" (*The Israeli Arabs*, 1974).

And the solution? Toledano concluded: "Israeli society must weaken the barriers [between Jews and Arabs], increase socio-economic intermingling, and create a mutual sense of respect" (ibid.). What Toledano was saying was that the policy of "goodwill, head-and-stomach" has not failed. We simply have not given the Arabs enough of it.

Other head-and-stomach experts pushed Toledano's myth of the "torn Arab." Thus, Dr. Yitzhak Ben Gad, Israeli columnist for the Philadelphia Jewish establishment weekly *Exponent*, wrote (December 26, 1975): "The overwhelming majority of Israel's Arab population has altered its standard of living beyond recognition. A traditionally closed Arab society has been transformed, through mechanization and technology, into a modern and developed one. As equal citizens in a democratic society, Israeli Arabs share with their Jewish compatriots the progress and benefits of Israel's economy. . . . On the one hand they are active and loyal citizens to their state of domicile— Israel. On the other hand, they cannot disavow their neighboring Arab brethren. . . . This conflict of *dual loyalty* is the greatest problem of Israeli Palestinians. . . . Only peace can normalize the situation of Israel's Arab citizen, when they can proudly affirm that they are Israeli and Arabs, both, without contradiction."

Of course this is nonsense, and the only frustration the young Arab feels is his inability to change "Israel" into "Palestine." There is no conflict of dual *loyalty*, only one of dual *authority*. On the one hand there is the Arab Palestinian authority to which he would willingly submit. On the other, there is the hated Jewish one he cannot—at present—escape. It is, however, more comfortable to think that the Arab attitude is not one of hate but of confusion. But if the latter exists, it is *not* within the *Arab* camp.

This brand of foolishness continued to be the typical, standard fare for Israelis. The Arab was equal; the Arab lived better than he had ever dreamed he could; the Arab was a loyal citizen —with a few problems, none of which could not be solved by the eternal materialistic solution: *more.*

The Israeli Foreign Ministry issued a pamphlet in October 1973 entitled *Minorities in Israel:*

Again the myth of equality: "The principle of equal rights for the Arabs of Israel has always been integral to the Zionist philosophy. . . . Israel's Proclamation of Independence (14 May 1948) affirms the principle. . . ."

Again the "head-and-stomach" irrelevancy: "The perplexed and impotent Arab of 1948 is gone. Today, a prideful, loyal Israeli Arab assesses his future soberly. The *fellahin* ["peasant farmers"] have become farmers versed in the most modern methods. . . . It is a magical metamorphosis. . . . The educated young generation are unrecognizably unlike their parents. . . . The roll of minority academics is steadily lengthening. . . ."

Again the myth of "confusion": "In the political con-

juncture of the Middle East, they often face a 'loyalty crisis.'
Does civic loyalty to Israel clash with their national conscious-
ness?"

Above all, *again the destructive myth:* "All the same, there is a
gradualness of integration, and year by year the tempo quickens
a little. The socioeconomic gap narrows all the time. Reciproci-
ty of suspicion is disappearing. The omens are not in-
auspicious."

This is the Israeli Establishment's version of the opiate of
the masses. Is it, perhaps, those Israeli materialists whose own
reflexes are so conditioned by material benefits who thus assume
that the Israeli Arab marches on his stomach?

And so, as late as November 15, 1974, Education Minister
Aharon Yadlin could tell a group of Israeli Arabs: "The State of
Israel expects its Arab citizens to be ambassadors of peace be-
tween Israel and her neighbors. . . . Israel is the example of how
Jews, Muslims, and Christians can live together in mutual re-
spect."

And then came Land Day and what should have been
perceived as the bursting of the ballooning myth. But no. With
every fiber of the state crying out the bitter failure and
bankruptcy of Israeli policy vis-à-vis its Arabs, Toledano, on
April 9, 1976, analyzed the problem for the *Jerusalem Post,*
saying: "There is no alternative to a policy of more far-going
integration of the Arab minority into Israel. . . . It means prima-
rily the opening of the dominant Jewish Israeli society, economy
and policy to Arabs who wish to integrate and lead full and
fulfilling lives in Israel."

The government, of course, agreed, a "senior cabinet
minister" telling the press (April 5, 1976) that "government policy toward Israel's Arab community requires no revision." He
insisted that "everyone recognized the need for speedier im-
plementation of programs to give the Arab citizen a wider role in
the life of the state. Educated Arab citizens have to be integrated
into the national endeavor."

And indeed, on May 23, 1976, the cabinet set up a
ministerial committee to study and implement proposals introduced by Toledano and super-dove Moshe Kol, minister of tourism. The proposals called for solving the Israeli Arab ferment by
"stepped-up integration of especially young intellectuals in em-

ployment, education, governmental and public services, and other facets of Israeli life." Kol also called for the establishment of a public council "for the fostering of Arab-Jewish relations."

Reaction by the "head-and-stomach" people was, predictably, favorable. Since it is simpler to feel that Arabs who throw firebombs at soldiers and shout "The Galilee is Arab" do so out of "frustration" over lack of integration rather than because they are Arabs and the state is *Jewish,* the simpletons and simplistic ones approved. Thus, the *Jerusalem Post* editorialized: "Israelis may quiver with rage at the inroads 'Fatah' slogans have made into the minds of many young Israeli Arabs, but it must be admitted that part of the fault lies in Israel's failure to provide suitable alternative channels of expression to his new force. . . .

"The key word that has been bruited about since the dramatic occurrences of March 30, is *integration.* . . . It is essential that the dominant Jewish society, economy and policy be opened to welcome Arab Israelis who seek fuller personal and communal integration into Israel."

It is interesting to note the difference between deluded Jewish reaction and that of even a "moderate" Israeli Arab. Mahmoud Abassi, Arab adviser to the Ministry of Education, is clearly a moderate, cautious Establishment Arab. He is a "good" Arab and his job guarantees this. He also approved the May 23, 1976 proposals but added a most pertinent comment to the Jewish Telegraphic Agency: "We want to be treated as equals *just as you expect Jews in the Diaspora to be treated as equals."*

Before the knee-jerk, reflexive approval, consider very carefully what Abassi said: He wants equality *of the kind Jews have in the Diaspora,* say, Canada or the United States. But the United States is not a state founded by and for a particular national or religious group. The United States was not founded as the home of the Swedes or Germans or Italians. It was certainly not founded as the sovereign state of a particular *religion.* Canada does not have a Declaration of Independence declaring it a Christian country or that the Anglo-Saxons have a right to "*their state."* The United States does not have a "Law of Return" granting automatic entry and citizenship to one people and not to others. In theory it makes no difference if Jews, Catholics, Protestants, Bulgarians, or Greeks are the majority in the United States, since all are *Americans.*

But Israel nourishes itself, not from its "Israeliness' but from its *Jewishness*. Its very right to exist is based on that Jewishness. It was because of the Jewish people's ancient claim to the land that the existence of a majority of Arabs was rightly termed irrelevant. It was because of a Jewish claim that Lord Balfour and the British government issued the proclamation supporting a Jewish national home in Palestine. It is because of its *Jewishness* that world Jewry supports Israel. How much money would world Jewry give to a United Appeal that raised money for an "Israel" whose Arab population was the majority and whose entire identity had changed overnight?

Of course Israeli Arabs were demanding "integration." Of course they wanted "more." Of course they wanted social and economic benefits. But not because that would satisfy them, not because that was *all* they wanted. They wanted to be *exactly* like the Jews, *including having the right to create an Arab "Zionist" state when they become a majority*, just as the Jews imposed their Zionism on them.

But how does one get through the head of a Teddy Kollek that his demand for water, electricity, and phone service for the Arabs of East Jerusalem may win him Arab votes but is irrelevant to the fact that they mock and hiss at his pathetic insistence that Jerusalem is "one unified city"? How does one persuade Kollek that his plan to "satisfy" the Arabs of Jerusalem by establishing a system of "boroughs" that will give them autonomy will only whet their appetite for full independence, jeopardize Jewish tourists in the "autonomous" areas of Jerusalem, and convince the Arabs of Jewish weakness?

To understand fully the mind of Teddy Kollek and his compatriots, one must consider an "event" that Kollek conceived of and carried out in April 1980. Fully aware of the emptiness of his "one Jerusalem" claim, Kollek, in conjunction with the American Jewish Congress, conceived of a "conference" of mayors from multi-ethnic American cities. Clearly, Kollek wished to tell the world: We have invited the mayors of Chicago, Pittsburgh, Cincinnati, and other cities to Jerusalem, *because we all have a common problem*. We all have people of different backgrounds and there is always a certain amount of friction. But just as Pittsburgh and Chicago solve their ethnic problems, so can Jerusalem, because our problems are similar.

The deception is so palpable that even former Deputy Mayor Miron Benvenisti was forced to demur. Benvenisti wrote: "The conference sponsors overlooked one little thing. The basis for their discussions was absolutely invalid. There is no comparison at all between Jerusalem's problems and those of American mixed cities. The minority leaders in America do not deny the legitimacy of the government and refuse to participate in its operations. To the contrary, they fight to integrate into the ruling apparatus . . . they seek a bigger slice of the American national cake. . . . The communal tension in Jerusalem stems from the fact that the Arab minority does not recognize the legitimacy of the government that was imposed on it. . . . While the minorities in U.S. cities seek 'good government,' the Arab minority seeks 'self-government'" (*Kol HaIr,* April 25, 1980).

It would be comforting to think that the nonsense is limited to the L.L.L. (Labor, Left, Liberal) of Israel. Alas, Begin, the Likud, (a block of political parties in alignment with Begin), and the "nationalists" all share, to varying degrees, "the Myth." Thus, despite riots, demonstrations, clashes, Land Days, polls that show Israeli Arabs denying the legitimacy of Israel, university students openly supporting the PLO on campus, and the election of a mayor of Nazareth who backs the PLO, Mr. Begin's new adviser on Arab affairs, Binyamin Gur-Arye, could calmly declare (April 25, 1980): "All the talk about radicalization of Israeli Arabs in their relation to the State of Israel is baseless."

Mr. Begin's old adviser on Arab affairs, Moshe Sharon, in an interview with *Maariv* (February 2, 1979), told the following anecdote to illustrate the prime minister's view of solving the problem: "Mr. Begin, as I told you, is a liberal. I often heard him chastise a minister: 'What?'! Your ministry discriminates against Israeli Arabs?!'"

Moshe Sharon himself is a classic example of the frustrations that make strong men weep and throw up their hands in despair. In the same interview he made the following explosive points: "A young Arab, intellectual and law-abiding, told me openly: 'When an Egyptian MIG is shot down, no Israeli Arab rejoices. When an Israeli Phantom falls—no Arab is sad.' That, to put it mildly, describes the hostile attitude of Israeli Arabs to the state."

And again: "The Arab is tied intimately to the Arab world
that surrounds him—in language, culture, religion, family, nation, and politics. Does this minority identify with Israel?
Absolutely not! And we dare not expect him to."

Finally. Finally, one hears plain, honest truth. Finally, one
expects to hear plain, honest solutions. Sharon continues:
"Once and for all we must begin a serious, deep, and ongoing
approach to solving the cardinal problems of the Israeli Arabs."
Dare we hope?

"The objective is to educate an Arab citizen who is law-
abiding, proud of his culture, and able to be absorbed into Israeli society. We must teach the Arab youngster more Hebrew
so as to be absorbed into a position. We must develop in
him a positive attitude toward creative work. . . ."

One hardly knows whether to laugh or to cry.

There is hardly any difference between Labor and Likud.
Begin's new deputy prime minister, Simha Erlich, set off on January 4, 1980, to meet the Arabs of the Jewish state. In Nazareth,
heart of the Arab Rakah (Communist Party) and PLO forces in
Israel, he told his audience: "I promise you that the government
sees in you a dear, loyal, and important community for the State
of Israel." He proved this at a symposium in Tel Aviv on March
20, 1980, on the subject of the "developing Arab village," proudly boasting: "Within one and a half years all the Arab villages
in Israel will be connected to the electric grid."

Perhaps the most depressing statement of all was the one
made by the chairman of the Knesset Foreign Affairs and Defense Committee, Moshe Arens, a staunch member of Begin's
Herut Party, who told a seminar (June 5, 1980) of his views on
Jewish-Arab coexistence. "We must," he said, "develop a prop-
erly pluralistic society where Jew and Arab *are equal in every respect,* including career opportunities. Life in Israel's democracy
should be made sufficiently attractive to deter the Arabs from
wanting to secede." It seemed that the madness of blindness had
struck down even one of the brighter Israeli figures. Labor,
Likud; there is little difference.

If whom G-d would destroy He first makes mad, the
Almighty must be exceedingly angry with His people. The frantic and frenetic search for a "solution" to a problem that is indeed a cancer in our body politic leads to suggestions and com-

ments that future generations will surely marvel at with a mixture of total astonishment and uncontrollable laughter.

● President Yitzhak Navon is upset over the serious Arab agitation in the Galilee. He is aware of the fact that from the Jewish standpoint there is a desperate need to settle Jews in that strategic northern region, where they are already a minority. This has led to a government program to "Judaize the Galilee." On September 13, 1978, while on a visit there, he noted that the phrase is offensive to the Arabs. "It is preferable," he said, "to use the term 'Jewish settlement of the Galilee.' It is more correct and also politically better." Of course. It is obvious that *that* will soothe the Arabs and prevent future Land Days in the Galilee . . . .

● Then Foreign Minister Yigral Allon was wont to hold an annual "Spring Jewish-Arab Gathering" at which—in the manner of some British colonial raja or pukka—he would speak to the assembled. On May 26, 1976, Allon said: "History decreed that Jews and Arabs should forever live side by side . . . always, within the independent State of Israel itself, there will be Jews, Muslims, Druzes, and Christians, *living together as citizens with equal rights. . . .*

"I believe that, in the future as in the past, *the Jewish majority and the Arab minority* will be able to live in understanding, cooperation, and mutual respect in the State of Israel, which arose to solve the national problem of the Jewish people. . . .

"To the extent that misunderstandings arise, it is necessary, and possible, to resolve them peacefully, in a spirit of understanding and goodwill, *without deviating from the progressive democratic laws which prevail in our country.*"

It is almost beyond comprehension that a foreign minister could have made such statements. One is faced with an agonizing choice: either he sincerely meant what he said and thus was both incompetent and bewildered, or he understood the nonsense he was saying and his contempt for Arab intelligence was profound.

"*The Jewish majority and the Arab minority* will be able to live in understanding. . . ." Note the assumption: that there will always be a *Jewish* majority in the state that arose to solve the *Jewish* "national problem." And what if through the peaceful cooperation, mutual respect, and understanding that Allon

called for the Arabs quietly and with many babies become the
majority in "the state which arose to solve the Jewish national
problem"? Would Israel then deviate from its "progressive democratic laws"? Would Mr. Allon then have advised the now *Jewish* minority to adopt the same acceptance of *their* status that he
so eloquently preached to his Arab minority?

Either the foreign minister of Israel was hopelessly confused
or a practitioner of deception. There is no guarantee of a Jewish
majority in a democracy—especially with a prolific Arab minority. Was Allon prepared to accept minority status graciously
and come each year to the home of the *Arab* foreign minister of
the new State of Palestine?

●   As the Arabs of Israel move steadily toward "radicalization" (an absurd term that attempts to deform their long-
suppressed natural feelings), we keep hearing more and more
pained Jewish reactions. The pain is always based on the premise that if only there would be goodwill, understanding, and
mutual trust, all would be well (and Jews could continue to enjoy the fruits of majority rule over the Arabs in safety). One of
the most dangerous Jewish offenders in this connection is the
Jerusalem Post, proponent of a confused and—from the Arab's
point of view—absurd policy that is neither meat nor milk, fish
nor fowl. In one of its rather typical editorials, the *Post* professed
"pained surprise" over the January 1979 declaration of support
for the PLO by the heads of the Arab councils in Israel. Since
that body was touted, for years, by *Post* men and those who think
like them as the "moderate leadership of the Arab community,"
the editorial (January 23, 1979) stated that such a statement
could only undo "the rudiments of mutual trust that have been
built up so painstakingly over the years by men and women of
goodwill in both communities. . . . What is needed on the Arab
side is a return to sanity by the upcoming generation of its central leadership."

The *Post* and those it represents can never, of course, believe
that to the average Arab, statements of support for the PLO are
the height of sanity. They will eternally refuse to believe that
"goodwill" is nonsense when the Arab believes that he, who was
once the majority in the land and is now a minority in a Jewish
state, has been robbed. The *Post* men and their Hebrew counterparts in Israel cannot believe this because to do so is to admit

that the very basis for their beliefs of a lifetime is a sham.

● Shimon Peres, leader of the Labor Party, is also, of course, a "goodwill, head-and-stomach" man, but he differs with the supporters of total integration. "We have failed, for twenty-eight years"—this in an interview with *Maariv*, March 26, 1976—"in regard to our Arab minority." And his prescription for Arab contentment and acceptance of Israel? *Separate* Arab development. Encourage and aid them to set up their own political parties. "Because we did not encourage them in this, they were forced to find expression in hostile political parties."

Ah, *that* is the source of the problem. Not Zionism, not the fact that the Arab feels nothing but hatred for the state that took away "his" land and made his people a minority in a foreign Jewish state. All we need do is allow him to establish his own *framework.* Question: Who prevented him from doing so all these years? Question: Will this separate party be *less* hostile to Israel than the present "hostile" parties to which he has gravitated? Question: How does separate existence breed love for the Jew? Will not a separate Arab party be based logically on a demand for separate existence and separation from Israel? Answer: Peres has not the slightest idea. His is one other side of the Israeli Coin of Confusion.

● The Peres idea was the subject of two articles in the *Jerusalem Post,* which merely proved the inflationary character of the Coin. Said Moshe Ater, Labor Party member, (July 12, 1976): "A precondition to peaceful cooperation between Jews and Arabs is . . . *deliberate segregation,* confining joint activity to essentials of mutual benefit."

But it was the second article by one Melvin Moguloff that surely is a candidate for the most fascinating political psychology article in many a day. Moguloff, described as a "social planner at one of the country's major public agencies," in an April 9, 1978, article, called for *separate but very equal* facilities. Economic and social conditions are the key for Moguloff, as befits a social welfare planner. Therefore, *if* we make sure that the Arab stomach is full and his head filled exactly like those of the Jews, it will be good. But, if not, "a large and articulate Arab community, in a democratic state, could not long accept second-class economic status."

What makes the Moguloff article fascinating, in a hideous

way, is the ending: *"Current government policies, if successful, seem likely to lead to the Arab community becoming the majority in Israel* [italics added]. Thus, an aggressive concern for equity between Arabs and Jews might be seen as insurance against the time when the Jews no longer enjoy majority status in Israel."

Three facts stand out as we read these lines—for perhaps the tenth time to be certain they really say what they do. One is the coolness and calm detachment with which the possibility— nay, probability—of the end of the Jewish state is discussed. Second is the numbing postulate that we should be careful to treat the Arabs well in the hope that when they become masters here they will reciprocate.

The third is the hideous part: How many other Jews in Israel, consciously or subconsciously, consider the ultimate end of the Jewish state and an Arab majority very likely and proba- ble? How many who contemplate that likelihood with calm fa- talism and dispassion would take to the barricades to prevent any effort to preserve the Jewish state by removal of the Arabs? How many would allow Zionism and the Jewish state to be sac- rificed on the altar of democracy?

For more than three decades, Jews in Israel, led by the "shepherds who do feed themselves," have lived with delusions, fed by fear and a sense of hopelessness. And so they put their faith in the myth. It took the Arabs to give the cleverest answer to it.

On July 4, 1974, Shmuel Toledano warned of problems ahead, "unless the Arab minority is totally accepted by the Jew- ish majority as an integral part of the state."

Three days later, in a most ungracious response to the benevolent Toledano, the Lebanese newspaper *Al Muhrar* re- jected the Israeli liberal's largess. The gist of the article, titled "Not by Bread Alone Does Man Live," was: Even if there were an opportunity to integrate the Arabs into Israeli society, this would not solve the problem, *since man does not live by bread alone.* He has other needs, and among them is *to live in honor in his own homeland.*

Of course, the Arabs are correct.

British colonialists used to scratch their heads in puzzle- ment over "native" rebellions. "What do they want?" used to be the Whitehall plaint. "When we came we found a jungle. They ate each other; they fought each other; they died young; they were poverty-stricken. We found a jungle and turned it into civilization." Of course, the reply of the "natives" was: "Yes, but it was *our* jungle, and now it is *your* civilization."

One would have hoped that Prime Minister Rabin, as he mounted the rostrum on that June day in 1976 to give his views on the Israeli Arab problem, understood that the heart of the Jewish-Arab problem in Israel is the same as that of the dispute between Israel and the Arab states. All Arabs, including those in Israel, believe that the Jews are thieves, robbers who came to an Arab Middle East and stole a part of it. It does little good to bemoan the fact that the Arab will not "compromise" or accept the arguments given by Jews (the bad as well as the very good). He is not interested in a British promise to Jews as embodied in the Balfour Declaration ("Who were the British to promise 'our' land?"); he is not moved by tales of Jewish suffering under the Germans or other Europeans ("Let them compensate Jews by giving them part of their countries"); and he is not even swayed by the oft-heard boast that the Jews turned a desert into a garden ("Yes, but it was *our* desert, and now it is *your* garden").

Even to begin to believe, in our time, that it is possible for two large nations to occupy the same land in peaceful coexistence when they differ in every possible aspect is an illusion of the first magnitude. When you add the fact that the present minority was once a majority, the hopelessness of the situation becomes even more apparent. And when the minority knows that it has massive support from brother Arab states with potential and power to "free" it; and when it sees a vast majority of the nations of the world supporting its cause; and when it knows that all but one of the superpowers are sympathetic and that the one supposed ally of Israel is slowly but surely moving to pressure and to weaken her fatally; when the knowledge that a "Palestine" will sooner or later exist alongside the Israel that the minority is struggling against, the hope of "liberation" becomes more and more a certainty in the breast of that minority.

The Declaration of Independence of Israel is not relevant to the Arabs of the Jewish state. Let the Jews have their declaration, they say; give us our independence.

CHAPTER 4

Israeli Arabs: Fathers and Sons (and Daughters)

January 28, 1980. Wise Auditorium at the Hebrew University in Jerusalem. Some fifty-five years after its founding, with emotional speeches and a deep sense of Jewish historical import, the first Jewish university in the Land of Israel, and the largest, watches as its students gather for a "cultural event." The hall is packed to overflowing with more than 600 students who are on their feet, singing the anthem. The auditorium fairly shakes as the loud, proud voices sing:

> *In the name of freedom, we shall give our lives,*
> *Arab Palestine is the land of our struggle*
> *We will accomplish the impossible . . . .*
> *We have seen the path from the Negev to the Galilee*
> *Our front will be triumphant.*

The "anthem." No, not *"Hatikva."* The anthem. Of *Fatah,* the guerrilla arm of the Palestine Liberation Organization.

The students of Hebrew University sit. On the stage a pantomime is being performed. A soldier—an Israeli—is torturing "Palestinians." Suddenly, three figures, faces covered by red *kafias,* leap upon him. As he lies on the stage, prostrate, hands outstretched, the three heroes strangle and stab him to death. As the pantomime reaches a climax, the students of Hebrew University are on their feet, cheering and applauding wildly.

The cultural evening ends with the moderator thanking the Popular Front for the Liberation of Palestine for its contribution of IL 10,000. . . .

The place is Hebrew University and the students do indeed

75

study there, most with generous scholarships. But they are Arabs—Israeli Arabs, and the vast majority are citizens of the state. They are studying to be attorneys and physicians and engineers and professors. But mostly they are studying to be the future leaders of the PLO and the "revolution." And, of course, they owe their education to the generosity and liberality of the Jews of Israel and the world.

On June 20, 1976, Prime Minister Yitzhak Rabin stood before his colleagues, members of the Labor Party, and spoke concerning the problems and future of the Arabs of Israel. In his hands he held papers—statistics—detailing the immense "progress" made by the Arabs of Israel since 1948. Among the figures that Rabin threw out to prove his contention of Arab advancement were those that dealt with education: In 1948, only 32.5 percent of Israeli Arab children were attending schools. Now the figure was 92 percent, compared with 60 percent in Jordan; 40 percent in Egypt, Iraq, and Libya; 20 percent in Algeria; and 15 percent in Yemen. Whereas the number of Jewish students had risen sixfold since 1948, the number of Arabs now studying in state schools had jumped *twelvefold.* More than 1,500 were now studying in Israeli universities (and several hundred were studying outside the country). In 1948 there were only 300 Arab teachers; in 1976, said Rabin, there were more than 5,000. Thanks to Israeli generosity, there were 241 kindergartens, 295 primary schools, 28 intermediate schools, and 80 high schools for Arab children.

In Premier Rabin's self-satisfaction one sees the bitter reality of Israeli self-delusion. Was Rabin seriously telling Jews that educational advancement would satisfy the Arabs and make them more sympathetic to the Jewish state? More to the point: *Did the prime minister of Israel not understand that it was precisely the educated Arabs of Israel who would be the most extreme, the most dangerous, the future leaders of the nationalistic revolution?* Did he not comprehend the tragic irony in the fact that the Israeli government and Jewish money were creating the Arab intellectual who would lead the revolt against Israel? The self-evident truth is that the figures that show the growth of Arab education are far greater cause for Jewish mourning than joy.

The *Jerusalem Post* (February 26, 1979) interviewed an Arab university graduate, a member of the PLO-supporting Abna-el-balad group in the West Galilee village of Kabul. He is the perfect example of the product that Israel's "head-and-stomach" policy makers helped to produce. Rabin and Begin would surely point with pride to the young Israeli Arab, a graduate of Haifa's Ironi Aleph High School (the only Jewish-Arab high school in the land), as well as of Haifa University's Department of Middle East History. Says this well-educated Israeli Arab: "A Palestinian state in the West Bank will not solve my problems. . . . The PLO is the only body that fights for me. . . . I do not feel this is my country. I don't care if I have more materially here than Arabs elsewhere. *I am willing to be poor if it is my country. . . .*

"I don't know where a Palestinian state should be, *but . . . of course I hope it will include my village."*

Let it be noted that his village is in the Galilee.

On Israeli campuses, Jewish students wear T-shirts that read "UCLA" or "Boston Celtics." But in May 1980 a group of Arab students took off their shirts to reveal their own brand of T-shirt which read: "The PLO represents us." That is the fundamental belief of all the Israeli Arab students, and if there are Jews who are shocked it is merely because of their own refusal to see.

The Arab students and intellectuals are the representatives of a new generation of Israeli Arabs, *one that rejects that very description.* In a Jewish Telegraphic Agency (JTA) article (May 5, 1977) Gil Sedan wrote: "Nor do they trouble to conceal their increasingly negative attitude toward the government of Israel, the country of which they are citizens. In the Arab village of Kfar Kana, just north of Nazareth, this reporter asked a young shopkeeper if he was Muslim or Christian. 'We are all Arabs,' was his reply."

A perceptive article in *Maariv* was titled: "From Israeli Arabs to Palestinians." That is the nub of the issue. These people now consider themselves Palestinian Arabs who, through tragedy, happen to live in Israel. It is not a situation they are happy with, and many are trying to change it.

The pity is that for years, the leaders of Israel (and, of course, the American Jewish Establishment) pointed to Israeli Arab passivity and acquiescence as proof of their loyalty to, and acceptance of, the Jewish state. Either they were fools or preferred to act as such. The real reason for Israeli Arab passivity lay in the very natural results of the events of history.

With the approval in 1947 by the United Nations of the Partition Plan, creating separate Jewish and Arab states in "Palestine," the Arabs, both within the land and without, prepared for what an Arab League official called "a momentous massacre which will be spoken of like the Mongolian massacres and Crusades." With British troops leaving, the Arabs were confident that they would decimate the Jews and establish Arab rule over the entire country. But while Allah proposed, the G-d of the Jews disposed, and the outcome of the fighting was quite different.

The Arab armies were thrown back, and not only did the State of Israel come into being, but an incredible panic swept the Arabs in the country, causing hundreds of thousands to flee. As the dust settled, entire formerly Arab villages and cities and regions stood empty of inhabitants and were now part of the new Jewish state. That which the Arabs could have had, were they prepared to accept the UN plan, was now lost to them. Instead of a tiny, grotesque Jewish state—in three sections, joined by two narrow checkpoints and with an Arab population constituting 40 percent of its citizens—there was now a much larger and more stable Israel with only 150,000 shell-shocked Arabs as its citizens.

But it was not only the quantitative loss that was so brutal. It was more than just the shock of being transformed from a majority into a minority. *The few Arabs of Israel who were left were now a people without leadership.*

The panicky mass exodus had seen the disappearance of the higher social classes. To quote a report by Uri Standel, issued by the prime minister's office: "The wealthy Arab landlords and rich merchants, the religious dignitaries, lawyers, doctors, engineers, writers, and journalists were the first to take flight, depriving the population of all centers of initiative."

The Arabs who were left were for the most part *fellahin,* feudal peasants, ignorant and illiterate. The last thing in the world they wanted was a political struggle. Knowing what they would have done to the Jews had the Arabs won the war (the rape of Jewish women and the severed sexual organs stuffed into murdered Jews' mouths were not isolated incidents in the riots of the twenties and thirties), they huddled fearfully, hoping just to live.

They did that, and more. From a group that faced unemployment in the cities, and famine and no source of credit in the villages, they evolved—with the help of the Israeli government—into the comfortable and self-assured Israeli Arab community of today (nearly 700,000 strong). But this took time, and for many years the Arab of Israel assumed a low profile. He was ignorant—he wished only to make a living. Not that he loved the Jews or their state. Hardly. It was rather that he was traumatized by defeat, a simple person without leadership, living (until 1966) under military rule that prevented him from freely moving about. Most importantly, he was part of the rural, feudal family structure known as the *hamulla*.

Until recently—and it is still a powerful factor in many villages—the Arab knew little individualism. Essentially rural, he belonged to a basic social village unit, known as *ahal* or *dar,* that can best be explained as "the extended family." This included the father, mother, all unmarried daughters, and all the sons with their wives and children. They all lived in the same village, in adjacent houses and sometimes under the same roof. Since the father owned the land that his children cultivated, he had complete control over them. They would hand over their earnings, and he supplied their wants.

The second factor that went into the de-individualizing of the Israeli Arab was the fact that even beyond the immediate "extended family," the Arab village was part of a structure based on kinship ties. Related families often lived in the same neighborhood and shared common economic and social problems. The heads of the *humullas* were its oldest members, their authority determined by their wealth and immediate family size. These elderly *humulla* heads held well-nigh dictatorial powers over the members of their clans. They determined who would receive land and who would progress up the socioeconomic ladder. And because, in the first years of the state, these patriarchs ruled the lives of their people, there reigned an illusory acceptance of Israel by its Arab citizens.

The truth is that the Jewish government understood from the first the venality and corruption of the old *humulla* patriarchs. They were conservative, suspicious people, interested only in their own welfare and position. For money and a promise of local power they were prepared to give the Jews what they

wanted: Knesset votes and submission. Of course, the old men
hated the Jews, but their guiding light was "What is good for
me?" They had little patience with and less understanding of
national aspirations, and, of course, any talk of social and economic reform was anathema to them.

The Israeli authorities in those years followed a two-
pronged policy: a military administration that severely restrict-
ed movement and unauthorized political activity, and, on the
other hand, a close working relationship with the old men of the
humullas. Large amounts of money went into patriarchal pockets,
and development funds were generously granted to "deserving"
villages. The Labor Party ingeniously created two Arab
"parties," both faithful *humulla*-led puppets, known as Progress
and Development and the List of Bedouins and Villagers. But all
Israeli parties tried their hand at buying Arab votes through the
venal old men. Thus, few found it odd that the Jewish National
Religious Party was able to garner votes in Arab villages. It was
hardly ideology but rather a clear indication of the real reason
for the apparent Arab "acceptance of" and "identification with"
the state of the Jews. It was *not loyalty to Israel but an "Uncle
Ahmed" mentality typical of early stages of minority submission.*

Of course, it had to end. The fraud of Israeli Arab acceptance of Israel was built on the fact of the feudal structure of the
Arab villages. But the days of that reactionary anachronism
were numbered, and ironically, it was the Israeli government
that, having the most to gain from its perpetuation, destroyed it.

There is nothing more menacing to entrenched, conservative feudalists than social and economic change, but that is
precisely what Israeli society and governmental policies brought
about in the villages. The very Arab educational revolutions of
which Israel boasts have destroyed the authority of the *humulla*
leaders by creating an educated, radical class that questions all
the social, political, and economic axioms upon which the ruling
patriarchs based their authority. It is not only that education
opened up windows to the world and allowed the young Arab to
see a vast spectrum of other social structures. It is not only that
education exposed young Arabs to radical, leftist, revolutionary
views that called for the overthrow of feudal privilege. It is
deeper than that.

Education—along with the fact that the young Arab was

Israeli-born and not a personal witness to the shattering trauma of defeat and fear of the Jews—led to a vicarious deep sense of shame and anger directed against the older generation of Arabs. The Arab who survived the 1948 debacle that permanently affected his thinking and drove him to collaborate with the Jews was now looked upon by his Israeli-born son as a traitor and boot-licking lackey. Born free, taking his citizenship and general rights for granted, educated, and open to radical ideas, he looked with contempt on his own father for kowtowing to the Israelis.

Thus, in February 1978, Israeli radio interviewer Edna Peer offered a live exchange between an Israeli Arab university student and his father. The son, a budding actor who told of having broken with his Jewish girl friend because she called Arafat a "murderer," was bitter toward his father. The latter is a quiet Arab, the kind of whom Israelis are fond. His local village's Histadrut (Israeli trade union) chairman, he is typically trotted out by all the Israelis who refuse to see the Arab reality. He is presented as "proof" of Arab loyalty. The son, knowing this and knowing, too, that his father's father was killed in Acre during the 1948 war, bitterly asked the father: "Do you know what I would have done if the Jews had murdered you the way your father was killed?" The son, not the father, is the representative of today's Israeli Arab. Every Arab school which Rabin and Begin and all the rest boast Israel has established will produce hundreds and thousands of such haters of Jews. The *hamulla* patriarch is an anachronism; the Israeli government saw him as a dam to stop the waters of Arab nationalism, but the dam has already burst. The Israelis might have gained twenty years had they attempted to preserve the Arab feudal structure. But since they chose to bring education and progress to the Arabs, they guaranteed the creation of an immediate generation of those dedicated to the active destruction of the Jewish state.

Of course, education is only part of the total revolution that has taken place in the Israeli Arab community. The Israeli government, which at first really believed that a well-fed Arab is a quiet, happy Arab, and which was also determined to show the world how liberal it was, consciously set about to raise the Arab standard of living. Two five-year plans, designed to develop the villages, succeeded in transforming the entire social, economic, and political structure of Arab life, at a cost of more than $50 million. Electricity was brought to almost every village, along with water and sewerage. New roads, houses, and clinics went up. Agriculture was revolutionized as the irrigated areas were expanded, especially in the villages of the Little Triangle along the Mekorot pipeline. New water sources were developed, old springs restored, and pipes laid to the individual villages.

Long-term loans and easy terms for agriculture were made available, and as a result mechanization developed rapidly. Tractors and combines replaced the old wooden plow and donkey and promoted the transition from subsistence to market crops. Israelis taught Arab farmers the latest methods of farming, diversification of crops, and land conservation. The Arab standard of living skyrocketed.

Easy credit and other government help saw a spectacular rise in new, spacious stone homes, equipped with modern sanitation, running water, gas cookers, refrigerators, and television sets. Close to 90 percent of all Arabs have electric lighting, and every village now is blessed with paved roads and easy access to the national highway system. Life was made better than the Arabs had ever dreamed, thanks to Jewish money and efforts. And the inevitable happened.

The rapid economic change that joined the educational advances brought about a *social revolution*. The difference between the young Arab and his parents is not measured in years but in *centuries*. The rural revolution sharply weakened the old feudal structure, as young Arabs were now able to apply for loans themselves and were no longer dependent on either fathers or *hamullas*. In addition, the sharp rise in living standards only brought forth rising expectations, whetting both the economic and political appetites, so that the young Israeli Arab stands like some modern-day Oliver Twist, facing his Jewish "benefactor" and demanding: *more!*

Israeli economic and educational advancement also led to a major social change—the rapid growth of the number of Arabs who daily leave their villages to work in Jewish towns and cities as well as the steady growth of an *urban* Arab population, with all the radicalism that this implies.

It is the town and city that produce unrest. Revolution,

Marx to the contrary, is not created by the rural numb and dumb. This is true in even advanced countries, and it is a hundred times truer in societies in which backward, conservative, feudal members of rural areas are suddenly thrown into the open, liberal, modern world of the city. When the Arab was exclusively an agricultural worker, he remained in his village. Mornings he awoke in his village; during the day he worked in his village; and as the sun set, he slept in his village. His world was circumscribed by it, his thoughts and actions molded by it and its *hamulla* heads. No agitator showed his head there for fear of losing it, and the ignorant Israeli Arab of 1948 had his wife (or wives), his children, his sheep, his field, his religion. Those, for him, were all that he needed, and he fully expected that his son would follow his life-style exactly, just as he had followed his father's, who had followed his father's.

But Israeli society could not be kept away. The growth of urban industry called for hands, laborers. The pay offered was far better than what might have been earned in the village, and gradually—and then not so gradually—the Arab began to leave each morning to work in Tel Aviv or Hadera or Haifa or Netanya. Today, well over 50 percent of Israel's Arabs work in towns—Jewish towns and cities. They see a different life-style, one that is quicker, more exciting. They see the stores and the clothing and the appliances. They see the women in short skirts and skimpy halters. The conflict between conservative and religious values and modern ones begins. The traditional value givers, the *hamulla* heads, are undermined. Moreover, as the opportunity for employment outside the villages grows, the power and authority of the father diminishes. This is true even when the son is not an intellectual but merely makes more money than his father, thanks to a job in the Jewish city. How much more so for the high school graduate, for the *university student,* whose dismay at his father's backwardness is reinforced by contempt for the corruption of the *hamulla* heads and deep shame at the readiness of the old generation to sell the national heritage for the pottage of Israeli lentils.

Today, under the impact of Israeli-induced modernization, there is a steady trend from the villages to the towns and cities. Probably some 40 percent of Israel's Arabs are now urban dwellers. Of course, in the cities the radicalization is even more rapid. In the cities there is no closed society, no ever-present father, no stifling *hamulla*. In the cities there are opportunities to meet Jewish girls, leftists, and intellectuals. In the cities one can see the Jewish world that runs Israel, the land to which the Arab is supposed to be loyal.

Israeli Arabs. Fathers and sons—and increasingly *daughters*. For the Israelis have liberated the Arab woman, too, in order that she may also vote for anti-Zionists and teach anti-Israel hatred. Thus, when the prime minister's office boasts that "the expansion of the educational system has helped to raise the standard of education of the younger generation of women" and "the fact that Arab women are coming into closer contact with the Jewish population is opening up new horizons," one gropes for an explanation for the smug satisfaction. The most that can be said for Israel's liberal policy is that it has created a new generation of Jew haters with due care to ensure that the source of the hate is equal, without discrimination because of sex.

To quote once again the young university graduate from the western Galilee village of Kabul who heads the PLO group Abna-el-balad: "We have very good young people in our village. The father no longer rules here. Now, each voter has his own ideas. We are trying to get rid of the *hamulla* lists. Ninety percent of the young people voted for us in the local elections. . . . My father wants to be left alone in peace and quiet."

The generation of the fathers, the Uncle Ahmeds, is dying, destroyed by the Israeli government's "head-and-stomach" policy. The father is dead; long live the son, and daughter, whom Israel created. They will do their best to destroy the Jewish state, and, of course, the Jewish state will continue to produce them. The very first generation of Israeli Arab university graduates immediately produced the El Ard anti-Israel movement in the early 1960s.

Indeed, even then there were those who saw and understood—and those who did, terrified by what they saw, put it out of mind. In *Midstream* magazine (December 1962) Nissim Rejwan, an Israeli writer, said: "One of the more alarming aspects of the Israeli problem is that the new generation of Israeli Arabs generally shows even less willingness, not to speak of eagerness, to accept the fact of Israel's existence than do their fathers and grandfathers. The so-called Arab *'intelligentsia'* in Israel, which

seems to embrace every literate person from university graduates to those who finished a few secondary classes, are in the
majority of cases swayed by the heady talk . . . about 'settling
scores with Israel.' *Many of them, it would appear, cannot reconcile
themselves to their status as a minority in a Jewish state and keep hoping
for some sort of savior."* Was anyone listening?

In the past ten to fifteen years, a professional, academically
trained stratum has arisen among Israel's Arabs. The rise of the
new Arab was a result of the bewildered and bewildering "policy" of an Israel that hopes to win Arab love through educational, social, and economic advancement.

What is the real result of the millions of dollars poured into
higher Arab education and the hundreds of millions spent on
secondary (high school) training? Consider: In December 1979
the Progressive National Movement (PNM) won the election for
control of the Arab Student Committee at Hebrew University.
In its platform the PNM called for:

● acceptance of the Palestinian Covenant (which calls for the
elimination of Israel)
● the creation of a "democratic, secular Palestine" in place of
Israel
● acceptance of terrorist activities as part of the Palestinian
struggle for self-determination

And, indeed, in 1979, students and visitors at the university
were startled to find mimeographed copies of the Palestinian
National Charter being distributed. Among other things in the
charter were Articles 19 and 20, which read: "The partition of
Palestine in 1947 and the establishment of the State of Israel are
entirely illegal. . . . Claims of historical or religious ties of Jews
with Palestine are incompatible with the facts of history. . . ."

The strenuous efforts of the leaders of the State of Israel
have produced a generation of Arab leaders and intellectuals
who are a source of everlasting irony: they are the products of
the Jewish state that they wish to dismantle in favor of an Arab
one.

And should one have any doubt, the immensely frank interview with Mahmud Muhareb should dispel all of them.
Muhareb, an Israeli Arab citizen of Lydda and at the time

chairman of the Arab Student Committee at Hebrew University, presented his views to *Maariv,* Israel's largest newspaper (January 20, 1978): "We, the Arab students in the university, constitute an indivisible part of the Palestinian Arab nation, and we struggle in its service and in order to achieve its goals.

"As for me and my personal lot, I am first and foremost a Palestinian, resident of Lydda. My Israeli citizenship was forced upon me. I do not recognize it and do not see myself as belonging to the State of Israel. The law requires me to carry an Israeli identity card and passport. As a Palestinian I would prefer Palestinian ones.

"With the final solution common to the Arabs of Palestine and Judea, Lydda will be in the sovereign boundaries of the democratic state. What will that state be called? Palestine, naturally. . . .

"We do not recognize the right which you call 'historic' of the Jewish people in this land—this is our fundamental principle. In this land only the Palestinian Arab people have the historic right."

Muhareb is a member of the PNM, one of the two major forces among Arab students in Israel. It is instructive that the other force, the "moderate" one, is Rakah, the Israeli Communist Party, which led the bloody Land Day riots against the government in 1976. But there is no essential difference between the ultimate hope of any Arab student in Israel: Arab sovereignty in every part of "Palestine" that is freed from the "conqueror."

There is nothing new or startling about this. The signs of Arab intellectual hatred of Israel and deep desire for its dismantlement were obvious to all who wished to see. The day the Egyptian army crossed the Suez Canal during the Yom Kippur War saw the surreptitious circulation of a flier that read: "With blood and spirit we shall liberate the Galilee." On the terrible night of the massacre of more than twenty Jewish high school students by Arab terrorists in the Galilee town of Ma'alot, in 1974, the nation mourned. But not all. The Arab students at Hebrew University held a noisy, joyous party in their Mount Scopus dormitories, built by funds from naive Western Jews who wanted to help the "Jewish state."

The next morning a Jewish student who had lost her brother during the "war of attrition" in 1970 complained bitterly to the dean of students. An investigation was begun and evidence gathered, but no disciplinary action was taken. The administration explained to the Jewish students that is primary role was to lessen tensions and preserve the delicate relationship between Arab and Jewish students. This declaration brought forth predictable results.

Within two weeks the Arab students were involved in yet another incident. Israel commemorates, annually, the terrible Holocaust that ripped away the lives of six million Jews. Known as the Day of the Holocaust and the Bravery, it was commemorated at Hebrew University by the lighting of memorial candles at the entrance of the dormitories. That night a band of Arab students smashed the glasses that held the candles. Even as an investigation was launched, the next week—Memorial Day for the fallen soldiers of Israel—saw similar desecrations of candles in their memory. Angry protests led to a decision by a university committee to suspend the students, but the university administration in a "gesture of goodwill" accepted the appeal against the "harshness" of the verdict and allowed the students to return to the benches of Israeli intellect. Not for nothing did the Arab students see in this retreat further proof of Jewish weakness. (It is pertinent to note that on Holocaust Day, 1980, more memorial candles were desecrated. One Arab student, Suliman Hasham, caught as he extinguished one of the lights, said: "There is enough light in the dormitories. We do not need candles.")

The pitiful weakness of the Hebrew University administration under President Avraham Harman inexorably led to greater brazenness on the part of the Arab students. During the latter part of 1974, terrorist activity reached a peak, and worried university officials met with the student organization to set up regular guard duty in the exposed dormitories. It was decided that all students who lived in the dormitories—including Arabs —would have to take a turn at guard duty. The Arab student organization immediately issued a statement that read: "No Arab student will participate in any activity aimed at a brother *fedayon* ["freedom fighter," the Arab term for the PLO terrorists], even if this refusal involves self-sacrifice—if this must be the price of the Palestinian revolution."

At a press conference called by the Arab students on De-

cember 1, 1975, three Arabs, Adel Mana'a, Riad Amin, and
Nabil Nahas, along with two of the apparently obligatory Jewish self-haters, appeared to explain their opposition. The Arabs
called the requirement "unjust because it involves a matter of
conscience." The conscience, of course, was their feeling that the
terrorists were fighting *their* battle and that it was a just one.
Meanwhile, two Arab students, fearing that they would be expelled from the dormitories, did agree to guard duty. On the
night of November 28, an attempt was made to set fire to their
room.

On December 23 some 200 Arabs and their radical leftist
Jewish friends from a group calling itself Campus gathered at
the university to protest. The banner they carried read: "We are
not ashamed to be Palestinians." The transformation from "Israelis" was becoming bolder.

A mass petition signed by Jewish students demanded that
the Arab students fulfill their obligations. At first the university
stood firm and agreed with the demand. Suddenly, however, it
announced that it had recognized "the crisis of conscience"
posed for the Arab student and agreed that those who could not
morally agree to do guard duty would be excused.

The victory led to similar demands for exemption at Haifa
University, where at least one-third of the students are Arabs. In
a struggle that saw threats on the life of the Jewish student in
charge of the guard-duty roster as well as two Arab students
from the villages of Isfiya and Deir Hanna charged with kidnap-
ping and threatening the life of a Bedouin student who was prepared to guard, the Haifa University administration agreed to
allow the Arabs to escape guard duty for a token monthly fee of
IL 30 (at the time less than five dollars).

The truth of the matter is that the Jewish demand to have
pro-PLO students do guard duty was in itself grotesque. What
emerged from this theater of the absurd was a Jewish university
allowing pro-PLO Arabs to study and enjoy scholastic benefits.
Jews demanded that the haters of Israel guard the Jews from
their own Arab brethren.

The combination of Israeli ghetto timidity and Arab
brazenness (one fed on the other) rapidly brought the campus,
for the first time, to violence. In the winter of 1975, the city of
Nazareth, hotbed of Arab nationalism, elected a Communist

mayor, Tewfik Zayad. Zayad, a bitter hater of Zionism and the Jewish state, became the focal point of a new upsurge of Arab nationalism. In particular he led the struggle against land expropriation (with full compensation) in the Galilee. That northern region of Israel, with an Arab population of more than 50 percent, posed a serious security threat to the Jewish state, and strenuous efforts were made to encourage Jewish settlement there. As mentioned earlier, the Arabs seized on the land issue to call for a general strike on Land Day, March 31, 1976, and in the resultant violence in which the Arab population of both the Galilee and the Little Triangle attacked police and soldiers with rocks and firebombs. Six Arabs were killed.

At Hebrew University, Arab students gathered on May 19, 1976, to commemorate the dead Arabs and to shout: "Down with the Occupation" and "The Galilee is Arab." An opposing Jewish group waved the national flag and sang Hebrew songs. Suddenly, from the Arab side, heavy stones began to fly. Witnesses later testified that the Arabs had parked a Cortina automobile, license number 755-982, nearby and removed sacks of stones which were thrown at the Jews. Four Jewish students were injured. One, Elhanan Blumenthal, was injured seriously and required a head operation.

The leader of the Jewish student body, Ariela Raudal, bitterly accused the university administration and President Harman of bowing to the Arabs. Raudal warned that the presence of 500 Arab students in the dormitories would lead to bloodshed and that the riot "was only the beginning."

And the Israeli government response to the clear threat from Arab educational advances?

In January 1976 the Ministry of Education released the findings of a fourteen-member team of Jewish and Arab "experts" on education, headed by leftist Mattatyahu Peled (who later became one of the spokesmen for Peace Now). The team called for reform of Arab education by basing it on the traditional and modern foundations of Arab culture, "stressing the particularity of the national character of Arab literature and history." There is, clearly, nothing more calculated to instill in the young Arab a greater sense of difference and feeling of injustice done to him than this program. And, of course, it would be done at Jewish expense.

Nevertheless, the Israeli government refused to bite the bullet. In reply to Arab Knesset member Zeidan Atshe's demand for an upgrading of the Arab schools, Education Ministry Director-General Eliezer Shmueli announced on September 27, 1978, that he had taken schooling in the Arab sector under his personal care. The ministry, despite budget problems, announced that it would spend an extra IL 20 million on Arab education.

Earlier, in June 1976, the first twenty-four Arab women graduates received their diplomas and licenses as Arab elementary school teachers from the David Yellin Hebrew Teachers College in Jerusalem. The program was sponsored and paid for by the Education Ministry, which was anything but lax in its diligent efforts to produce the educated and intellectual Arabs who would lead the struggle to do away with the David Yellin Hebrew Teachers College, the Israeli Education Ministry—and Israel.

Thus, Prime Minister Begin's adviser on Arab affairs, the Ministry of Education, and the Jewish Agency announced, in March 1978, that a new state-financed fund had been set up to award one hundred scholarships to outstanding Arab university students. Studies were being made, it was announced, to widen the scope of the fund to cover outstanding Israeli Arab *high school* students as well, if enough Jewish money could be found.

The most powerful weapon the PLO has in Israel is the education provided by Jews, with Jewish money, for the Israeli Arabs. The Jewish state trains teachers who, increasingly, either teach or turn a deaf ear to strident Arab nationalism. And how could it be different? In 1937 the British Palestine Royal Commission Report claimed that Arab teachers were turning government schools into "seminaries of Arab nationalism." A former Arab education official in Palestine wrote: "An Arab teacher could not, even with a severe stretch of the imagination, have been expected to foster loyalty to a government that, in his opinion, was daily undermining the national existence of his people" (A. L. Tibawi, *Arab Education in Mandatory Palestine*).

The very same words could be—and are—said by Arab teachers serving under the Jewish government of Israel. And they, actively and passively, train the new, educated, hostile, hating generation of the PLO.

In December 1979 *Maariv* carried an exposé of the growing open hostility toward the state manifested in Arab government schools. It quoted an official of the Education Ministry: "Political subjects are raised in class and teachers utter slogans that deny the very existence of the state. These are commonplace occurrences." The superintendents whose job it is to check and prevent such incidents are themselves, in many cases, in sympathy with the statements. Writes *Maariv:* "At a meeting of superintendents three years ago, one said: 'I am a Palestinian Arab and as such I will educate the children.'"

Among the incidents reported by *Maariv:*

● On a trip to Jericho by a school in Araba, the teacher shouted at two Bedouins serving in the Israeli army: "You should be ashamed of yourselves wearing those uniforms and serving in the army as the Jews rob you of your land."

● In Rama, on Yom Ha'atzmaut (Independence Day), a teacher told his class, "Those Arabs who celebrate the Jewish Independence Day are traitors to their homeland."

● On Independence Day, 1977, as the Israeli flag was being raised, one teacher in Sakhnin said: "This flag raising is in honor of the day of servitude and not of independence." The same day, in the village of Sha'ab, three teachers refused to rise for the flag raising and asked others to do likewise.

In general, the flag has become the symbolic target of Israeli Arab teachers and students alike. In Tayba, one teacher refuses to teach about the Israeli flag since "the two blue stripes are symbols of the occupation and the desire to expand to the Nile and Euphrates."

● On June 18, 1978, students in Turan ripped the flag to pieces. The principal admitted there had been similar incidents in the past and apologized for not reporting them. According to *Maariv:* "There have been cases of flag burning, the drawing of the PLO flag on blackboards, and hate-filled compositions. In none of these cases was there an adequate response by administration or faculty."

● In November 1978 Prime Minister Rabin visited Nazareth to speak to high school students. The Arab students asked him questions that in both content and tone shocked the country. Said *Maariv* in an editorial: "If anyone thought that the pro-

PLO sentiment was limited to the other side of 'the Green Line' [the territories], yesterday's meeting between Premier Rabin and Nazareth high school students should have brought him up short."

● In February 1978 four high school students from the villages of Tayba were accused of attempting to set fire to two buses and of painting anti-Zionist slogans. When they were taken to the village to reenact the deeds, hundreds of students stoned the police and prevented them from finishing their mission. When the mayor, Abdul Hamid Abu Ataya, appeared in court with scores of students, he threatened a general strike unless the students were released.

It is, thus, little wonder that in a survey of Arab high school students in June 1974, fully 84 percent stated that they favored the establishment of a Palestinian state. (Of the rest, almost all refused to venture an opinion). The high school students are the target of and greatly influenced by the Arab university students, and because most other careers are limited, the university graduates gravitate toward teaching, where they convey their bitter anti-Israel feelings. High school students are invited to the campus. In one interesting development, after the openly anti-Israel rally at Hebrew University's Wise Auditorium, the Arabs asked for the hall again for February 10, 1980, to meet with high school students. In light of the previous meeting, the school declined to grant the facility, but a "spontaneous" Arab demonstration persuaded them to change their minds.

In March 1978 Arab students at Hebrew University invited high school youngsters from Tayba to spend the weekend at the "Hadassah" dormitories of the school. A wild party broke out, with the students smashing sinks and toilets. Bitter Jewish students complained that it was not the first time. It was clear that the actions were more than exuberance but a political expression of hate and contempt for the state.

The rise of the new generation of educated Israeli Arabs who did not know the bitter taste of defeat and who openly moved toward confrontation with Zionism and the Jewishness of the state was itself given enormous impetus by the Six-Day War.

Again, ironically, it was Jewish military victory that the Jews turned into yet another political defeat. For the first time in nineteen years the Arabs of Israel were able to meet and talk with other Arabs who were not Israelis, who called themselves "Palestinians," and who openly spoke of the day when the hated Jews would leave. The Israeli Arab suddenly realized that he was neither meat nor milk, fish nor fowl. He was not an Israeli, but now he was struck by the awesome realization that he had not been a "Palestinian" all those years either! He was looked upon by the West Bank "Palestinians" as a traitor who cooperated with, and accepted, Israeli citizenship from the Jews who had stolen the land from his people. In one fell swoop, all the factors that went into creating the new radical Israeli Arab came together. Things would never be the same again.

Not only were there new contacts with the West Bank "Palestinians," but this was also the beginning of joint cooperation. Thus, Israeli Arabs participated in a "Palestine Week" held in 1978 at the Universities of Bethlehem and Bir Zeit. They helped organize it, and they printed and distributed a leaflet calling for support of the PLO. In defiance of the law several Israeli Arab students have begun studying in schools in the liberated territories. Indeed, Hanna Nasir, the PLO-backing former president of Bir Zeit College (near Ramallah) who was deported by Israel in 1974 for incitement, told a Kuwaiti newspaper in January 1979: "Despite all Israeli efforts to prevent young Arabs from within the Green Line [Israel] from both studying and teaching at the college, we have three lecturers there today from the region occupied in 1948 [Israel] plus several students.

"One of the beautiful things is the renewal of ties between all members of the Palestinian people living in the land of Palestine, and this makes it easier to fight against the conquerors."

This is quite true. The opening of the borders between the State of Israel and the liberated areas was seen by the incredibly obtuse Israelis as allowing the better-fed Israeli Arabs to demonstrate the benefits of Israeli occupation. Of course, a child could have known that exactly the opposite would occur. The Israeli Arabs were suddenly given the opportunity to meet, regularly, with their *own people* who were struggling for what the Israeli Arab understood to be a common goal: freedom:

The mayor of Hebron, Fahd Kawasma, said (January 22, 1979): "The Israeli Arabs have remained foreigners and their

lot remains ours. There is no possibility of blurring the fact that
they and we are part of the same people, and the fact that they
live in Israel does not make them less Palestinian."

In his newspaper interview, Bir Zeit President Nasir added:
"The destiny of the Arab College at Bir Zeit is to be the nucleus
around which is built the Palestinian state." Indeed, the Arab
students being trained in the Jewish universities of Israel see
themselves in the same light. They are the seed of the future
"Palestine" leaders in that area of "Palestine conquered in
1948." They give leadership and examples to high school students and are the PLO leaders of tomorrow.

The irony is that the most extraordinary rise in Arab
brazenness has taken place under the supposedly tough Begin
government. *Maariv* reporter Yosef Tzuriel commented on this
as long ago as April 27, 1978: "The rise of the Likud to power
created a certain amount of tension in the first months among
Arabs of Israel and the territories who expected a firmer policy
against them. *But after a short while it became clear that the new government was as liberal as its predecessor, if not more so.*"

The last two years have seen an inevitable rise in Arab student hostility toward the state. After winning the elections for
leadership of the Arab students at Hebrew University, the PNM
opened an office in the student dormitories on Stern Street,
hanging out an eye-catching sign: "Progressive National Movement." How a group such as the PNM was allowed to run for
office or its members remain as students rather than be prosecuted for sedition would seem difficult to explain. Bear in mind,
however, that this is a university that allowed an Arab student,
Fares Saur, a member of a terrorist group that planted a bomb
in the school cafeteria, to continue his studies after finishing his
jail sentence. The school explained that the criteria for acceptance to the university were purely academic.

In its publication *Tachadi* for December 1978 the PNM
wrote of its opposition to "any settlement with a recognition of
the Zionist entity in any part of Palestine." The student author
called for a war "beginning with leaflets and demonstrations
and concluding with armed military struggle." Above all, the
PNM made this point crystal-clear: "The struggle is not limited
to the 'occupied territories.' We must widen it to all parts of the
Arab motherland."

The PNM, running for control of the Arab student body,

had distributed literature outlining its program and goals in which they demanded that "the right of national self-determination for the Palestinian people also includes the masses in [Israel's] Galilee and the Triangle." And so in January 1979 several Arab students distributed a pamphlet calling for support of the PLO and the disappearance of the "Zionist entity." Moreover, some Arabs fired off a cable to the Damascus meeting of the Palestine National Council to voice their support of the PLO's struggle against the ever-present "Zionist entity."

A furor arose in Israel; more "shock"; more demands for expulsion of all PLO-supporting students from the school. The universities did nothing, but tough General Avigdor Ben-Gal issued "stay-at-home" orders to six of the students. The orders kept them limited to their villages and were to be in effect for three months—enough time to make them heroes and thus allow them to return and continue their incitement.

The six came from six different Israeli villages: Tamra, Araba, Kfar Yasif, Musmus, Sandala, and Umm al-Fahm. It is instructive to look at two of the students so that we may get a clear picture of the insanity of the Israeli policy, as reported by Yosef Valter in *Maariv* (February 16, 1979).

Masoud A'jabria, twenty-four, is completing his M.A. at Hebrew University in international relations while going to law school.

Besides Masoud, there is his brother, Sa'id, learning chemistry at the Mizrachi-religious-sponsored Bar-Ilan University; a sister, studying at a teacher's seminar in Hadar Am, and five younger brothers and sisters are attending high school. Naturally, someday they will go on to a university. Yosef Valter visited the family and reported: "From a brief conversation you find that all of them think and speak like Masoud, the older brother." That is a starkly frightening sentence when one remembers that the editor of the Hebrew University student paper, Arye Bender, recalls a conversation he once had with Masoud A'jabria. Said the Arab: "In order to achieve a Palestinian revolution we must shed rivers of blood."

Jamal Mahajana, twenty-one, comes from Umm al-Fahm. His is a small Arab family, with only six children, four of high school age, and one a teacher. Mahajana is a product of the integration Israeli myopics preach. He studied in the mostly

Jewish Afula high school and says, "I was not discriminated against." And so, having received the same education his Zionist neighbors received, and having been accepted into Hebrew University while 50,000 poor Sephardic Jews remain outside, Mahajana says of his telegram to the PLO in Damascus: "We emphasized that we are Palestinian Arabs living in the State of Israel and, like others, we claim that the PLO is the sole representative of the Palestinian people. . . . The Zionist regime is an oppressive regime. . . ."

The total lack of any coherent and consistent policy on the part of Israel toward the Arabs was seen two weeks later, when the national Arab Student Union announced that it, too, saw the PLO as the exclusive leader of the Palestinian people. No one was arrested, no one placed under house arrest. Little wonder that in the year that followed Arab boldness increased.

Arab students held an unauthorized demonstration at Hebrew University in November 1979 to protest the planned expulsion of Shechem's PLO mayor Bassam Shaka. When the school suspended the leaders of the demonstration, the Arab students announced a massive—illegal—protest. The rector, Yisroel Meshulem, a rather spineless academician, fearing a Jewish-Arab confrontation, pleaded with the Arabs to cancel the demonstration *and promised to rescind the suspensions.* The Arab protest was held, nevertheless, and as the students shouted, "We are all Arafat," and "The state is all ours," a fight broke out involving chains, rocks, and knives. Three Jewish students were injured. A Jewish student group was formed called Students Who Are Disgusted.

At Haifa University, on May 4, 1980, 150 Arab students marched through school buildings, disrupting classes and shouting against "Israeli fascism." Three days later a swastika and the words "Death to the Jews" were painted on doors at Haifa's Technion.

At Haifa University, the Arab students published a paper called *Bian,* in which, among other things, they said: "We are an indivisible part of the Palestine Arab people and the PLO is our sole legal representative. . . . Zionism is a racist, colonialist movement. . . ."

The young Arabs of Israel. The fathers are dying. The sons remain, and they will have sons and daughters—*many.* The

young, educated, modern Arab. The Golem of Israel, created by
Jews who believed that by caring for his body and expanding his
mind, they would lead the Arab to accept being a permanent
minority in a Jewish state.

If examples of Israeli blindness were not so prevalent, no
one would believe them. But consider:

In January 1979 Knesset Education Committee chairman
Ora Namir paid a well-publicized visit to the schools of Umm al-
Fahm, one of the centers of Israeli Arab hate. Passing a wall on
which had been painted "Long live Fatah," she told the Arabs
that "we are committed to doing everything we can to make
Arab schools equal to Jewish schools," despite a government
decision to freeze and cut spending levels for Jews.

And then Mrs. Namir, a Knesset member and a leader in
Israel, said: "The fact that you do not have enough latrines in
the schools is, for me, even more tragic than not enough class-
rooms. You will have the budget. But you will have to promise
me that the latrines will be first."

Not by latrines does an Arab live, and he will never trade
his national passions for them. The latrines we give him he will
take. But the education he receives from Israel he will use to
bring closer that day when Jews will be a minority and he can
generously offer *them* the latrines.

CHAPTER 5

The Demon of Demography

In May 1976 the Israeli Arab poet Awani Savit was briefly arrested for having written and publicly read seditious poems following the Land Day Rebellion. One of his poems reads in part:

> *Oh, shedders of blood.*
> *How did you ever believe you could murder my people?*
> *It is an impossible task.*
> *If you killed six, why we can bring into the world that same day*
> *sixty more. . . .*

The great Arab weapon in the battle against Jewish Israel is: babies. In an article in the newspaper *Ha'Aretz* (March 10, 1978), leftist Natan Yelin-Mor wrote: "One of the Arab notables once told me, following news of the death of several young Arab terrorists: 'If they would listen to me they would stop all military actions that cause only losses and suffering. We have to sit quietly, to work, and to bring forth children. In this way we will become the majority in the not-to-distant future. And then there will be no Israel as we know it.'"

The Arabs have not stopped that terror, but they have babies at an explosive rate. And so, according to the 1979 Annual of the Israeli Central Office of Statistics, the Israeli Arab population should triple in the next generation if current Arab and Jewish reproduction figures continue. That would mean that around the year 2000 there would be four million Jews in Israel and no fewer than two million Arabs. The Arabs would constitute one-third of Israel's population! A similar projection was made in March 1978 by Dr. Moshe Hartment of Tel Aviv University to the Knesset Committee on Aliyah and Absorption,

99

who said that even if Israel were to give up all the liberated territories and return to the pre–June 1967 border, the Arabs would constitute between one-quarter and one-third of Israel's total population. One need only consider how many Arab Knesset members would be elected and what would be their power in conjunction with that of the leftist Jewish members of the Parliament.

All this stems from several factors. On the one hand, the Israeli Arab birthrate is the fourth highest in the entire world (larger than India's), numbering between forty and forty-five per thousand. This contrasts sharply with the Jewish birthrate, which is between seventeen and twenty-two per thousand. But there is more to this. For not only do the Arabs of Israel have many children (an average of seven or eight per family versus fewer than three per Jewish family), but thanks to Jewish medical facilities their babies survive to become adults. Thus, their survival rate is the highest in the world. This means that their natural increase is an astronomical 3.5 percent a year, and they more than double their population every seventeen to twenty years. (The Jewish increase is a mere 1.5 percent annually.)

But there is yet another factor, even more meaningful. The huge birthrate has itself produced the phenomenon of the youngest community in the world. Nowhere does one find such a high percentage of young people as among the Arabs. The median age for Arabs in Israel is fifteen, meaning that fully half of them are below the age of fifteen; two thirds are under twenty-one. The implication for future generations is obvious. An ever-greater percentage of Arabs are now entering the childbearing years than are Jews. The Arabs will have a huge number of people of childbearing age for many decades to come as their tremendous numbers of young people grow and themselves have large numbers of children.

The Jewish median age, on the other hand, is much higher —close to thirty—and all that is implied for future Arab growth can be seen, in reverse, for the Jews. This, plus the fact that the Jewish death rate (7.4 per 100) is higher than the Arab death rate (5.6 per 100), prompted the Central Bureau of Statistics in March 1980 to paint the grim picture of an Arab population tripling in just one generation, while the Jewish growth would be less than 40 percent!

All this makes a mockery of the frantic call of the doves for return of the liberated lands, for the most powerful of their arguments is that of population. "To keep these lands and make them part of the Jewish state," contend those doves, "is to jeopardize the 'Jewish character of Israel.' The influx of hundreds of thousands of Arabs into Israel would see their percentage rise dramatically and, thanks to their birthrate, the majority that Jews now enjoy in Israel may very well end."

It is a theme played over and over by those who easily don the mantle of liberal and progressive thinking. In an article in *Midstream* magazine (June–July 1976), Yair Kotler, a senior editor of the Israeli newspaper *Ha'Aretz,* summed up that position: "If Israel were to annex the occupied territories, the population ratio of 'Greater Israel' would be 60 percent Jews to 40 percent Arabs. Then, sooner or later, the impressive Arab birthrate which holds a world record would overtake the Jewish population. If that were to happen, how could you prevent catastrophe?"

Similarly, former Israeli Professor Amitai Etzioni wrote of the demographic problem posed by the liberated lands in a 1968 article, "Israel's Colonial Temptations." Said Etzioni: "Israel is both a Jewish and democratic state. How is it to maintain its Jewish tradition with a population that is 45 percent Arab, a people whose numbers are increasing at a greater rate than the Jews? If the Arabs are to be given full citizenship rights, would this not give them a majority one day . . .?"

Countless articles and warnings have been thundered at all the governments of Israel concerning the demographic demon that would be involved in the annexation of the territories. Figures of all kinds, statistics, numbers, projections, have been produced, all warning of the need to rid ourselves of the territories because of the Arabs who go along with them. Indeed, just a few months after the 1967 war, the Peace and Security Movement issued a statement warning that annexation of the territories would force Israel to lose either its Jewishness or its democracy, since the enormous Arab population and birthrate would eventually make the Arabs a majority.

Surely, in the face of the clear Arab population threat within the State of Israel itself, it is worse than a delusion to believe that giving away the territories frees Israel of an Arab demographic threat. It is demagoguery of the worst sort, the kind that deliberately hides the truth. Giving up the liberated lands will do nothing but gain Israel a relatively brief span of time before the same demon shows up again, while giving up precious territory that brings the enemy within a few miles of Israel's heartland. With or without the territories, Israel faces the reality of Arab population explosion and it refuses to face that fact.

In this the "hawks" are as hapless as the doves; they have no answer for what to do with either the Arabs of Israel or the liberated lands. Begin and the hawks simply do not reply to the simple question "What do you do with the million Arabs of the territories?" just as no one replies to the same question about the Arabs of the state. Those who demand annexation of the liberated lands, no less than the "doves," blithely ignore the question of Arab population or fall back on evasive replies. They simply have no answers.

Back in 1949, when Prime Minister Ben-Gurion defended his signing of an armistice with the Kingdom of Jordan and thus his implicit recognition of its control of Judea and Samaria, he said: "A Jewish state in existing reality . . . in western Eretz Yisrael [that is, including Judea-Samaria] is impossible if it is to be democratic, for the Arabs in western Eretz Yisrael out-number the Jews. . . . How then will it be a Jewish state? We want a Jewish state even if it is not in the whole of the country. . . ."

To this, opposition leader Menachem Begin replied: "We —a minority in Eretz Yisrael? If we accept that assumption then there are many parts of Eretz Yisrael which should not have been included in her boundaries. . . ." One senses Begin's in-dignation, but he has not replied to the question. He did not answer in 1949, and to this day one awaits a rational reply.

Instead, we hear evasions such as: No clear demographic projections are really possible (why it is not made clear); the past is no guide to the future (why not is again not spelled out); Jewish immigration to Israel will make up for the higher Arab birthrate (a delusion of major dimensions). The truth is that, having no answer to problems, the "hawks," no less than the "doves," avoid them.

Thus Ariel Sharon in June 1979 told the Knesset that

"there is no danger that we will ever be a minority in the land," even if we annex the territories. He gave no figures of his own to answer a projection by the Israeli Central Bureau of Statistics showing the Arabs of Greater Israel making up 48 percent of the population by 1995.

What is even worse is that the proponents of annexation so avoid reality that they blithely speak of granting Israeli citizenship to the Arabs of the liberated lands!

Sharon was interviewed in the *National Observer* (February 2, 1974) by Lawrence Mosher. In discussing the Arab population of the liberated lands he said: "Here I see three possible solutions. One is to offer Israeli citizenship to the Arabs, which I think would be good and normal. I don't see any demographic problem here [*sic*]."

Eliezer Livneh, one of the hawks of the Greater Israel Movement, writing in *Midstream* magazine (October 1967), presented several views on what to do with the then newly liberated territories. He then presented the view that he enthusiastically espoused: "A third school of thought demands that Israel simultaneously incorporate all the new territories into a democratic Jewish state and that it undertake an ambitious program to resettle the refugees. . . ."

Livneh made it clear that he understood that only a certain number would resettle elsewhere. And the others? "The remaining refugees must be granted Israeli citizenship and their economic, cultural, and social level raised to Israeli standards." Naturally, the hundreds of thousands of Judea-Samaria-Gaza Arabs who were *not* refugees at all would also be granted citizenship.

How could Israel, the Jewish state, possibly absorb the Arabs? Typically, an answer is given that avoids answering. Wrote Livneh: "Zionist thought [*sic*] always took into account the probable existence of a large number of Arabs in the Jewish state. As originally conceived by the UN, the Jewish sector of Palestine was to have had an Arab minority of 45 percent. Had the Arabs not fled the area in huge numbers in the 1948 fighting, they would soon have formed a majority of the population."

How blasé and utterly unresponsive! And had they not fled and had they been the majority, what would have happened to Israel, to Livneh, to *Midstream*? And since the 1967 Arabs showed *no* inclination to flee, from where would Livneh's miracle come? And what "Zionist thought" ever really seriously considered the problem before fleeing into evasion and blessed avoidance of the pain?

Yuval Ne'eman of the Hatchiya Party has spoken of "dual sovereignty" for the Arabs of the liberated areas. In an interview in *Maariv* (July 19, 1974), he was asked what citizenship the Arabs there would have. His reply: "As they wish, Israeli or Jordanian. . . . They would have the right to vote for one of the two parliaments, according to the citizenship of their choice." When asked if they would be able to serve in political capacities, Ne'eman replied: "Yes, according to their citizenship. *Should they achieve senior political posts in Jordan, they may turn Jordan into a Palestinian state.*"

The incredible fact is that the interviewer did not follow up with the logical question: And should they achieve senior political posts in Israel . . .?

The flight from reality is most clearly seen in Begin's autonomy proposals. (Few people seem to know that the autonomy concept eventually endorsed at Camp David was Begin's idea, not Sadat's or Washington's.) In his various points Begin lists:

"Point 14: Residents of Judea, Samaria, and the Gaza district . . . will be granted free choice (option) of either Israeli or Jordanian citizenship.

"Point 15: A resident of the areas . . . who requests Israeli citizenship will be granted such citizenship in accordance with the citizenship law of the state.

"Point 16: Residents of Judea, Samaria, and the Gaza district who . . . choose Israeli citizenship will be entitled to vote for, and be elected to, the Knesset, in accordance with the election law."

Labor Party leader Yigal Allon in a blistering attack on the proposal called it a "farce" and asked a Labor Party meeting (March 5, 1978): "Who will guarantee that there will not be found hundreds of thousands of Palestinian Arabs who will willingly accept Israeli citizenship and thus [that] the delicate Jewish-Arab demographic balance will [not] automatically shift from a Jewish state with a sizable Arab minority to a binational state?"

Begin and the "hawks" have no answer. The "doves" do: Give up most of the territories with the Arab population. Not only is this an irresponsible giving up of Jewish Eretz Yisrael, not only is it the creation of a dagger in Israel's heartland as Arab sovereignty returns to within fifteen miles of Tel Aviv, Herzliya, Ramat Gan, Petah Tikva, and Netanya; *it also does nothing to solve the population problem.*

That population problem is the greatest threat to the survival of Israel, and it exists with or without the liberated lands. What madness makes us persist in avoiding it? What terrible thing binds our will so that we do not muster our courage and resolve to solve it?

The refusal to deal with the problem honestly is clearly seen in the June 1979 speech by Sharon, in which he mocked the warnings of Arab population growth and "proved" that since World War I the Jews had grown more than the Arabs despite their birthrate. Now even Sharon knows full well that all this happened almost solely because of Jewish immigration and the flight of more than half a million Arabs from the country.

Only a demogogue or an ignoramus could refuse to admit that on the eve of the establishment of the Jewish state in 1948, almost 40 percent of the population within its projected boundaries were Arabs and that more than 500,000 fled. How many more Arabs would there be in Israel today had they *not* run away? Who can refuse to know that in the four years between 1948 and 1952 the Jewish population almost *tripled,* thanks to the huge *aliya* of both European Holocaust survivors and of 650,000 Jews from Arab countries whose religious fervor and Zionism moved them to go to Israel? Who cannot admit that only for those reasons did the Arab population shrink to barely 11 percent of the total population? And who can deny that since then the Arab population has achieved a remarkable rise as reported in Central Bureau of Statistics figures? "The natural increase of non-Jews is so great that it overtakes the percentage rise of the Jewish population despite the immigration to Israel between 1952 and 1978 of nearly one million people" *(Maariv,* March 28, 1980).

From where will such aliya come today? The Arab nations are depleted of their Jews, Soviet Jewry rushes in huge numbers to the West, not to Israel. Will the assimilated and affluent French, English, and American communities emigrate to Israel in the millions?

Indeed, the reverse is true. Most of the projections of the

Jewish population in Israel in the year 2000 have been based on various figures of immigration totaling between 50,000 and 60,000 a year. This figure has now dropped to 25,000 or 15,000 a year. The truth is that the *net* percentage of immigration growth is closer to *zero* and probably below that. The reason? Along with immigration to Israel, there is *emigration from the country*. Jews from the Exile not only do not desire to come to Israel —even trouble spots such as Iran and South Africa find Jews seeking the shores of American, European, or Commonwealth nations rather than Israel—but Israelis are leaving in dangerously large numbers.

At least half a million Jews who lived in Israel have left and now reside in the United States and Canada. According to the Knesset Committee on Aliya and Absorption, some 2,000 Israelis leave every month, and many who plan to emigrate will not admit it, preferring to get a tourist visa, list their reason for traveling as "vacation," and then hope to find some way to remain in the country. The weekly newspaper for Israelis in New York, the Sunday-morning television show, and the three-hour daily radio program testify to the phenomenon. The neighborhoods in Los Angeles and New York where Hebrew is heard on all sides are chilling evidence of the reality of *yerida* ("emigration").

And, of course, emigration feeds on itself. As more Israelis leave Israel and settle in the West, the psychological barrier of shame that once existed is broken. Once Israelis were literally ashamed to admit that they wished to emigrate. Today, with half a million who have done so, that shame is gone. More and more can rationalize their intention to leave by pointing to the army service they have given, the high taxes, the inflation, the economy, the annual reserve duty.

And once one has a relative or friend in America, it becomes much easier to obtain good advice and aid in emigrating. One need only speak to young Israelis to realize the staggering number of those who seriously think of leaving. Nor need one belabor the obviously negative effect the sight of all those Israelis has on the efforts to persuade Western Jews to come to Israel. Certainly, many a Western Jew who has toyed with the idea is shaken by the number of Israelis who prefer *his* country.

And so, if Tel Aviv University professor Moshe Hartman warns of the need for an annual immigration net rate of 80,000 in order to keep the present percentage advantage of Jews in "Little Israel," where will that come from? It is nonexistent— *and the Arab population peril exists.*

There are those who claim that modernization will decrease the Arab birthrate. In answer to this one can only point to the fact that this may indeed be true, but it is more than matched by the drastic drop in the Jewish birthrate.

In 1978 Minister of Absorption David Levy, a Sephardic Jew and father of eleven children, pointed to the urgent need for immigration because "Israel's biggest contributors to Jewish natural increase—the Sephardic couples—are producing fewer and fewer offspring as time goes on."

And says Zvi Eisenbach of the directorate at the Central Bureau of Statistics: "Levy is right on target, for the fertility rate of Asian-African Jewish women in Israel has plummeted from almost 6 offspring in 1955 to 3.66 in 1976" (*Jerusalem Post*, March 7, 1978). Since then, the general drop in the Jewish birthrate has continued, from 3.2 children per family in 1976 (for *all* Israeli women) to 2.7 in 1979. Whereas 75,066 Jewish children were born in 1976, only 69,600 births were registered in 1979, despite the increase in the Jewish population. The spectacular drop in the Jewish birthrate since 1948 has been almost solely due to the negative Ashkenazic influence on the Sephardic women.

This influence, both directly through social workers urging Sephardic women to learn birth-control methods and indirectly through the desire to imitate the supposedly more "cultured" Ashkenazim, has led to more than use of the Pill. According to Central Bureau of Statistics figures, there was a drop of 9 percent in the number of Jewish marriages between 1975 and 1976 (it was also pointed out that divorces went up by the same amount, 9 percent). This trend continues. Despite the increase in population, 28,583 Jewish weddings were performed in 1975, but only 24,500 were recorded in 1979. Tradition for the Sephardic Jews was shattered on all sides, leading to further decline in the birthrate. The average male Israeli married at the very late age of twenty-seven and the female at twenty-three.

This phenomenon was aided by a blatant preferential factor in Israeli life. Young Jewish men and women who reach the age of eighteen must serve in the army, the men for three years.

The young soldier is sent back into civilian life at the age of twenty-one, and only then can he begin his career. The Arab is free from military service. He is free to work and make money at eighteen and to marry early—another factor that is not immediately perceived in the cold statistics of the Central Bureau.

And then, of course, there is abortion, almost exclusively a Jewish phenomenon in Israel. Even before the Knesset passed the murderous abortion law a few years ago, the Ministry of Health admitted that there were around 40,000 abortions a year. To quote the *Jerusalem Post* (March 10, 1978): "Many physicians and sociologists believe the actual number is much higher. With the new liberalized abortion law already in the books, this rate of 'natural decrease' will grow even more sharply." Indeed, and so much more so that it is estimated that each year close to 100,000 Jewish babies are legally murdered in Israel. As the younger generation of Sephardic Jews comes more and more under the influence of leftists and the secular educational system, its traditionalism, the greatest factor in large families, will be eroded even more.

This decline in Jewish birthrate more than matches any drop in the Arab birthrate which will take generations to be meaningful. Dr. Moshe Hartman goes even further and claims: "Contrary to expectations, industrialization and urbanization has not reduced the Arab birthrate, which is among the highest in the world" (*Jerusalem Post*, March 3, 1978). The reason is clear. The tremendous economic growth given the Arab sector by Jewish liberalism has made it possible for the Arabs to have children without economic struggle. And, of course, that is the result of the Israeli welfare-state policy which, in the words of Ora Shem-Or, "encourages greater reproductivity in the Arab sector thanks to the monthly grants paid for each child" (*Yediot Aharonot*, May 8, 1978).

The Jewish subsidizing of the Arab birthrate is only one more disastrous aspect of a policy that stems from fear of world reaction to "discrimination" and liberal guilt feelings that, once again, are at odds with and overcome both Jewish tradition and common sense. What is even more outrageous is the statement by Dr. Hartman before the Knesset Committee on Aliyah and Absorption: "Whereas in all countries suffering from overpopulation, there exists a policy of family planning, we have no such thing *because of political reasons" (Maariv,* May 24, 1978).

It is, of course, true that any such plan would never be adopted and cooperated with by any Arab local council, for they all realize that population growth is a powerful weapon. But the fact that the Israeli government hesitates to attempt such a policy, out of fear of its effect on the Israeli Arabs, shows how strong the growing Arab minority has already become. That fact is surely not lost on the Arabs of Israel.

Let it never be forgotten, too, that the Israeli Arabs' willingness to revolt and express their hatred of Israel and Zionism is directly related to their exploding and *young* population. Both the intellectual fuel and the unfortunate cannon fodder of revolution come from young people. It is from them that political extremism emanates, and they are most open to its siren call. Every revolution is begun and fought by young people. The enormously high percentage of them among Israeli Arabs is ominous.

Not only has the Israeli government no policy for reducing the number of Arabs; over the years it has agreed to bring more into the country or turned a blind eye to their illegal arrival. Immediately after the 1948 war, under the agreement signed in Rhodes, areas in the Triangle were added to Israel, along with 30,000 Arabs. In addition, as a goodwill gesture designed to encourage "peace," 40,000 Arabs were allowed to return from Lebanon, France, and Cyprus under a "reunification-of-families" scheme. Among those allowed to return were vicious anti-Zionists such as Greek Orthodox Bishop Maximus Hakim and Communist leaders, who, it was hoped, would be a "moderating influence"!

Thousands of residents of the northern Arab villages of Gush Halev (Jish), Rami, Kfar Yasif, and Eilbon were allowed either to return legally or to remain after having illegally crossed the border, often with the aid of "well-meaning" Jews.

Indeed, large numbers of more "well-meaning" Israelis today demand the return to their homes of the Arabs of Ikrit and Bir'im villages, despite the warning by Knesset member Amnon Linn: "That would be a green light for a mass campaign to let all the displaced Arabs inside Israel go back to their 1948 [border] homes as part of the *Harakat el Awda*—the return movement." More important, it would open the door for a campaign to allow hundreds of thousands *outside* Israel to do the same.

In the city of Jerusalem, the government has spent a fortune to ensure its Jewish majority (one more example of the ludicrous contradictions in a state that is supposedly devoted to reassuring the Arab that he is equal). Despite all the money and effort, however, the Jews are losing the battle, and one of the reasons is illegal infiltration of Arabs from the territories, especially from the area around Hebron. There are some 15,000 to 20,000 of these Arabs living in the Old City as well as in the villages just outside Jerusalem. Not only does this mean 15,000 to 20,000 more enemies of Israel inside her borders (and their inevitable army of babies), but as the Jewish Telegraphic Agency (JTA) *Bulletin* of October 2, 1975, reported: "Air photos taken recently by the city authorities revealed that the little villages around the city have become an ever-thickening Arab wall between Jewish West Jerusalem and the Judean desert. . . .

"The nature of the Arab expansion does, however, alarm some residents of the newly built Jewish quarters on the outskirts of the city. These quarters had been intentionally built in the northern, eastern and southern extremities of the Jerusalem Jewish belt around the Old City. As the Arab villages expanded, they stretched out toward the new Jewish quarter, drawing an Arab chain around the Jewish housing projects."

Why does the Israeli government allow the Arab demographic noose to tighten around Jewish Jerusalem's neck?

Left-leaning Gil Sedan, a JTA writer, explained it this way: "The city, deeply preoccupied with a plague of illegal construction by Israeli contractors, can hardly find the time and manpower to deal with this problem in the Arab sector. . . ."

Are Sedan's incredible lack of proportion, his misplaced sense of priorities, his characterizing of the Jewish "danger" as more acute than the Arab one, merely a total failure to understand the Arab menace? Hardly; in a final burst of political commentary he writes: ". . .the expansion of [illegal] Arab suburbs in Jerusalem is something Israel will have to learn to live with—unless it wants to . . . act counter to the repeated Israeli argument that Arabs and Jews can live in harmony in Jerusalem."

Of course, the talk of harmony is ludicrous. The Jewish buses and cars, on their way to the new Jewish neighborhood of

Neve Yaakov, which are stoned in Bet Hanina and Shu'afat; the attacks on children, the plague of burglaries and fearful women in East Talpiot, which stands across from Jabal Mukabber and Arab-A-Sawahre; the tension in the Jewish quarter of the Old City—all attest to the Arabs' hatred of their Jewish "occupiers" and are just a brief hint of what Jewish men—and women— might expect from an Arab victory.

Sedan, the liberal, *must* condone illegal Arab infiltration and building, *must* turn a blind eye to Arab violence, because deep in his heart he is ridden with guilt concerning the *Jewish* emphasis of Israel and Zionism. And so, too, the deputy mayor of Jerusalem, Miron Benvenisti, presiding over a schizophrenic policy under which millions are spent on Judaizing the city while the fact that Arabs are illegally settling there is ignored. He told the JTA that he was "in no way perturbed by the increase in Jerusalem's Arab population." His party's leader, Shimon Peres, on the other hand, told a party forum on August 25, 1977: "I do not want to wake up one morning to discover that Jerusalem is subject to the demographic fate of Galilee." What Peres was telling his party members, including all the Israeli Arabs he hoped to attract, was that he did not want to see too many Arabs in Jerusalem. But it was Labor that sat quietly by—and did nothing—as the Arabs illegally settled.

The Likud government is just as hapless. "The growth rate of the Jewish population in Jerusalem is declining steadily despite governmental policies aimed at increasing the number of Jews who live in the capital"—the words of Gideon Patt, Likud minister of housing. Does he recommend the removal of the illegal Arabs? Of course not. And so millions will be spent annually in a losing battle to keep Jerusalem "Jewish," because the Jewish leaders are striken by guilt and fear.

In any case, Jerusalem with its 120,000 Arabs (more than one out of every four in the populace) spotlights another aspect of the demographic demon. Not only are the Arabs increasing at an explosive rate, but they are concentrated in definite areas. In those Israeli areas that border Judea-Samaria, which has already been promised "autonomy," the Arabs make up much more than their 18 percent of the national population. In Jerusalem they are 27 percent; in the Triangle 50,000 Arabs sit along the old pre–1967 "Green Line" border, cheek to cheek with relatives who live in the "autonomy" region of Samaria, and in the Galilee 300,000 Arabs already make up a majority in a region that touches Lebanon, the Golan Heights, and Samaria. The Galilee—Israel's future Northern Ireland-Cyprus.

The Galilee. Where Arabs outnumber Jews by a small percentage but where the Arabs make up 75 percent of the hill areas. From the slopes of the Nazareth hills up to the Lebanon border there are more than one million dunams (a quarter of a million acres), almost exclusively Arab. Where the Arab birthrate grows by between 4 and 6 percent a year, among the very highest rates in the world. Where the Arab population will double in less than fifteen years. Where in a six-mile radius around the lonely Jewish town of Carmiel there are twenty-seven non-Jews for every Jew.

The Galilee. Of which Shimon Peres said: "The areas in Israel that are still unsettled, or settled only in a certain manner, are and will continue to be a subject for special attention beyond Israel's settlement policy. The Arab countries which covet areas inhabited by Jews will be all the more greedy for the completely uninhabited regions and parts where there are no Jews."

The Galilee. Where Arab growth gives birth to Jewish fright and flight. Where the army must build parallel roads that bypass Arab villages so that Jewish women will not have to go through them at night. Where in Upper Nazareth apartments stand empty because Jews have left the town or refuse to go there. Where in the past twenty-five years 10,000 Jews have come to Kiryat Shmona and left; one-fifth of its homes stand empty; in July 1979 some 500 families, including 70 teachers, threatened to leave.

The Galilee. An area of which Yehoshua Ben-Porat wrote (*Yediot Aharonot*, August 28, 1965): "Another reason offered was that 'the claim has been repeatedly made that Galilee was not intended as part of Israel according to the Partition Plan, and this continues to feed the hope that a plebiscite will be held in the area, which is after all Arab and not Jewish.' Thus 'the problem of Galilee is a Jewish problem . . . it is an Arab empire within our borders . . . and those who believe with the government that military rule alone will liberate [Galilee] are simply mistaken.'"

The Galilee. Where the city of Acre threatens to "go Arabic." And so *Maariv* writer Menahem Rahat (May 9, 1977) spoke of "the worrisome forecast that sees Acre possibly losing its Jewish character and returning to being a city with a definite Arab population. This forecast is based not only on statistics that clearly show a trend among Acre Jewish families to leave the city, along with a reverse trend on the part of Arab families in the region to move there. It is also apparent from the declarations of various Arab personalities in the city who speak of the 'Arabization of Acre.'"

The Galilee. Where the Jews build a small outpost, Tel El— 53 Jews in the midst of 40,000 Arabs. Where Dr. Amnon Sofer of Haifa University tells of the Arab village of Sakhnin which has grown to 12,000 people, adding 500 new ones every year. "To keep up with that it is necessary to establish two *moshavim* ["Jewish settlements"] a year in that area," says Dr. Sofer.

But that is not happening, and Israel faces the real truth of Arab demography. Of course, the ultimate threat is that of the Arabs quietly achieving national majority, which will allow them to take control of the Knesset and legally abolish the Jewish state. The population figures are all in their favor.

In 1976 the U.S. Library of Congress, in a study of the Arab-Jewish population, predicted that even if Israel were to give up all the liberated lands, the Arabs within the State of Israel would become a majority in 100 years. *That was based on an annual net immigration of 25,000.* Israel is nowhere near such a thing, and with economic chaos already in the land, great efforts will be needed to keep the number of emigrants from exceeding the number of new arrivals. Seventy years is a much more practical figure for that Arab majority. Why should the Arab grow more moderate? In the face of the figures that show him moving toward becoming a huge minority and eventually a majority, why should he voluntarily throw away his opportunity to rule rather than be ruled or even to *share* rule? What are 70 years or 80 or 100 to the Arab? If Jews could dream of the return to Zion and a sovereign Jewish state for 1,900 years, why do we think that the Arab cannot dream and hope and work toward his return for a century? Why do we think that, in his own way, the Arab cannot be his own "Zionist"? In the past, among all the Zionist leaders who deluded the people and themselves, one man, Ze'ev Jabotinsky, came closest to understanding. But not close enough.

In his classic essay "An Iron Wall," he wrote: ". . .there is not even the slightest hope of our ever obtaining agreement of the Arabs of the Land of Israel to 'Palestine' becoming a country with a Jewish majority. . . .

"In our peace proclamations we try to convince ourselves that the Arabs are either fools easily deceived by a milder interpretation of our aims or a tribe of mercenary materialists ready to give up their rights to the Land of Israel in exchange for cultural or economic advantages. . . .

"As long as the Arabs preserve a gleam of hope that they will succeed in getting rid of us, nothing in the world can cause them to relinquish this hope, precisely because they are no rabble but a living people. And a living people will be ready to yield on such fateful issues only when they have given up all hope of getting rid of the alien settlers. . . ."

Jabotinsky was absolutely correct. But then he, too, stumbled. He concluded: "Then only will they begin bargaining with us on practical matters *such as guarantees against pushing them out.* . . . I am optimistically convinced that they will indeed be granted satisfactory assurances and that both peoples, like good neighbors, can then live in peace."

It is distressing to find a logical, perceptive man like Jabotinsky writing such nonsense. Alas, the virus of self-delusion strikes even giants of intellect. Did not Jabotinsky realize that guarantees against pushing the Arabs out would eventually lead to an Arab majority through the peaceful means he applauded? Could he not grasp the fact that it is precisely by living as "good neighbors" with political rights that the Arabs can "Palestinize" the Jewish state? Jabotinsky, the product of nineteenth-century liberalism and committed to "national minority rights," could not face the contradiction between that and a Zionist state. He, too, fled from logic and painful reality.

And so, of course, the ultimate threat is the majorityship of Arabs in the State of Israel which will turn the Jewish state into an Arab one. The threat, however, is not limited to that. Jews do not have the dubious luxury of waiting seventy or eighty years to become a minority. Ora Shem-Or put it this way: "We dare not assume that the Arabs will wait until they are an absolute majority and the state will fall into their hands as a ripe fruit. The minority of a million today is not like the minority of a few million tomorrow. As they grow in numbers and the relative difference between them and Jews declines, so will grow the pressures. The confrontation will come years before we reach the 'red line'—the line of equality in population."

The confrontation will come as the Arabs of Israel constitute one-quarter or one-third of the state. Riots and rebellion will be seen on television screens all over the world. Bombs will go off, and bloody clashes between soldiers and Arab civilians will take scores of lives. The "moderate" Uncle Ahmed Arabs will disappear from the scene, and demands for the incorporation of the Galilee and the Triangle into a "Palestinian" state will be heard. World opinion will be galvanized against Israel, and American Jewry will be torn by debates. In the Knesset the twenty-five or thirty Arab members will disrupt sessions with demands for autonomy and proper representation for Arabs. *Aliya* to Israel will dwindle to a trickle, for who will wish to leave a non-Jewish land for one that is headed in that direction? On the other hand, there will be a tremendous rise in emigration from the country as talented people flee, causing a serious shortage in manpower in the armed forces and in technology.

Demands for a greater share in the state, for the right to live in Jewish cities, for the right to hold top jobs, and for total equality for the Arab in Israel will lead to mob confrontations and make whole areas of Israel unsafe for Jews to travel. The frustration and self-control of the Sabra will explode, and he will, more and more, ask why he must suffer for this Zionist-Jewish concept that means so little to him anyhow. Greater intermarriage and intermingling on top of his fear of war and tension will lead to greater support for a binational state. Jewish support for the state will dramatically drop off, for it will no longer be the Jewish state.

Long before the arrival of an Arab majority in Israel, there will be prior demands—all gaining force through the annual, immutable growth of Arab population: demands for greater political power and representation in Knesset and cabinet; demands for "autonomy" in the Galilee and Triangle; demands for the annexation of those areas to any "Palestine" state that might arise; demands for the return of the "Palestinian" refugees to their homes and property in Israel.

Demography and democracy. Both combine to prick the illusions and delusions. Both force the Jew to look honestly at the Jewish state and at Zionism. Both force him to choose his destiny. There is a contradiction, and the voices of both are loud and clear. There is the Jewish voice of the distinct, unique Jewish nation and state. And there is the Arab voice of "Palestine." Between them there is an irreconcilable difference.

CHAPTER 6

The Ultimate Contradiction

There is an ultimate insoluable contradiction between the State of Israel that is the fulfillment of the 2,000-year-old Jewish-Zionist dream and the modern nation-state that sees all its citizens as possessing equal rights and privileges. There is an ultimately immutable clash between that part of Israel's Declaration of Independence that created the *Jewish* state and the part that promised "complete equality of social and political rights to all its citizens," even though they be Arabs and not Jews. There is—let it be said once and for all—a potential confrontation between the Jewish-Zionist state that was the millennial dream of the Jewish people and modern concepts of democracy and citizenship.

We are pained, embarrassed, thrown into intellectual agony. We hasten to avoid such talk. It is unnecessary, dangerous, irresponsible, better left unspoken. Nonsense! *Far better to meet the issue, deal with it boldly and courageously, explain it to our children and ourselves, than to have it explode in our faces tomorrow.*

There is nothing for which the Jew need apologize. A people that has suffered ecumenical agony and that has been deprived of the rights that other nations demand for themselves owes no one an explanation. The Middle East sees Islamic republics in which the Arabic quality and the Muslim character of the state are inscribed in the constitution; who shouts about Arabic "racism"? Africans insist upon the blackness of their state, and exclusiveness of culture and identity are the foundations of scores of nations. Who apologizes? The Zionist state *is* Judaism, the need for a land of the Jews where the people can escape Holocaust and build a distinctive Jewishness that will flourish.

The very kernel of Jewish longing for a homeland through nearly 2,000 years of exile was the belief that the Jews were a separate and distinct people. In a world in which we recognize the right of self-determination for Papua, who will challenge Jewish rights?

Moreover, the Jews constituted a unique people in that they were at one and the same time a religion and a nation, a religio-nation, which had lived as a unique society and culture in its own land—Eretz Yisrael. On the one hand they suffered unparalleled horrors and massacres in their wanderings in foreign lands. They knew no peace in any country in which their numbers grew large and their quality shone through. There was no society, religion, or economic or social system that gave them permanent haven and rest. Jews were burned to death, drowned, cut to pieces, converted to death, Inquisitioned to death, Crusaded to death, Islamized to death, pogromed to death, and Auschwitzed to death. The Jews learned a bitter lesson in their twenty centuries of being strangers, of existing as a minority. The lesson? It is not good to be a stranger. Never be a minority. Never again!

As impolite as it may sound, the Jews learned, after rivers of blood, not to trust to the tolerance and mercies and hospitality of others. They no longer wished to rely on the armies and the police and the swords of others to protect them from holocausts. Enough of being strangers. The Jews wanted to live. The Jews wanted their own armies, their own protection, *their own home.*

And, of course, the Jews wished to preserve their unique spiritual identity. No minority culture can grow, normal and healthy and vibrant, in foreign soil. "How can we sing the song of the L-rd in a foreign land?" The Jew wanted a home of his own in which to be *Jewish* and not remain a hyphenated nonentity of Mosaic persuasion. The Jews were a separate and distinctive people seeking to live a separate and distinctive life in its own separate and distinctive state, a people that had tasted all the promises and guarantees and mercies of a hundred majorities. Never again.

Determined not to be killed off, they came home to the land they had lost twice before. They would not lose it a third time—through war or peace, through sword or "democracy."

It was on the basis of their uniqueness that the Jews founded political Zionism. It was on that basis that they approached Turkey and then Britain for help in allowing them to establish a national home. It was on that basis that the Bible Christian instantly understood the demand, and so too the League of Nations and later the United Nations. It was on the basis of being Jewish, the same Jewish people that had once lived in that same land, that the Jews demanded a land in which other people lived, trespassers. There could not have been any other moral or logical basis. And it was as the *Jewish* state that Israel came into being. The very assumption of a *Jewish* state guaranteed that it cannot permit the Arab minority to become a majority. The most fundamental law of the state is the linchpin in that effort. It is the Law of Return that grants automatic entry and Israeli citizenship to any *Jew*. That is the key to the insistence that Jews will be a majority that controls the Jewish sovereignty, political power, military might, and destiny of the country. Would Israel allow the Arabs through peaceful democracy to become a majority? If that question can be asked, no Arab is really equal. If that question can be answered in the affirmative, there is no Jewish state.

But it is more than that. It is the specific and unique *atmosphere* that is created by a *Jewish* state. The language, the religion, its holidays, the heroes, the ties to the outside Jewish world, the very air, become Jewish. The Jew in Boston or Rotterdam, Melbourne or Johannesburg, Moscow or Montreal, feels that Israel is "his," and his right to it is stated by the Declaration of Independence as being deeper than that of the Israeli-born Arab. It is not by material benefits alone that a man or woman lives. He, she, both, need to feel that the land is *theirs*, their political, cultural, spiritual home; that they *belong*. No Arab can say that about Israel as he sings the *"Hatikva"* or listens to the Jewish Agency, United Jewish Appeal, and World Zionist Organization speeches. "Oppression" need not be physical. It can be, and usually is, the atmosphere of living under someone else's majority rule, never being truly "home." That is the Arab plaint.

If the Arab is unhappy about this, one can understand. It is never easy to be a lodger in someone else's home. But his unhappiness will not be resolved, for the Jew will not turn a lodger into an owner. If the Arab would rather live in his own home and atmosphere, he is welcome in any of the twenty-plus Arab states that exist. Israel cannot, and morally dare not, change its Jewish character. For Israel to change that Jewish character would be to turn those who created it on the basis of the Jewish historical right into liars and thieves.

It would be more than admitting that "Jewishness" was used in the past only in order to take away Arab land. It would be a cynical slap in the face to world Jewry which gave of its energies, funds, and in many cases, lives for the dream of a Jewish state. It would be a despicable cutting off of all obligations to oppressed and persecuted Jews who see in today's Israel their trustee and defender. The Israeli who was once in need of a home and who found it in a state that was pledged to help him would now—no longer in need—selfishly cut the lifeline for others.

The Jew has no moral right to an Israel that is a non-Jewish state. But in a Jewish state let no one insult the Arab by insisting that he is equal and that it is "his" state, too. It is this ultimate contradiction between the Jewish character of Israel and the democratic right of the Arab to aspire to all the rights that Jews have—including to have an Arab majority in the land—that will never give the Arab rest or allow him to accept the status quo.

From the very beginning non-Jews understood this far more easily. Most Jews instinctively sensed the contradiction but could not give up the idea of a Jewish state, and so they repressed the reality. But Gentiles conversant with the problem had no such difficulties. Alvin Johnson, president emeritus of the New School for Social Research, discussed the "Palestine" problem in January 1947, one and a half years before the establishment of Israel. Writing in *Commentary* magazine, he stated: "It would be no simple matter to establish and maintain a Jewish majority in Palestine. . . . It is entirely realistic to say that the Arabs of Palestine do not want to live as a minority under the Jews, no matter what formal guarantees are given of minority rights. . . . *A national minority must expect to be oppressed.* Even if it is no more oppressed that the Sudeten Germans and Slovaks in Czechoslovakia, *the minority will consider itself oppressed.* . . . I submit, the Arab-Jewish problem in Palestine cannot be solved under the scheme of majority-minority nationalism."

Thirty-two years after Johnson made his precise observations, the majority-minority situation he warned about was in existence—more than three decades of Jewish majority rule with formal guarantees to an Arab minority.

In 1979 a survey of Israeli Arab thinking was undertaken by the Arab-Jewish Center at Haifa University. In light of the "remarkable accomplishments" and "advances" made by Israeli Arabs, the results of the poll are of more than passing interest.

• No fewer than 50 percent of the Arab citizens of Israel queried openly admitted that they reject Israel's right to exist.
• Some 64 percent consider Zionism to be racism.
• The same proportion, 64 percent, called for abolition of the Law of Return.
• Finally, whereas 87 percent of Israel's Arabs demanded that Israel give up all the land liberated in 1967, an astounding 59 percent also called for a rollback to the *1947* boundaries.

The head of the survey, Dr. Sami Samouha, stated that the results made it clear that the point of issue between Jews and Arabs in Israel has nothing to do with the pace of integration of Arabs into the life of the state. "The dispute centers above the Jewish-Zionist character of the State of Israel. Sooner or later the Israeli Arab will demand substantive changes in the character of the state."

Dr. Samouha was saying that in a Jewish state, whose entire character and destiny are tied to Jewishness and Judaism, the Arab citizen can never feel equal or part of it. Dr. Samouha is, of course, absolutely correct. He, *as an Arab*, understands this. Would that the Israeli leaders were as perceptive.

The Jew, like it or not, must choose: *unswerving adherence to a Jewish state, or the democracy of the Western liberal world which gives the Arab the right to change the country into an Arab state.* More and more Israelis are forced to face this reality as being at the heart of the Arab-Jewish conflict. And others, having realized how terrible the dilemma, cannot bear to choose a Jewish solution. They either flee reality and devise a patently evasive or absurd answer, or they make their choice: democracy! A growing number of Hellenized Israelis declare that if there is a conflict between Jewishness and democracy, they choose democracy and the end of the Jewish state.

Of course, the evaders of reality still constitute the majority. They flee the reality of the Arab teacher in Araba.

Araba, the Galilee Arab village. Na'ama Saud is a young Arab Sabra. He teaches school, teaches the young Arab generation of Israel. A reporter for *Maariv*, Yisrael Harel, asks him (May 28, 1976) whether he accepts the fact of Israel as a Jewish state with himself as a minority with equal rights but no national ones. Saud replies: "Today I am in the minority. The state is democratic. Who says that in the year 2000 we Arabs will still be the minority? We are today about half a million Arabs in Israel. Today, I accept the fact that this is a Jewish state with an Arab minority. But when we are the majority I will not accept the fact of a Jewish state with an Arab majority."

Who is listening? Who *wishes* to see the dual threat to Israel —demographic and democratic? Certainly not Israeli leaders. In 1976 all the blindness, deafness, and contradictions that characterize the problem were in evidence in the person of Prime Minister Yitzhak Rabin.

On April 14, 1973, Rabin was Israeli ambassador to the United States. In a press conference in Tel Aviv, he made the following significant statement: "The process of Jewish rejuvenation is based on the rise of a state whose great majority is Jewish and which will be founded on Jewish values. *Therefore, I doubt if she could hold too large an element of non-Jews.*"

Three years later, Rabin was prime minister of Israel and in an angry mood. The Land Day Rebellion (March 30, 1976) had left a shocked country in its wake. Rabin, in a Knesset speech, furiously attacked the Rakah Communist Party, instigator of the Land Day riots, for attempting "to tear up the fabric of cooperation between Jews and Arabs built up over the past twenty-eight years." A prime minister whose view is based on Israel as a *Jewish* state that cannot accommodate "too large" a number of Arabs blames the Communist Party for destroying "a wonderful relationship"? What can we say? What can Rabin possibly take the Arabs for?

Then, on May 6, 1976, Rabin spoke to the annual meeting of Tel Aviv senior high school students. There he proclaimed:

"The majority of the people living in a Jewish state must be Jewish [*sic*]. We must prevent a situation of an insufficient Jewish majority and we dare not have a Jewish minority. . . .

"There is room for a non-Jewish minority on condition that it accept the destiny of the state vis-à-vis the Jewish people, culture, tradition, and belief. *The minority is entitled to equal rights as individuals with respect for their distinct religion and culture but not more than that.*"

Rabin did not elaborate on how one prevented an Arab minority from becoming too large or becoming a majority. Nor did he analyze what positive impact his words might have on the happy Arabs of Israel.

On May 24, 1976, Rabin met with the heads of the Arab village and town councils to learn what was troubling them. Angry Arabs left the meeting after Rabin had again limited them to the sphere of a religious and cultural group. And then, on June 6, the same group—widely regarded as the "moderate" leadership of the Arabs in Israel—drafted a memorandum in which they challenged Rabin's definition of Israel as a "Jewish-Zionist state in which lives an Arab minority with distinctive culture and religion."

Not at all, said the moderate Arab leaders: *"The State of Israel is a binational state [Dawle Thunaiya Kawmiya] with a Jewish majority and Arab minority."* The implication was clear. Tomorrow, it could be an *Arab majority* and a *Jewish minority*. The Arabs were openly resenting the Jewish-Zionist foundation of Israel, to the "shock" of such as the pathetic *Jerusalem Post*. One gets a stunning insight into the confused minds of the Jewish liberal, reading the June 9 editorial of a paper that prides itself on its progressive struggle on behalf of Israel's Arabs. It is a mix of classic southern-plantation paternalism and confusion: "In response to grievances harbored by the Arab community the government has opted for a policy which would encourage far-going Arab integration into Israel and close the gaps between the two communities. *This is an enlightened minorities policy* [*sic*]. . . .

"Israel was established in accordance with the 1947 UN partition decision as a *Jewish* state. . . . It may therefore be essential to reiterate to Israel's Arab citizens that while they have the inalienable right to fight for greater equality and more opportunities—a fight in which many Jews will enlist on their side

—Israel is and will remain irrevocably Jewish."

Pity the confused liberals. *"Israel will remain irrevocably Jewish."* And suppose the Arabs become a majority? Can the liberal leopard change its spots? Will the *Jerusalem Post* and all its ilk refuse to allow them to vote? Would this be any way for a liberal to behave? And so, in ideological panic, the *Jerusalem Post* refused to think about it and, in the best tradition of southern paternalism or British colonialism, offered the Arab an "enlightened minorities policy."

What may be most significant about the Arab memorandum was the fact that its four drafters were all "moderate" Arabs linked to the Israeli Labor Party. They were Hana Muwiz, council head of Rama; Tark Rafik Abdul Hai, head of Tira; Jamil D'raba, head of Sakhnin; and Ahmed Msalha of Daburiya. For years these men had been "loyal" Israelis, dutifully following the Zionist line. What caused them to change? *Had they changed?* The answer is no, they had not.

The longtime Israeli expert on Arab affairs Tzvi El-Peleg wrote, after the Land Day Rebellion: "They [the Arabs] knew how to conceal the enmity and at the proper time to allow it to burst forth. As long as the time had not yet arrived for the enmity to come into the open, everything went peacefully. Correct relations, elaborate hospitality. . . ."

But now the time had come, and the real Israeli Arab stood up to proclaim partially his true desires. Of course, Rabin learned nothing. In June 1976 he stood at the well-publicized Labor Party symposium, and after, again, going through a litany of self-praise ("Israel can be proud of her attitude toward the Arabs of Israel in the practical conditions in which she finds herself"), and after reciting the compulsory "head-and-stomach" figures that proved how much progress the Arabs had made in Israel, Rabin proceed to state yet again the two impossible pillars of his policy. Said the prime minister: "Israel is a Jewish state" with "full equality of rights for all non-Jewish citizens with respect to their separate cultural and religious identities."

Of course the Arab wanted more. Of course the Arab resented, *hated,* the fact that a *Jewish* state doomed him to perpetual minority status, never able to control his homeland. Of course, the right to have babies and vote gave him the right in a democracy to become a majority and change the character of the state. Did not Rabin understand that? How did he propose to prevent such a situation: Does "full equality" for the Arabs mean that they have no right to bear as many children as they wish, who will then elect enough Arabs to the Knesset to change "Israel" to "Palestine"? Or does "full equality" perhaps imply "with limitation on their rights to vote"?

No one dealt with any of this at the meaningless symposium. The Jews frantically avoided thinking about it as they tried desperately to persuade the Arabs how good things were for them. One incident, however, underlined the real situation. Said one of the Arabs present, attorney Jamil Jalhoubi: "If everything is so good, why are things so bad? We must recognize the rights of the Palestine Arab nation that lives in Israel. There has been economic progress, but not by bread alone does man live."

The basic impossibility of Arab integration in a Jewish state and the fundamental reasons for an Arab-Jewish conflict that are insoluble are recognized every so often by various Israelis who can never bring themselves to come up with the solution. Thus, Moshe Sharon, former adviser on Arab affairs to Menachem Begin, stated (June 22, 1979): ". . .The Arabs of Israel feel they belong wholly to the Arab nation, which opposes Israel, and yet live in a Jewish state with whose political goals they cannot identify and whose social and cultural values they do not share. . . .

"To identify with this state means regarding its Zionist character, its Jewish culture, and its political and Jewish national goals as their own. No Arab in Israel can do so. . . . The preference is to see some radical change in the character of the state . . . in which the roles would be reversed: a Palestinian Arab majority would rule over a Jewish minority. . . . In the present state of affairs, integration cannot work in this country. . . ."

And, in a personal viewpoint, Sarah Hoenig wrote, following the Land Day Rebellion (*Jerusalem Post*, April 5, 1976): "We should see last week's Arab riots for what they were—outbreaks of hostility against the Jewish state, pure and simple. . . . Unless we come to grips with the fact that the basic cause for the riots is Arab unwillingness to accept the Jewish state despite its nearly 28 years of independence, we shall be deliberately beclouding our vision.

"Why, after all, should the Arab nationalists acquiesce in the continuation of Israeli sovereignty as an irreversible fact when they have just succeeded in destroying the Lebanese state as it had been for over 40 years?"

Back in December 1951, Judo L. Teller wrote a perceptive article in *Commentary* in which he pointed out: "It must be remembered that the Arabs in Israel are not just a minority in the usual sense of the word. They are a defeated enemy with all that this signifies in mutual fear, resentment and suspicion. . . .

"In Haifa, a Jewish teacher exorted his pupils to be 'good citizens of Israel and loyal sons of the Arab people.' Michael Assaf, writing in *Hamizrach Hachadash*, branded this a doctrine of incompatibility. In the context of current events, Assaf said, a 'loyal Arab' must wish to drive the Jews unto the sea. . . .

"They cannot consider themselves simply Israelis, differing only in religion and language from the Jewish majority of their co-nationals—for that state in its very lineament is the expression of *the desire of that majority to create a land that should be its own. . . .*"

This is the heart of the problem, and as long as Israelis refuse to betray the raison d'être of the state, its Jewish character, there is no solution. Dr. Subhi Abu Ghosh, an Arab official in the Ministry of Religions, was quoted in an article in *Present Tense* (Spring 1975): "Israel has to decide whether its Israeli or its Jewish aspect predominates. I am an Israeli, but I cannot be a Jew. The problem of the Arab minority is one for the Israeli establishment, not one for the Arabs themselves."

The anti-Zionist publication *Israel and Palestine*, published in Paris, understood all too well the contradictions in general Israeli thinking as well as the particular confusion in Prime Minister Rabin's statements. In referring to the persistent "head-and-stomach" declaration as well as Rabin's insistence that Israel is a Jewish-Zionist state, the May 1976 issue stated: "It was proved once more that a full belly is no substitute for freedom. . . . Israel's Arabs consider themselves now to belong to the Palestinian people which lives in the occupied territories and in the Arab countries. . . . Rabin's speech amounts to a statement that the present oppression is an attribute of this state's roots and character. . . ."

It is the Jewish character of Israel which the Arabs will never accept, and it is the Jewish character of Israel which is threatened by the political rights given to the Arabs by a schizophrenic Declaration of Independence and the ideologically torn and confused Israeli liberal leaders. Writing in *Midstream* magazine (January 1968), Joel Carmichael reasoned: "And if the Arab community within Israel achieves parity and is democratically represented in the organs of government, it is hard to see how an Israeli government could avoid the curbing of two rights that it is bound to regard as fundamental, and that have always been so regarded by the historic Zionist movement —the right to control both immigration and land development. If an Israeli Arab community roughly the size of the Israeli Jewish community were to be fairly represented in government, there is, of course, no reason to think it would tolerate the promotion of these two cardinal goals of the Zionist movement." Mr. Carmichael was being charitable. The Arabs would not tolerate the Zionist movement and the Jewish state.

A brief glimpse of what the Arabs have in mind can be garnered from a disingenuous proposal by an Israeli Arab leader. On June 28, 1976, Rashad Salah Slim, head of the Israeli village of Eiblin, drafted a memorandum in which he suggested that the name of the state be changed to "Israel-Palestine" and cover all the territory on *both* sides of the Jordan, including the country of Jordan. Free immigration would be given to all Jews and Arabs (including, of course, the Arabs who fled their homes in 1948). Voting would be based on one person, one vote. Of course, this is little more than a more cynical version of the PLO's call for a "democratic, secular Palestine," which translates into an Arab state. Slim's unique contribution is the name. Such a state would by its population automatically become the twenty-second Arab state, but the name "Israel" would remain in a hyphenated version (for at least the first six months).

Of course, the Arabs want "democracy." Their numbers mean the end of the one Jewish state in the world. The mad Jewish insistence that Israel is committed to this "democracy" is but the latest in Jewish tendencies toward suicide.

The Jew must decide whether he is prepared to sacrifice the Jewish state on the altar of "democracy" that is a cynical weapon in the hands of Arabs who have trampled on its banner a hundred times over in the past. The Jew must recognize that *no* Arab wishes to live in a *Jewish* state and that "democracy" is his weapon in putting an end to that state.

There are, of course, those Israeli Arabs who say that they *do* recognize the State of Israel and do see it as their country. Let no one rejoice prematurely. The Arabs who say this are simply accepting what they see as a *realistic* position. Israel exists, and they live there. The fact does *not* make them happy, for there are not two Arabs in the country who would not prefer to see a miracle occur and Jewish rule be displaced by Palestinian rule. But although they would prefer a Palestinian state in what is now Israel, they believe that this will not occur in the foreseeable future. They are not prepared to jeopardize themselves by saying the things that so many students do. But this is so, not because they differ with the sentiments expressed by the "radicals"; they are simply more "practical." Every Arab reserves for himself the right to work toward that glorious day when he will be the majority and at least by democratic, legal means will make his "Israel" an Arab state.

And so, the Arab who proclaims Israel's right to exist and his acceptance of citizenship and belonging to Israel is playing the same game that has been played for some time in regard to Jerusalem.

Sadat or Carter or some other gentile world statesman proclaims his fealty to the concept of "one Jerusalem," and Jews rejoice. For Jews also proclaim their demand for one, unified Jerusalem, and if the Egyptian and American presidents also do —why, there is proof that they support the Jewish position!

Nonsense. It is a game, the kind of Middle Eastern game of semantics in which men of deception, duplicity, and evasion are experts. Of course Sadat is for "one Jerusalem." But his concept is that of one unified *Arab* Jerusalem. Of course the American say they support a unified city. But if that unified city is an Arab one, they will support *that*. Jews are fearful of demanding precise and exact definitions lest their worst fears be realized, and so they join the game. "One Jerusalem"—all things to all people.

It is the same with the "Israel" that Arabs in the country claim to recognize and accept. "Israel" to the Jew means the *Jewish* state, irrevocably, permanently. Not so to the Arab. Yes, he recognizes a state called "Israel," which *today* is a Jewish state. But the "best" of the Arabs, the most "moderate," the most willing to accept the right of Israel, the Jewish state of today, to exist, *do not recognize that right as absolute*. They recognize the right of Israel, the Jewish state, to exist as long as a majority of its citizens prefer an "Israel" as the "Jewish state." But the most "moderate" and good Arabs are not *Zionists*. Should there eventually emerge an Arab majority in the country, every one of them—*swearing loyalty to "Israel"*—will go to the polls and vote out its Jewish character. They will, undoubtedly, vote to change its name too, but that is not really relevant. Every Arab in Israel reserves for himself the right, as a democratic majority, to abolish the *Jewish-Zionist nature of the country* that he would now dominate. Every Arab demands the right at least to work peacefully toward the day when the Law of Return is abolished and Israel will be a de facto Arab state.

The almost hysterical obeisances to "democracy" on the part of Israelis and their frantic insistence that Arabs enjoy democracy in an Israel that is committed to democracy are simply astounding. *Clearly, the more they pledge themselves to "democracy," the more bound they are to their commitment; the more impossible it will be for them to deny the Arab the right to put an end democratically to the Jewish state.* The Western-influenced Jewish Hellenists of our time dig their own pit of doom. Thus Labor Party Secretary-General Haim Bar-Lev, visiting South Africa in June 1980, was asked to compare the minority situations in South Africa and Israel. According to the Jewish Telegraphic Agency (June 10, 1980): "Bar-Lev observed that while he was not familiar with the South African situation, he felt that there was no comparison. In Israel, where there was equality before the law, both Arabs and Jews had to vote and sat in the same Knesset."

Is Bar-Lev a fool or a knave? The thought of a comparison with the pariah of the Western World—South Africa—turns him into a defender of democracy and of the rights of Arabs to do away with Zionism, as they sit "in the same Knesset" with the future Jewish minority. And so, in the end, he digs his own pit. He deceives not one Arab but contributes to the dismal Jewish self-delusion that will explode in our faces one day in the not terribly distant future.

On June 27, 1980, the former Labor Party director-general

of the Foreign Ministry, Gideon Rafael, wrote an impassioned defense of democracy in Israel. But, more important, he blistered the "fanatics" and "extremists" with their "antidemocratic virus." Rafael is a firm believer in democratic rights for the Arabs of Israel. He calls on "the supporters of the democratic way of life" to be "on constant alert to weed out the growth of antidemocratic tendencies. They must warn against cheap slogans and deceptive shortcuts. They must strengthen the understanding that democracy, with all its shortcomings, outshines the deceptive glitter of autocracy."

Rafael is guilty of the worst of cheap slogans. His bitter condemnation of honest "extremists" is a cover for his fear of facing the frightening question: Would he allow the Arabs of Israel to exercise their glorious democratic rights in order to put an end to Zionism?

Will that democratic "shortcoming" also outshine "autocracy"? The inherent contradiction of the Rafaels is not lost on the Arabs. What they fail to understand, however, is the genuine confusion of soul in those modern-day Hellenists who are really gentilized creatures of the West. The very real conflict between the Jewish values and Western ones unifies them. They are truly troubled souls, and so they attempt to avoid thinking about the real question, all the while hysterically waving high the banner of total democracy they hope they will never have to test. The promises they make to the Arabs are really anesthetics for their own troubled consciences. In the end they will be forced to choose, when, thanks to their own previous moral cowardice, they will have brought Israel to the very brink of tragedy.

A Jewish state versus the Western, gentilized one of total equality for Arabs and Jews. A growing Arab population that uses democracy to turn Israel into "Palestine." One cannot emphasize too often or too strongly that *this* is the core of the problem. But the tragic dwarfs who guide Israeli policy are too terrified to see. And so they choose to avoid reality.

Teddy Kollek, the greatest proponent of the illusion of "one Jerusalem," appoints mini–advisers on Arab affairs. One of them, Aharon Sarig, described his task (February 28, 1978) as being to "close the enormous gap" between East (Arab) and West (Jewish) Jerusalem "in everything connected with educational facilities, housing, and cultural institutions as well as the entire infrastructure, including roads, water, and sewerage pipelines, street paving, and lighting." This, he hopes, will " *increase the feeling of Jerusalem Arabs that they are part of the city.*"

Kollek, himself, in San Francisco in June 1980, ruled out, naturally, any Arab control of even part of the city, as well as *joint* rule of the city by Jews and Arabs. How, then, does the former Viennese, now Jerusalem, burgomaster propose to make the Arabs happy in a city that will never be theirs? The answer: "boroughs." "Large cities must be divided up into smaller districts to give people more feelings of identity and responsibility. This would give the Arabs the *feeling of running their own affairs.*"

Is it possible Kolleck actually believes this plan?

The Arabs will not have sovereignty; they will never be allowed even *joint* rule with Jews—but he will give them "*the feeling* of running their own affairs." What can one say concerning such contempt for the Arab mentality?

The Arabs deserve better. They deserve our recognition as a people who cannot be bought with sewerage lines or "feelings." At a celebration of Jerusalem writers commemorating the eleventh anniversary of "Unified Jerusalem," an Arab writer spoiled the evening for Teddy Kollek by deviating from the script. Said Muhmad Abu Shalabay: "This will be another Belfast. We must divide the city into two parts and have the eastern city be the capital of the Palestinian state."

The Arabs and their leftist Jewish comrades know better. Dr. Ismail Sabri Abdullah, an Egyptian university professor, wrote a book in 1969 called *Fi Muwajahat Isra'il* [Confronting Israel] in which he pointed to the fact that there was not an *Israeli* nationality but a *Jewish* one, and this was the cornerstone of the state: "The main obstacle in the way of forming a distinct *Israeli* nation is the Zionist [read: Jewish] link. For Israel cannot become a nation unless she finally ceases to consider herself the homeland of the Jews. The concept of an *Israeli* nationality inevitably negates *Jewish* nationalism."

What the Arab was saying was that the Jewish foundation and character of Israel prevented the Israelis—the *Arabs* of the state and the Jews—from creating a common, equal *Israeli* nationality. That, of course, is true. For the Arab of Israel to feel equal, the state, as the first and basic step, would have to give up its specific *Jewish* character. Is that what Jews want?

How important it is to understand that the Israeli Hellenists are troubled people, torn by their essential Western concepts and the desire to hold onto the Jewish state. They are upset when an Elmer Berger, renegade Jew and one of the key Jewish lobbyists against Israel, says: "This exclusivist Zionist nationality concept has always been the source of conflict in Palestine and it remains so today. By definition, the State of Israel's Zionist 'Jewish people' nationality base cannot accommodate any number of 'non-Jewish people,' nationals who might, in normal democratic procedures, threaten the 'Jewish character' of the state."

There are, of course, Jews who have no problems with such statements. Ironically, they are the Jews over whom Kollek and Rafael and Bar-Lev and Rabin turn apocalyptic. They are the Jews who see not the slightest problem in choosing. When confronted with the choice of Jewish survival through the Jewish state or a democracy that would turn it into an Arab one, they naturally and quite Jewishly opt for Jewishness.

Of course, they say, we insist upon a Jewish state with a Jewish majority and Jewish sovereignty and Jewish control of its own destiny. Of course we have learned our lessons of the Exile well. Of course we do not trust the Arabs to be kind to us and protect us. Of course we know what they did to us in the past and would do tomorrow, again, if they could. Of course we will never agree to be a minority again. Of course we have learned our Holocausts well. Of course Judaism demands a Jewish state —Jewish in spirit, culture, identity, and destiny. Of course there is no room for an Arab who is not prepared to accept the permanent limitations of a minority.

So speak those whose Jewish consciences are clear and who do not quake at the cry of "racism."

In 1933 David Ben-Gurion debated, with British Labor M.P. Josiah Wedgwood, the question of Zionism versus democracy in Palestine. Ben-Gurion, hardly a paragon of consistency, told Wedgwood: "When we are faced on the one hand with democratic formulas and on the other with the vital concerns of masses of workers, we give priority to the practical problems."

One suggests that the Ben-Gurion challenge be rephrased and made our national statement: "When we are faced on the one hand with a democratic demand to allow our enemies to take from us our state, and on the other wish to build that magnificent Jewish land that will be a haven for the Jewish body and a home for the soul, we choose Zionism; we choose the Jewish state; we choose Judaism."

The Arab Report, a propaganda sheet published by the Arab Information Center in the United States, wrote on November 15, 1975: "The essence of the political doctrine of Zionism is the concept that Jews are one people and the corollary that Jews must have a state of their own. . . . In a country in which there is a law called the Law of Return, permitting a Jew who has never been to Palestine to return, and a policy prohibiting a Palestinian from actually returning to his home . . . how can a country like that be described as a democracy?"

How amusing to read this and then to contemplate such Arab "democracies" as Saudi Arabia, Syria, Jordan, Kuwait, Iraq, Egypt, Algeria, *ad infinitum.* But that is not really relevant. The real issues is whether the Jew will accept the stark reality of the ultimate and insoluble contradiction or whether he will choose the Jewish state over democracy or fall victim to the Hellenism and guilt born of assimilated Western concepts.

The frantic pangs of assimilated conscience bode ill for the Jewish state. In an article for the Jewish Telegraphic Agency (June 10, 1976), Uzi Benziman wrote: "Israelis nowadays find themselves forced to face up to issues which were swept under the carpet for many years. . . . Israel was created to enable the Jews to have their own independent state where they would implement the Zionist vision of a restoration of sovereign national life. But relations between the Arab inhabitants and the Jews living in and immigrating to Israel were never sufficiently defined and clarified. . . .

"The real problem, after all, is rooted in the very definition of the state as a Jewish country which allows the Arab minority to have its own life. . . . Relations between Jews and Arabs are complicated because the majority represents a unique entity that embodies a religion and a nationhood, while the minority belongs to a larger, supranational entity. . . . *A new definition of the Israeli nation is needed.*"

What does Benziman mean by a new definition of the Israeli nation? Is he saying that in order to bring peace to Israel,

the state must "de-Judaize" itself, throw off the Zionist definition of Israel as a *Jewish* state? Is he calling for the cutting of ties
between Israel and Jewishness, Jewish people and Jewish tradition and culture? Is he saying that *all* people who live in Israel
now be looked upon as *Israeli nationals,* regardless of whether
they are Jews or Arabs, and the "Israeliness" now be measured
in the same way "Britishness" is?

There are not a few Israeli Jews who say yes. They are the
ones who see not the slightest reason to be Jewish, since the term
holds absolutely no religious or national meaning or value for
them. They are the Sabras or near-Sabras (along with the usual
sprinkling of Jewish self-haters), the Hellenists of our time.
They are the people to whom Judaism as a religion means nothing, and so the most fundamental pillar of Jewishness collapses.
But neither do they have even the superficial reasons to be Jewish that are the staffs of the Jews of the Exile and of certain
elements in Israel. These latter, though having thrown off religion, remain Jews for one or two other fascinating reasons:
goyim and *chulent.*

Goyim—gentiles. Vast numbers of Jews in the world remain
Jewish only because the Gentile does not permit them to do otherwise. "What forty eight prophets and seven prophetesses
could not do—turn the Jews to penitence—Haman's ring did,"
say the rabbis. Anti-Semitism, the bloody, murderous, ironic
reason that millions of Jews remain so.

Chulent—the Sabbath concoction of potatoes, beans, and
meat that cooks all night on the stove. It is the symbol of the
Jewish culinary and other social traditions that millions of Jews
who have left tradition still remember. Nostalgia! I remember
Zayde; I remember the Friday-night candles and wine.
Nostalgia, a weapon of conscience that binds and holds the Jew
to a people in which he would otherwise not see the slightest
unique value.

Goyim and *chulent:* hardly logical or deep reasons to remain
Jewish, but powerful, nevertheless, and effective.

But what do we say to hundreds of thousands of Sabras
who have never lived as a minority and who do not know the
lesson of *goyim,* the Gentiles? And what of all those who do not
have *chulent* or nostalgia to grip them and make Jewishness important, for whatever reason? What of all the dry bones of Israel

who have neither Jewish skin nor flesh nor veins nor spirit? What of all the gentilized Hebrews, products of a secular Zionism, socialist or otherwise, who aimed at creating a nation exactly like all other nations and succeeded so magnificently, of which the universal crime, social upheaval, and permissiveness that now grip the state are eloquent proof?

For these people there is not the slightest relevance to being Jewish, and their "Israeliness" means exactly as much or as little to them as "Danishness" or "Swedishness" or "Uraguayanness" to citizens of those countries. To the gentilized Hebrews there is only one major imperative: to live, and as much as possible without problems.

And if "Zionism," that link between Israel and Jewishness, is the cause of so much grief—annual reserve duty, high taxes, terrorist threats, inflation, insecurity—why, who needs it? And so thousands who can leave the country, and the Uzi Benzimans, suggest "a change in the definition" of the state.

There are scores of variations on the theme of de-Zionizing and de-Judaizing Israel. Each of them involves making the state less Jewish, in the absurd hope that that will satisfy the Arabs. Thus, a group called Shutafut ("Partnership") is established by a Jewish intellectual as a "union for creating conditions of partnership between Arabs and Jews." Question: How does one create a "partnership" in which one of partners insists that he be the senior one? Surely by making *both* equal coowners in the business—and there goes Zionism. Is that what Shutafut wishes?

Of course, the true absurdity in this is that the Arabs do not want partnership in the land they sincerely believe is theirs, especially when they believe that time and conditions are on their side. Why, the very rise of such a group convinces them that the Jews are fearful of the future, for otherwise why should they—who control the state—bother to try to make the Arabs "partners"? Certainly they, the Arabs, would never do such an insane thing if they were a majority. The Arabs do not want *shutafut,* partnership; they wish to control the land they will call "Palestine."

In reality, Shutafut's political program is vague or nonexistent. For all practical purposes, it reverts to the old "head-and-stomach" philosophy of helping Arabs to a better life as a means of having both sides reach "goodwill" and "coexistence." Nevertheless, although its "program" is politically vague and meandering, its entire spirit breathes "de-Zionization." Almost instinctively, the group seems to understand that a Zionist Jewish state and Arab-Jewish "love" are contradictions. And so, while its practical projects are those of "head-and-stomach," the real goal is the surrender of the exclusively Jewish state in favor of an "equal" partnership in which Arabs will love Jews.

Shutafut is one more in a long chain of liberal Jewish efforts to give up their own rights in hope of winning the love of others. The inevitable failure of the effort will stem from the fundamental contempt that the Gentile has for a Jew who, having no *self*-respect, can clearly never respect *him*.

Among the love and coexistence projects that are the first steps toward the de-Zionizing of Israel, Shutafut started a shaggy commune of a sort near Latrun, to be known as Neve Shalom. (Among the leading lights were one Bruno Hassar, an Egyptian Jew turned Catholic, described as "the prophet" of the commune, and Reconstructionist rabbi Jack Cohen.) There, in August 1977, as part of a week-long program to train counselors for joint Jewish-Arab children's summer camps, a Jewish-Arab poetry reading was held on the theme of "love of homeland." The Jews, naturally, spoke of love and peace. Fawzi Abdullah, an Arab poet, had other things in mind. His love of homeland was sincere—he wanted his land. And so the poem he read was called "Land Day," in which he condemned the Jews for taking Arab land. The Arab poet, he decided, had a national task: the writing of "historical documents." That meant describing the "wounded homeland" in which the Arabs were divided into "a minority within it and refugees without."

Partnership, indeed.

Shutafut will never bring peace to Israel, but it is doing two things quite successfully. It is helping to weaken and eventually will poison the concepts of Zionism and Jewish nationalism, especially in its effect on young Jewish students and liberals in the United States. Their simplistic and intellectually questionable approach, based on the magic words *love, peace,* and *coexistence,* finds fertile soil in the minds of young people, themselves victims of rootlessness and intellectual shallowness.

Second, Shutafut helps prepare the way for the breaking

down of the barriers that, until now, mostly prevented intermarriage and assimilation. Without any kind of plan to prevent the Arabs from politically taking over the Jewish state, the Hellenists of Shutafut, through de-Zionization, work vigorously on programs that destroy the uniqueness and separateness of the Jew. This must inevitably duplicate the intermarriage and assimilation that decimated Jews in Germany, from where the founder of Shutafut stems.

The truth is that even without groups such as Shutafut, assimilation has begun to grow in Israel. Held back for decades by Arab-Israeli conflict, by strict geographical separation between Jews and Arabs, and by strong traditional as well as anti-Arab feelings, it has begun to spread in recent years, those reasons having begun to weaken. Intermarriage and the breakdown of uniqueness have risen. This in itself makes the growing Arab population a threat to the spiritual existence of ever-growing numbers of Jews.

But the work of Shutafut and other groups of its kind will surely escalate the process. Surely, the joint Jewish-Arab workshops, summer camps, retreats, clubhouses, and visits to homes will do precisely what such things did during the eternal Jewish struggle for minority rights in every land of the Exile. Jewish youngsters with no Jewish education will see no differences between themselves and Arab youngsters. Friends will become lovers. Jewish women will find coexistence with Arab men in bedroom retreats, and the already nonexistent intellectual reasons not to intermarry will be reinforced in the name of "brotherhood" and "goodwill." Shutafut and other groups such as Interns for Peace (an organization with much money and support from the U.S. Reform Jewish movement, the American Jewish Committee, and other Establishment giants) all nourish the myth of "head-and-stomach" coexistence as well as moving toward the de-Zionizing of Israel. But most of all they are the prime drivers on the road to Jewish-Arab assimilation. For intermarriage and assimilation cannot thrive through separation. The first need is to break down barriers and to intermingle. That is being done by Shutafut and Interns.

There are indeed many who see nothing wrong with this. They are the masters of illogic who call for a "solution" to the Jewish problem of assimilation in the Exile by struggling hero-

ically to create a Jewish state in which Arab-Jewish mixing will
lead to Jewish disappearance in a joint "Israeli" identity. Black
humor aside, they are people who are faced with a Jewish value
versus a universal one; being essentially gentilized Hebrews,
they opt for universalism.

*Jewishness versus universalism. A Jewish state versus a Western,
liberal, equal one. Zionism or open democracy.* Ultimately Israel will
have to choose.

In an offhand remark in June 1976, Prime Minister Rabin
wondered how much longer "will we be able to prevent Nazareth Arabs from settling in [Jewish] Upper Nazareth?" Immediately, angry residents of the Jewish town signed a petition
that stated: "We came here to provide our children with a Jewish education and to raise them in a Jewish—not Arab—atmosphere." The Jewish residents, all immigrants, were making
the eminently logical point: to live next to Arabs in a mixed
atmosphere, they could have remained in Morocco.

Veteran *Yediot Aharonot* writer Shlomo Shamgar found his
liberal instincts repelled by the Jewish reaction. On June 27,
1976, he angrily wrote: "I cannot understand how Jews who
know what happened to our people because of such reactionary
views can so arrogantly reject neighbors of this or that nationality or religion. . . . The Arab is tolerated at best, as a neighbor in
the country but not in the neighborhood.'

Shamgar, of course, revels, in his self-righteousness. Will he
tell us what he thinks of a state that by law is *Jewish* and what
he thinks of European states that call themselves *Christian?* What
would Shamgar say to a state whose law of immigration applies
only to non-Jews? Will Shamgar agree to a democratically
elected Palestinian state in place of Israel? Shamgar is one of
those whose terror of thinking about the contradiction between
democracy and Zionism forces his feelings of guilt to erupt on
behalf of Arabs in Upper Nazareth housing projects.

The Arab-Jewish problem in Israel has nothing to do with
lack of integration, jobs, education, or toilets. It has nothing to
do with stomachs or heads. It is the desire of a minority (once a
majority) that was humiliatingly defeated to be sovereign in
what it considers its own land. It is the problem of a Jewish state
that says nothing emotionally, spiritually, nationally, or culturally to the non-Jewish Arabs. It is a question of a state with

a bewildered Declaration of Independence drafted by confused and bewildered men—whose universal values clashed with their Jewish ones, leaving them troubled and guilt-ridden. It is the problem of a democratic option that can eliminate the Jewish state at the ballot box.

It is a question of democracy. It is a question of demography. It is a question we must ask ourselves: Are we prepared to commit national suicide?

No two peoples so different in every way can possibly share the same country. The world is filled with examples of the rise of nationalism and separation that promise for Israel the horrors that today are international realities. We need only look at a world torn by particularism to realize the folly of the belief that Jews and Arabs can coexist in Eretz Yisrael.

CHAPTER 7

One Worlds

The frantic Israeli efforts to come up with workable plans for Arab-Jewish coexistence in Israel are all based on a need to believe in the validity and truth of the following proposition:

It is possible for two peoples who differ in everything that constitutes a people—nationality, religion, ethnicity, culture, language, and common historical experiences over 3,000 years; it is possible for these two peoples, one of which has lived in the land as a majority for six centuries while the other was mostly absent for 1,900 years; it is possible for these two peoples, after the former minority has, in the wake of decades of hate, violence, and war, become the majority and ruler, and the former majority, overnight, has become a small and powerless minority; it is possible for these two peoples, after the former minority has acquired total sovereignty and national power in the land that the former majority always claimed as its own; it is possible for these two peoples who live in a land that the present minority believes to be entirely its own and that the present majority insists is its birthplace, its home, its property, its right, and therefore proclaims in it a state of its own, belonging to all the members of its nation wherever they may be; it is possible for this state to breathe the religion, nationhood, culture, ethnicity, language, and destiny of only one of the two peoples; it is possible for the minority to have massive population and educational growth that assures it of becoming at least a third if not a majority of the country in the future; it is possible for the nations surrounding this state to be related in blood, religion, nationhood, culture, ethnicity, language, and destiny to the minority, vowing to erase the sovereignty of the majority state; it is possible for the majority in the state to grow increasingly isolated and bitterly attacked throughout the world; it is possible for the minority to sense the growing weakness, insecurity, and divisions in the state, even as in the territory bordering the areas in which they live offers have been made for autonomy, *and with all that:* it is possible through goodwill and economic and social progress for both peoples to live together peacefully, with the minority feeling loyalty and civic attachment to the state that belongs to the other, with no dreams of someday taking it over.

If I were an Arab, I would laugh. Being a Jew, I weep. The state is the vehicle and home of the nation. From time immemorial the two have been synonymous. The city-state of Greece was the home of a particular people. All the citizens (with the rarest of exceptions) were of the same nation, religion, culture, language. Again, with the rarest of exceptions, there were no German-Athenians, Italian-Athenians, Hispanic-Athenians, or Afro-Athenians in Athens, no "hyphenated" citizens. All Athenians were Greek; all came from the same background with common blood and shared historical experience. This was the natural and normal state of affairs in the ancient world, and logical it was.

The nation, a collection of tribes, themselves derived from clans and families, was one large common family joined by the thickest and most binding of elements: blood. Everywhere it was the same. The Land of Moab was the state of the people of Moab and of no one else. In it, all spoke a common language, Moabite; in it, all worshiped a common god, Kmosh; in it, all remembered their common ancestor, Lot. No two nations "shared" Moab. It was normal and logical. A family needs a place to live and be safe from the elements; it acquires a house. The house belongs to that family and to no one else. It is the family that establishes the rules and regulations of the house. It is their name that is given to the house. So was it with the extended family, the nation. The nation gave its name to the land, and strangers who arrived did not become citizens and coowners of the land merely by dwelling there. It was the one family-nation that owned the land and that established the rules. One who was not a member of the family might be a guest, a welcome visitor, or even a tolerated resident—*but he was not a citizen: the land was not his.*

It was only relatively recently that a new concept emerged, the nation-state of modern times. Suddenly it was not membership in the *nation* that gave a person rights and ownership, but residency and domicile in the *land*. Whereas once the one nation-owner gave its name to the land, now the land gave its name to the residents thereon, regardless of their lack of common racial, religious, cultural, ethnic, linguistic, or historical ties. And so, the Austro-Hungarian Empire proudly boasted of its Austro-Hungarian "citizens," Serbs, Croats, Poles, Rumanians, Hungarians, Czechs. The boasting came to a loud end with the assassination of the Austrian archduke by "citizens" who preferred to be independent Slavs, or Poles in a sovereign Poland, Rumanians in a Rumania, and Hungarians in a Hungary.

World War I marked the beginning of the end of the belief that a multinational state could exist without violence, blood, and force. "Self-determination," a modern-day attempt to return to the original nation-state, became the watchword. Wilson and the Allies carved out whole new countries from old ones, with the hope of having each nation live under its vineyard and fig tree, in its own sovereign state where *it* could set its own destiny. It was an admission of the inevitable conflict between two peoples sharing the same land.

Since state after state remained with sizable national minorities, it was decided to write into the peace treaties that followed the war "national minorities guarantees," and a whole body of international law arose to protect those nations within larger nations. Of course, they failed. Bloody communal conflict and constant tension were the lot of Central and Eastern Europe between the two world wars. Indeed, it was the presence of sizable numbers of ethnic Germans in Poland and Czechoslovakia that afforded Hitler the opportunity to aid his "oppressed" compatriots, attack those two nations, and precipitate World War II and the Holocaust.

Following the war, universalists and federalists of various kinds arose. Throughout Europe, nationalism appeared to be under attack and the call for a European community of nations was led by Jean Monnet, who, along with many others, predicted the demise of nationalism. The rise of communism and its call for proletarian internationalism merged with astonishing advances in science and technology that supposedly would level cultures, blur differences, shrink the world, and make it one. It was an illusion.

Internationalism is not the wave of the future, and the Talmudic axiom "Man is near unto himself" is translated in modern geopolitical terms into an epidemic of nationalist and separatist drives. The power of separatism is inevitably greater than that of amalgamation, as the pulls and pressures of religion, race, national entity, and creed exert a far more emotional pull on the souls of men than the nebulous international call for federation or the artificial coming together of peoples with little or no common history of suffering or sharing.

It is the nature of man to feel closer to the most limited and narrow circles of people. Just as the family, in almost all cases, takes precedence over the nation, so does the nation easily win more loyalty from its citizens than the "world." And within the modern state, whose boundaries are so often artificial creations that overrun and bisect entire tribal or national entities, lumping together many distinct and separate nationalities or religions by fiat, there is ferment today as the pull and tug of nation, tribe, religion, and just plain difference lead to demands for separate power, sovereignty, and state.

Sometimes it is the case of two different national groups sharing the same country, one a majority and the other a large and powerful minority. The example of Cyprus comes readily to mind. Sometimes it is religion that divides and leads to bloody rioting or wars; consider the Hindu-Muslim conflict that led to the partition of India into two states, one Hindu (India) and the other Muslim (Pakistan). Sometimes it is a bitter language struggle that is also the tip of the iceberg in a nationality conflict; Canada and Belgium are cases in point. *Many times it is just "difference."*

The world today is rent and riddled with conflict between parties sharing a common territory and demanding full control of the area, "autonomy," removal of one of the conflicting groups, or division of the land into separate parts. It is unheard of to see two sharply differing national groups that share the same territory—one a majority and the other a minority—living peacefully amid the placid acceptance by one of permanent minority status. No, the *differences* between entities lead to demands for separate sovereign territory or separate autonomy so that they may live their own unique national, cultural, religious, and social lives. The fact that they may, and usually do, go to civil war with *themselves* once they have achieved their own sovereignty does not detract from the pull of the magnet of sovereignty. Differences, per se, lead to hostility. Sometimes it is the minority that demands power and sovereignty. Sometimes it is the majority that oppresses the minority to protect its power and sovereignty. But whatever the result, the cause is the same. Differing national, religious, or cultural groups do not live in peace with each other.

The innumerable cases, today, of agitation based on differences exist not only in the "unsettled" areas of Asia and Africa, but in ordered and settled Europe and the Western Hemisphere. They transcend ideology and do so easily; the great irony of our age is the failure of communism even remotely to bind the world's proletariat into one common unit. Nationalism has easily conquered communism, and the conflict between China and Vietnam is little more than a direct continuation of the national struggles between them that have gone on for ages. It matters little whether emperor or commissar sits in Peking or Hanoi. And it is the angry *nationalism* of China over the humiliations suffered at the hands of Czarist Russia in the nineteenth century that weighs far more in Peking's mind than the Marxist-Leninist proletarian bonds. Chinese identity and the bonds between Chinese wherever they may live are far more important to the "Communists" of China than the international ties of communism the world over. Similarly, Yugoslavia looks to itself, and Tito placed his own national interests first, the interest of the International a distant second.

The separatist drive is alive and well enough to stun us in such stable areas as Great Britain, where Scots and Welsh who have suddenly begun to mutter things about independence even manage to win seats in the British Parliament. France is shocked to hear Bretons and Corsicans demanding freedom, and bombs go off in Paris to underline those demands. And if calls for freedom and independence are born of separate national, or religious, or language differences, how much more impossible is it

to expect peace and harmony and acceptance of minority status
from an Israeli Arab who is different from the ruling majority
Jew in every possible way? And when one adds to this the fact
that the Arab minority was once a majority in the land, what are
the chances for harmony and peace? Such is the reality of the
Jewish majority–Arab minority situation in the Land of Israel. A
look at just some of the myriad separatist movements and conflicts in the world—most far less abrasive than the Jewish-Arab
one—will go a long way toward dispelling dangerous illusions
and delusions concerning the possibility of Jewish-Arab harmony in the Land of Israel.

It is a survey that is necessarily cursory and incomplete, for
there is simply no room in this book for a detailed description of
all the disputes. It is enough, however, to put the Jewish-Arab
conflict in proper perspective: a deadly battle with only bloody
encounter as long as the Arabs remain in the land.

THE MIDDLE EAST

In Israel's backyard are not only first-class exhibits of
"coexistence" between various differing groups but also classic
proof of how Arabs treat a differing group within their midst,
even when that group is Arab. It takes little to project from that what
life would be for *Jews* in a country that has a large, powerful
Arab minority—or majority.

Lebanon: Christians versus Muslims

No one knows exactly how many people have been killed in
Lebanon since the civil war there began just a relatively few
years ago, but 50,000 would be a conservative figure. Nor do we
speak of the tens of thousands maimed and wounded, the hundreds of thousands who fled their homes, the untold amount of
property damage.

The antagonists in Lebanon all speak the same language:
Arabic. They share the same culture, come from the same national ethnic background. *They are all Arabs, one people in every way
but one:* some 55 percent of the population is Muslim and the
rest, Christian. That has been enough to cause a bloody five-
year war, to cause de facto partition of Lebanon into Christian
and Muslim enclaves, and to breed hate and vengeance. It has

been enough to bring about an incident such as that of the village of Aishiya.

Aishiya is a Christian Maronite Village in southern Lebanon. On October 21, 1976, Lebanese Muslims, supported by PLO terrorists, attacked. Nadil Nassen, a Christian Arab, survived and described the attack: "They slaughtered us like sheep. They raped women, smashed skulls, and murdered children in their mothers' arms. Women and children hiding in fruit orchards and caves around the village were found and murdered, one by one, by knife and dagger." Nadil reported seeing a thirty-five-year-old woman named Mary Samih and her seven-year-old son tied to a tree and their heads hacked off.

On September 28, 1976, the Associated Press reported an attack on the Christian village of Ras el-Harf, ten miles east of Beirut. Quoting the Christian Phalange radio station, the AP said that Muslim forces overran the village, "stormed its church and monastery, and blew up its cemetery. 'Skeletons were dug brutally out of graves and thrown into the main street of the fallen village,' said the radio station." It should, of course, be pointed out that the Christian Arabs were every bit as brutal in their attacks on Muslims.

The very Lebanese system is testimony to the hostile divisions of the various communities and their fears and suspicions of each other. Its eventual breakdown is proof of the ultimate inability of the Arabs to accept coexistence with "different" groups—even though they themselves are Arabs.

The constitutional law of 1943, when Lebanon attained independence, provided for official recognition of the diverse communities and guaranteed them just representation. By consensus, the president (the real power) was always to be a Maronite Christian, as befitted the largest religious community. The prime minister is always a Sunni Muslim, despite the fact that the Sunnis are not the largest Muslim community in the country; they are, however, the most advanced. In turn, that has led to friction with the larger Shiite Muslim community, which believes that it deserves more, at the expense of both Sunni Muslims and Christians. (Under the constitution, the Shiites "get" only the post of Speaker of the House.)

The Sunnis have yet another grievance. In 1920, for political reasons, the colonial French government that ruled Syria-

Lebanon at the time amputated a large Sunni Muslim region of Syria and attached it to Lebanon. This move, which transformed the Sunnis from majority to minority status, has been a source of bitterness ever since.

In any event, all the government posts, from the highest to the lowest, were distributed by numerical strength of religious communities. Thus, the Parliament was run on the basis of six Christians to five Muslims, and within each religion there was yet another breakdown according to sects. This incredibly complex and burdensome system came into being in the hope that if each group received its "proper share," all would learn to coexist.

Of course, the civil war proved that this was a hopeless delusion. The instant the Muslims felt they had an opportunity to seize control of the country, they attempted to do so. And so Arabs, who differ in nothing but religion, slaughter each other. The reason? The Arab Muslims demand a state in which *they* will wield power. They are not prepared to live under the rule of others, no matter how narrow the differences. Each group seeks its own sovereignty, a cultural and political entity to call its own. *Differences between groups, per se, engender friction, conflict, hostility, hatred.*

Iraq and Iran: Kurds versus Arab Muslims and Muslim Non-Arabs

Millions of Kurds live in the border area of Iraq, Iran, and Turkey. They are Muslims but not Arabs. They make no secret of their demand for an independent Kurdistan. Because of this there have been sporadic uprisings in both Iraq and Iran with heavy fighting and loss of life. Particularly in Iraq, where at least 25 percent of the population is Kurdish, the rebellion has threatened the territorial integrity of the country. The Kurds attempted to revolt against the former Iraqi monarchy too, but in 1970 and again in 1973 a truly serious war broke out against the Ba'ath government in Baghdad.

The ostensible demand was for autonomy, but the Kurds made no bones about their eventual hope: a Kurdish republic carved out of large chunks of Iraq, Iran, and Turkey. The Iraqis poured all their power into a total effort to crush the Kurds, and when the shah of Iran ceased his support of them, by 1977 the revolt was smashed. The legacy of hate, however, remained. In September 1977 the London-based Anti-Slavery Society charged that the Iraqis were torturing and dispossessing Kurds. The Kurds, for their part, still dream of their state.

Meanwhile, a similar scenario is being played out in Iran. With the fall of the shah, the Kurds in western Iran near the Iraqi border raised, again, the banner of autonomy. Bloody battles took place in July 1979 near the towns of Serow, Marivan, and Kermanshah, culminating months of struggle. On July 30, the Iranian Kurdish spiritual leader, Sheikh Ezzedin Hosseini, appealed to Tehran to work out a compromise that would grant the Kurds self-rule. Fighting continues to this day.

Iran: Persian Muslims versus Arabs versus Afghans

In June 1979 the Arabs of Iran tried to seize the chief port city of Khorramshahr, demanding autonomy for the Arabs of Iran's southwest province of Khuzistan. In the first week thirty-seven people were killed and in the next month hundreds more were either arrested or shot as the Arabs sought autonomy from the Persian majority. The fact that both groups are Muslim had not the slightest effect on the struggle.

In the desolate area where Iran, Afghanistan, and Pakistan converge live the Baluchis. They call the land Baluchistan, to the dismay of the three existing states. They are Sunni Muslim, all of the same tribal, historical, and cultural background. Artificial borders mean little to them, and the Iranian Baluchis, of whom there are more than half a million, have openly supported their Afghan brothers against the Soviets.

More important, there is a growing move for a Baluchi state to be carved out of the three-nation area they inhabit. At the end of 1979 Baluchis and Iranian Islamic revolutionaries clashed in the city of Zahidan. At least eleven died and eighty were wounded in three days of fighting. The Iranian government, which is Shiite Muslim, looks nervously at the ethnically and sectarianly different Baluchis. And so does Pakistan.

Pakistan: Pakistanis, Baluchis, Pathans, Bengalis, Biharis, Shiites

In 1971 Pakistan suffered a humiliating trauma. In a short but decisive war, rebels in the eastern half of the country, aided

by Indian troops, crushed the Pakistani army and seceded, to
form a new state called Bangladesh. Originally, violent fighting
between Muslims and Hindus, which left thousands dead,
forced the British in 1947 to partition the subcontinent into Hindu India and Muslim Pakistan after it was found that nothing
could persuade them to live together peacefully.

The problem with Muslim Pakistan, however, was that
there were two huge areas of Muslims in the subcontinent, separated from each other by more than 1,000 miles. And so, partition created "two Pakistans-that-were-one," separated by a
huge expanse of India. Pakistan, having been born of the inability of Muslims and Hindus to live together, proceeded to go to
war with itself over other differences. The Pakistanis of West
Pakistan differed in everything but religion with the eastern
Bengalis. Difference led to hostility, violence, war—Bangladesh.

No sooner had Bengalis achieved majority independence
when they found themselves with a minority of their own: Urdu-
speaking non-Bengali Muslims, known as Biharis. Some
250,000 of those unwanted people (said Bangladesh President
Mujibur Rahman: "Let the world purchase an island for
them") sat in fear in Bangladesh as 200,000 Bengalis were
trapped in West Pakistan and rounded up for internment
camps.

Pakistan faced yet another "Bangladesh," this time to the
west. The largest number of Baluchis live on the Pakistani side
of the region they call Baluchistan. A separatist nationalist
movement there, the United Baluchi Front, is led by Mobashir
Hassan Kesrami; the World Baluchi Organization of Oulfat
Nazzram has its headquarters in Baghdad. In 1973 serious fighting broke out between Baluchi rebels and government troops.
What may be an even more serious problem is the Pathan or
Pushtu national movement, whose tough mountain fighters inhabit the area of the Khyber Pass and other parts of Pakistan
and Afghanistan.

And as all these Sunni Muslims war because of national
and ethnic differences, Pakistanis of the same ethnicity and nationality met in 1980 in bloody confrontation in Pakistan's capital, Islamabad. More than 10,000 Pakistani Shiites with clubs
and stones battled police over the imposition of a Sunni religious
tax, known as the *Zakat.* The Shiites, who make up 15 percent of

Pakistan's eighty million population, felt threatened by the strong fundamentalism of Pakistan's Sunni Muslim President Zia.

Syria: Sunnis versus Alawites versus Druzes

Syria is "blessed" with an abundance of religious sects. The majority of the population is Sunni Muslim (65 to 70 percent), but the country is controlled by the Alawite sect, a Shiite off-shoot. On August 31, 1979, an Alawite religious leader was assassinated in Syria's largest port city, Latakia. Thousands of Sunni Muslims demonstrated against the government, and 2,000 troops had to be brought in to quell the revolt. At least five people died.

Since then, a growing rebellion against the government has spread to every city in Syria. It is led by the Sunni Muslim Brotherhood, and the roots of the rebellion are in the rise to power of the Ba'ath Party in 1963.

For decades the Sunnis controlled Syria; the Alawite and Druze sects were powerless. Both the Druzes and Alawites, who bitterly resented their lack of power, flocked to the then-outlawed opposition Ba'ath party. At the same time the Alawites and Druzes found in the army jobs shunned by the more affluent Sunnis. When the Ba'ath, with army support, overthrew the government in 1963, the Alawites liquidated the Druze officers in the army and proceeded to take power from the Sunnis. (It might be noted that the Druzes were also victims earlier of a large-scale massacre in their mountainous area, Jebel ed Druz, some thirty years ago. Lest one weep, let it be known that some of the most vicious slaughter of Christians in Lebanon was perpetrated by Druzes and Sunnis.)

The Alawites enacted measures against both the wealthy and middle classes (mostly Sunnis and Christians) as well as against the power of the Sunni Muslim clergy. The almost daily bombings in Syria, today, are the Sunnis' response. Syria— where two groups, both Muslim, both Arab, differing *only* in sectarianism, kill each other. The reason? They are different and they both want power.

Egypt: Muslims versus Copts

The Coptic Christian Church split from Rome in the year

451, and in Egypt it claims no fewer than six million adherents, a large minority that pales, however, in comparison to the other thirty-four million Egyptians—almost all Muslims. The Copts have always lived in insecurity in Egypt, and the recent upsurge in Muslim fundamentalism has caused serious friction.

In March and April of 1980 Muslim student riots in the university city of Asyut, which is half Christian, led to the death of at least one student and injuries to and arrests of many others. The Muslims demanded that no Copts be appointed to government posts and imposed other restrictions. Harassment was so bad that the pope of the church, Shenudah III, canceled all non-religious Easter celebrations and retired to a monastery in the western desert to protest harassment by fanatic Muslim groups.

Two years earlier, Shenudah and forty-four bishops had cloistered themselves in a Cairo church for a five-day fast. The focus of that protest was a proposed law approved by Sadat's Council of State, the highest judicial body of Egypt, stipulating death for any Muslim who converted to another faith and for anyone who encouraged him to do so—clearly aimed against the Copts and their efforts to proselytize. Churches in Asyut were stoned, and the Coptic community in Houston, Texas, protested to President Carter. According to the Associated Press (September 11, 1977), there had been a rise in Egyptian "demands for a return to the strict traditions of the early days of Islam."

The growing violence against the Copts led to planned anti-Egyptian demonstrations by Copts in America and Australia. The government issued a veiled threat against the Copt protest that would endanger "national unity and social peace," and Sadat, in a nationwide broadcast from Parliament, spent almost twenty minutes condemning the Copts for disrupting the national unity. The Copts are as Egyptian as their Muslim counterparts. Why the tension and threats? They are a large minority, they are educated—and they are very different.

Turkey: Muslims versus Muslims, Armenians, and Orthodox Syrians

In December 1978 mobs of thousands of Sunni Muslims in the Turkish city of Kahramanmaras charged through the streets, screaming: "A *jihad* ["holy war"] for Allah!" Two days later, more than 100 Alawites were dead, more than 1,000 were wounded, and thousands had fled in panic. Said Interior Minister Irfan Ozaydinli: "The fighting sprang from enmity and hatred that had accumulated over the years."

Despairing of a solution (in July 1980 another eighteen Alawites were killed in Corum, a city where their sect makes up 30 percent of the population), thousands of Alawites fled to Syria to join their Alawite brothers; there they can defend themselves against *Syrian* Sunnis.

Others, however, have fled as far as Holland, which has a large (100,000) Turkish immigrant worker population (itself causing friction in that European country). Several score Alawites arrived in 1980 in Almelo and Enschede and went into hiding with other Turkish families.

They join thousands of Syrian Orthodox Christian Turks who fled eastern Turkey for Holland out of fear of persecution by Muslims, *especially Kurds*. Their main refuge is the Dutch town of Hengel, but they won headlines on Good Friday 1979 when 135 of them occupied the Roman Catholic St. John's Cathedral in Bois-le-Duc to demand permission to remain in Holland, lest they be killed in Turkey.

And, in 1977, the Armenian Secret Army for the Liberation of Armenia murdered the Turkish ambassador to the Vatican, the fifth Turkish diplomat to be killed by the group, whose goal is vengeance for the massacre of Armenians during World War I and an Armenian state. The massacre of more than two million Armenians by the Turks in that war has never been forgotten, nor has the short-lived independent Armenia that followed the war. On June 14, 1977, the president of the Federation of Turkish-American Societies wrote an angry letter to the *New York Times* condemning "the mad search for identity by certain Armenians." Mad or not, the point was well made. Sixty years afterward, the Armenians still seek a separate state and power of their own.

This is the Middle East, where Muslims and Arabs appear to be incapable of living in peace with anyone—including themselves—who is "different." Sometimes it is religion, sometimes ethnicity, sometimes language. Sometimes they are a majority, sometimes they are a minority. But always there is the inability to live with the difference. Across the ages come the prophetic words: "And thou shalt call his name Ishmael . . . and he will be

a wildman: his hand will be against every man and every man's
hand against him" (Genesis 16:11–12).

And if this is so, what madness holds us in its grip and has
us believe that they will live with Jews who differ from them in
every way, who "stole" their land, and who appear today to be
weak and retreating? Israel heads inexorably toward another
Cyprus.

Cyprus

Cyprus is an island that in 1960 gained independence, but
no peace. No sooner had the struggle by the Greek Cypriots
against the British ended than they turned their attention to the
Turks. For centuries a large Greek majority of some 80 percent
had lived uneasily next to a Turkish minority of about 18 percent. The demand of the Greeks for independence always carried with it a corollary: *enosis,* union with the Greek motherland.
To the Turkish minority, the thought of living under the Greek
Cypriots as an 18 percent minority was bad enough; the thought
of being part of Greece was terrifying. And so the independence
plan called for a "bicommunal" state—not a federation, but a
state in which the Turks would get proportional representation
with appropriate vetoes of important issues—including *enosis.*

Archbishop Makarios, the Greek Cypriot leader, attempted
to subvert the agreement in 1963, touching off an ugly war between Greeks and Turks with the Turkish army, just across the
waters, ready to step in. In 1974, when the Greek colonels in
Athens did attempt to establish total Greek rule over the entire
island, the Turkish troops invaded and put an end to bicom-
munalism. They succeeded by force, fear, and harassment in
forcing the Greek Cypriots to go to southern Cyprus, while
Turkish Cypriots resettled in the northern part of the island.
Decades of bitter fighting led to a solution by transfer of population. Today, Cyprus is in effect two states, each homogeneous,
each the sovereign land of a people who could not live in peace
with the other.

There are differences from, but striking parallels with, Israel. In both cases, two peoples differ in national, ethnic, cultural, religious, and linguistic qualities. In both cases, the minority has powerful ethnic brethren outside the country, but
nearby, who sympathize with their plight. In both cases, the

minority is between 18 and 20 percent of the total population. That is all bad enough, but for Israel there is even a worse difference. *The Greeks were always the majority* and the Turks never claimed the land had been stolen; the most they sought was their *share* of the land. The Arabs of Israel claim that *since* they were once the majority, *all the land was stolen from them.* Israel moves inexorably toward Nicosia.

Asia

India: Bengalis, Tripurans, Assamese, Muslims, Hindus, Andhras

Indian army Major R. Pajamani told reporters: "I wonder whether My Lai [the South Vietnamese village that was the scene of a massacre] was half as gruesome as here." It was June 8, 1980, and the scene was the village of Mandai in the northeast Indian state of Tripura. As many as 2,000 Bengalis had been savagely slaughtered by Indian Tripura tribesman who raped and burned alive women and children. Tens of thousands of hysterical Bengalis fled from the province. The cause? The Tripura Upaijati Yuua Samiti led a drive demanding the expulsion of all Bengalis who had emigrated from East Pakistan (now Bangladesh) since 1947. The influence of the Muslim Bengalis had reduced the Hindu Tripurans to a minority in their own state.

Five months earlier, similar riots began in the neighboring state of Assam, whose indigenous Hindu population is descended from Burma's Shan tribes. Millions of Bengalese have fled to Assam over the years, and according to a United Press International dispatch (April 6, 1980): "The Assamese call the Bengalis a threat to their own culture and political life and fear being outvoted in their own state. Assamese students are spearheading a campaign to have Bengalis deported from the state."

In the Assamese riots, mobs armed with swords, spears, gasoline cans, and bamboo sticks stormed Bengali villages, killing hundreds, burning homes, and driving tens of thousands to flee to safety in neighboring West Bengal, an ethnically similar state. The West Bengalis retaliated, blocking the narrow corridor that is the only access to Assam from the rest of the country.

Assam, Tripura, Nagaland, and other northeast states are "seething with extremist demands for national self-determination," according to UPI (April 22, 1980).

India itself was born in the bloodbath of a horrible Hindu-Muslim civil war in which countless numbers were killed. Eighteen million Hindus and Muslims fled their homes in a massive exchange of population as they sought safety with their own kind. But India remained a country with astronomical problems.

The truth is that India is an artificial state that stands on the verge of falling apart. There are at least a dozen major regional languages, with Hindi the most common in the north. But Hindi is incomprehensible in the south of the country, where Indians speak one of the Dravidian languages. In 1978 the government made an effort to make Hindi the truly official language of the country, causing the chief ministers of the four southern states to meet in Madras and condemn the government for its efforts "to covertly impose Hindi" on people who speak another language. The southern Indians warned: "This conference voices its apprehension that any further attempt to impose Hindi is likely to erode the confidence of the non-Hindi-speaking people in the government." It was a blunt warning that underlined India's fragility and divisions. For it was the bloody riots between linguistic and ethnic groups that forced India's first prime minister, Nehru, to redraw the map of the country to give each major language group a state of its own. It is clearly a stopgap measure, a patchwork designed to gain time. But the bloody communal rioting in India today shows the inevitable ascendancy of division over forced, artificial unity.

Indeed, even the general Muslim-Hindu problem that was thought to have been solved with partition in 1947 still haunts India. Millions of Muslims still remain in India, and in August 1979 fifteen people were killed and scores injured as a bomb went off at a Hindu religious ceremony in Jamshedpur, and Muslims and Hindus battled in the streets.

And, as a kind of immutable footnote: To solve language and ethnic tensions, the forty-five million Telegu-speaking Indians were given their province of Andhra Pradesh.

It took twenty-five years, but in 1973 bloody fights broke out as the people of the wealthiest part of the state, Andhra, rioted to demand separation from the poorer part, Telengana.

Sixty died as mobs smashed, burned, looted, and shut down the state known as "the rice bowl of India." Differences, where the two competing rivals are large enough, lead to hostility, division, and separation.

Sri Lanka: Buddhist Sinhalese versus Hindu Tamils

Just twenty-two miles to the southeast of India lies the large island of Sri Lanka, formerly Ceylon. In August 1977 two weeks of mutual slaughter between the ten million-strong Buddhist-Sinhalese majority and the three million Hindu Tamils killed 54 (officially) and left 25,000 Tamils homeless. Said a shaken official: "I have seen the beast in man, I have seen men burned alive and women raped and houses set ablaze."

Led by the Tamil United Liberation Front, the Tamils seek a separate Tamil Ealam state in northern Sri Lanka, near their fifty million Tamil brethren in South India. Ironically, the Sinhalese may be unwittingly aiding in just that. Their attacks on the Tamils sent tens of thousands fleeing in an exodus of fear to the northern part of the island. What is happening is the de facto partition of the island. Militant Tamil separatists killed at least a dozen police in 1979.

By February 1974 the situation had grown so bad that the government announced that talk of partition was to be a criminal offense. No one believed that the government could jail three million people. And the violence continued.

Philippines: Muslims versus Christians

More than 2,000 people were killed or wounded in 1978 in the war in the southern Philippines between Muslim secessionist rebels and government forces. According to Deputy Defense Minister Carmelo Barbero, some *60,000* people have been killed in the first seven years of the uprising. About 100,000 Filipino Muslims, in addition, fled to the nearby Muslim Malaysian state of Sabah to find refuge with their fellow religionists.

Yes, the Muslim presence is felt in Southeast Asia, too, and the Manila government has been forced to spend more than half a million dollars a day on the revolt. The Filipino Muslims in the south number about two million, mostly on the island of Mindanao. When the Spanish conquered the islands in the sixteenth century, those Muslims who resisted and were called

Moros (Moors) were driven south. There they fight today for a state to be known as Bangsa Moro, and the bloodletting continues.

Thailand: Buddhists versus Muslims

On September 22, 1977, two grenades exploded at a ceremony attended by the king and queen of Thailand and their two daughters in Yala province. The royal family was unharmed, and the government accused six Muslim secessionists of the attempted assassination.

Muslims in the three southern provinces near Muslim Malya, Pattani, Yala, and Narathiwat have fought for years for the secession of the provinces with their million Muslims. They are led by the National Liberation Front of the Pattani Republic.

Burma: Buddhists versus Muslims

No fewer than 100,000 Muslim refugees fled into Bangladesh in the first half of 1978 from Burma, where they claimed the army "had waged a campaign of terror against the country's Muslim minority." The exodus caused a serious rift between the two countries when the president of Bangladesh, Major General Ziaur Rahman, accused Burma of "an inhuman eviction of Muslims."

The "Overseas Chinese": Vietnam, Cambodia, Indonesia, Malaysia

The "boat people" of Vietnam for the most part are not Vietnamese but *Hoas*—Vietnam-born ethnic Chinese—and the Chinese who live outside China proper, in every country in Southeast Asia, are a hated minority. For the most part this stems from the fact that their diligence and hard work have enabled them to control the commerce of the cities. Jealously is a deeply ingrained trait in man. When the object of this jealousy is "different," you have the makings of bloody communal conflict.

And so between March and June 1978, 90,000 Chinese fled Vietnam after official harassment, prompted by a desire to "Vietnamize" the economy. In China the refugees would face difficult conditions, at least among their own people. An

Associated Press dispatch (June 2, 1978) quoted a Western diplomat: "They prefer China, where they are not a hated minority, rather than Vietnam, where no matter what they do they will be looked down on."

Since then, hundreds of thousands of Chinese have fled as Vietnamese nationalism easily overcomes any fraternal proletarian Communist feelings. For 2,000 years the two people have hated each other. Communism is simply irrelevant in the face of ethnic differences.

In Cambodia, where half a million Chinese lived until the Khmer Rouge horror, the new government moved against the Chinese. According to the AP (August 18, 1976), there are special "cooperatives" that are "reserved for the Chinese where the discipline and security are tighter, the work more grueling, and the rice rations often less than given ethnic Cambodians." At least two special villages were established into which Chinese were herded. One was called Phum Chen Youm, "the village where the Chinese cry."

In two Muslim-dominated states slaughter of Chinese has taken place. In the late sixties one of the worst single massacres in history took place, as *millions* of Chinese were slaughtered in Indonesia. The government claimed a Communist plot had been uncovered to take over the government, but the Indonesians used the opportunity to eliminate the Chinese community of which they were bitterly jealous because of their economic domination of the country.

The other country was Malaysia, where today economic prosperity papers over a smoldering volcano of racial tension between the Malays and Chinese. The Malays make up about 50 percent of the population but hold less than 10 percent of the country's capital investment. The Chinese, who constitute 10 percent of the country, control some 35 percent of the economy.

The country underwent a bloody period of Communist insurgency in the fifties. The revolt was as much Chinese versus Malay as ideological, since the Communists were almost all Chinese. Finally, crushed by the British, Malaysia was able to survive only because the predominantly Chinese Singapore wisely seceded, thus changing the ratio of the country from a totally impossible fifty-fifty balance to its present one of near-impossibility.

Indeed, six years after Malaysia came into being, young Malays in May 1969 swarmed into the Chinese district of the capital, Kuala Lumpur, and—with knives and spears— hacked to death every Chinese they could find. Houses were burned, cars smashed; at least 300 died. Today, as a government policy of preferential treatment helps the Malays catch up, the economic boom distracts most people. But as a foreign diplomat told *Newsweek* magazine (March 12, 1973): "The problems that produced 1969 are still there." Quite true. For all the other problems are based on the essential dilemma: two competing national-religious groups in the same land who are *different*.

Western Europe

Nothing more clearly illustrates the power and reality of the *differences* and the desire of the "different" for their own autonomy and sovereignty than the incredible upsurge of separatism in advanced, progressive, stable, Western Europe. There— where twenty years ago people spoke of economic and political union of a united western half of the continent—*today, there is a veritable rise of tribalism.* In Spain, it is Catalonians and Basques; in France, Corsicans and Bretons; in Belgium, Walloons and Flemish; in the United Kingdom, Irish, Scots, Welsh; in Yugoslavia, Serbs, Croats, Albanians, Macedonians. No amount of international pressure can ever overcome the power of difference and the desire for separate power to decide one's future and destiny. Consider:

Spain: Basques, Catalans, Galicans, Andalusians

The death of Franco may have also been the prelude to the eventual demise of Spain as we now know it. At least two and possibly five areas are focuses of demands for autonomy and separatism.

In the first six months of 1980 more than sixty people were killed in the area of northern Spain in which live the Basques. They dream of an independent state to be known as Euzkadi, and the terrorist group ETA (Basque Homeland and Liberty) is a serious and deadly force in the land. The Central government in Madrid, in a desperate effort to stop Basque terrorism (as an example, on July 24, 1979, Basque bombs went off at Madrid's crowded airport and two main railroad stations, killing 7 and injuring 113, including many tourists, who were the main target), agreed to an autonomy plan that it hoped would satisfy the Basques. Of course, the move only encouraged separatist sentiment (more than half the elected Basque Parliament was either for independence or for much more "autonomy," and the ETA, whose members train in South Yemen, keep blasting their bombs). The retreat of the Madrid government as it allows the flying of the red, white, and green Basque flag (the Ikurrina), control of police, and education (in the Basque language) will guarantee an eventual Basque republic.

The second major candidate for separatism is Catalonia, the northeast province of six million people, with proud Barcelona as its capital. In 1932 the Catalonians won a measure of local autonomy known as the Generalitat. Franco abolished it, and after his fall the demand for its restoration erupted. The Catalan flag—yellow with four red stripes—began to fly, and stickers appeared: "I am a Catalan" and "Read, write and speak Catalan."

The Madrid government agreed to the reactivation of the Géneralitat, and thousands welcomed back, from a thirty-eight-year exile, the Catalan leader, José Tarradellas, who led them in the Catalan national anthem, "Els Segadors." He told a crowd: "We must be the vanguard of freedom and democracy of all the people of Spain." These include the Galicians in the northwest and the Andalusians in the south and the Canary Islands—all clamoring for "autonomy." Said the pro-Franco paper *El Alcazar:* "This paves the way for the disintegration of Spain."

France: Basques, Corsicans, Bretons
The border between Spain and France separates more than two countries. In the words of the French Basque separatist group Eneata ("Ocean Wind"): "It is a crime against nature and a wall of shame, like the one dividing Berlin." What the group means is that the frontier is artificial, for it divides the Spanish Basque country from the French Pays Basque, and the day will come when "Spanish Euzkadi is liberated. . . . French Euzkadi will join us" in a single Basque state. The reason that violence against the French has so far been limited is that the ETA in Spain needs the French Basque region as a sanctuary for

escape from Spanish police and soldiers. But there is little doubt that the day of the French Basque is coming.

In April 1980 nine Corsican terrorist blasts rocked Paris and Nice; in January of that year armed members of the Corsican People's Union (UPC) seized a hotel in Ajaccio, Corsica's capital; hundreds of bombings attributed to the Corsican National Liberation Front have destroyed fuel tanks, freight stations, and offices. Moderates demand "autonomy," angrily pointing to the French policy of dumping former Algerian settlers, known as *pieds noirs,* in Corsica Said Lucian Alforsi, one of the leaders of the Corsican national movement,: "If it goes on like this, we shall be a minority in our own homeland." The "extremists," who blew up an Air France Boeing 707 airliner at Ajaccio Airport, are more honest; they openly call for Corsican Independence.

The French government will hear of neither independence nor autonomy and has vowed "to protect the unity of the Republic." But police are killed in Corsica, terrorism has reached the mainland, and the Corsicans wish the French well in the unity of France, but they claim that they are *not* French and not part of that unity. They are *different;* they want *their* state.

At the end of the fifteenth century, the French annexed Brittany. Today, 500 years later, the demand for autonomy is the loudest it has been in decades. Some 2.7 million Bretons are stirring, and one day before the visit of French President Valéry Giscard d'Estaing in 1977, bombs smashed government offices and the radio-TV license fee center in Redon and Rennes. In October of that year, a Breton bomb knocked out a TV relay station.

The Bretons are demanding "autonomy" as a first step. They are demanding that the Breton language—a Celtic language related to Gaelic and Welsh—be taught in the public schools. In Brittany today "Uncle Tom-ism" is dying a lingering death. Says the sixty-five-year-old mayor of Cast: "Better they learn English or German. What interest is there in learning a language they will never use?" Young Bretons, like folk singer Alan Stivell, sneer at the "Uncle Pierres." These young Bretons are pushing an ethnic sense of identity. "Our grandparents were proud when we spoke French," said a newspaper editor in Quimper. "Now our children are proud when they speak Breton."

The Breton nationalists have made contacts with the IRA. France will lose even more of its stability and "unity of the Republic" in the years to come. The Bretons are not French. They are *different*.

Britain: Asians, Blacks, Scots, Welsh

It used to be said as one looked at the worldwide expanse of British real estate, that "the sun never sets on the British Empire." The sun has no such problem today, as Britain has shrunk to the dimensions of a tiny island. And even that shows disturbing signs of disintegration.

In April 1980 a full-scale race riot (some termed it an "uprising") occurred in the generally placid southwest English city of Bristol. So violent was the outbreak that the police fled the area, leaving the St. Paul's region of the city to the mercies of the mob. It was a riot of blacks against whites, and the remarkable thing is that, in the words of one account, "it took them and the whole country by surprise."

In terms of color, Britain for centuries was a homogeneous nation. "White as an angel is the English child," wrote poet William Blake, and until World War II he certainly was. Britain recruited tens of thousands of Commonwealth nation people to help it fight the Nazis, and in the postwar labor shortage it allowed in many West Indians to take the menial jobs that the white British did not want. In 1948, with the empire falling apart, the British desperately tried to imbue it with a sense of "Britishness." And so the British Nationality Act was passed, declaring all Commonwealth citizens to be also citizens of the United Kingdom. Britain was never the same.

Waves of nonwhites flowed freely into the country so that, today, *official* figures list some two million of them, representing 3.5 percent of the population. But most British scoff at this, for the government conveniently ignores the number of illegal immigrants. Thus, if the government claimed that 43,000 nonwhites immigrated to Britain in 1978, police estimate that some *90,000 more* arrived illegally.

In general, the nonwhite residents by 1979 were broken down as follows: West Indies, 620,000; African Asians, 180,000; African Africans, 110,000; India, 430,000; Pakistan, 240,000; Mediterranean (Cyprus), 160,000; Oceania/Asia, 130,000; Bangladesh, 50,000. It is interesting, of course, to note that some of the immigrants came because of ethnic persecution in their old homes (the Asians expelled from Africa by blacks; those from Bangladesh who fled Bengali–non Bengali clashes).

The immigrants tended to gather in major urban areas, so that more than 10 percent of the population of London is non-white. Sections of Bradford, a textile center, look more like India than the Midlands, and some Birmingham (England) schools look like those of Birmingham, Alabama.

There is hate in England, today, on both sides. Despite a Race Relations Act that makes it illegal to incite racial hatred, in 1978 bloody rioting took place in Notting Hill; in 1976 racial clashes occurred in London, Manchester, Birmingham, Liverpool, and Blackburn. In June 1976 and again in April 1979 vicious riots took place in the London suburb of Southall, which houses the largest concentration of Indians and Pakistanis. And in the almost all-black neighborhood of Brixton one can see the smoldering anger and hatred.

The white British see the nonwhite influx as another symptom of their national decline. The difficult economic times, and social depressions combine with the feeling expressed by an attorney who revisited his old neighborhood of Peckham, now racially mixed: "I was amazed. I felt completely alien. I felt *pressure.*" In a word, many white British feel that they are losing "their" country.

It does little to point out that by law those nonwhites are as "British" as Blake's "white angel." The "Blacks out!" graffiti, the regular clashes, the growth of the neo-Nazi National Front, which has sizable support in the troubled areas—all point to the growing problem.

For years, the British smugly accused the United States of racism and prejudice in regard to its nonwhites, but that was when less than 17 percent of the United Kingdom was nonwhite. Things have changed, and Conservative Member of Parliament John Stokes could rise and warn of "a takeover of this country by alien peoples." In 1968 people scoffed, but today they remember the words of Enoch Powell, a member of the House of Commons: "We must be mad, literally mad, as a nation to be permitting the annual inflow of some 50,000 dependents [of immigrants] . . . . As I look ahead I am filled with foreboding. I seem to see the River Tiber foaming with much blood."

The struggle in Northern Ireland is too well known to require detailing here. It is an ongoing battle that began in 1690 with the Battle of the Boyne, and the partition of Ireland into one independent Catholic state and another predominantly Protestant dependency never wrote *finis* to the struggle. Two important lessons can, however, be learned from the bloodbath:

1. The two Irish opponents are similar *in every way* except religion. This has not prevented atrocity and horror.

2. For decades the Irish question appeared to be settled and the Irish Republican Army seemed to have faded away because of apathy and indifference on the part of the population. Deep differences may indeed lie dormant, but they do not die. They merely await the proper moment.

The discovery of oil in the North Sea brought hope to economically beaten Britain and also an upsurge in a Scottish movement of independence. Suddenly, the Scottish nationalists jumped from a group that had received 2 to 3 percent of the popular vote to one that garnered 30 percent. The reason was clear: economically depressed Scotland was faced with the possibility of a huge income from the oil, all of which lay off what would be *its* shores *if it were independent.* That, and the knowledge that it was tied to an England with serious political, social, and racial problems that Scotland did not need, suddenly gave a frightening urgency to London's need to soothe the Scottish separatist beast. The House of Commons, after bitter debate, approved limited home rule for Scotland in 1978, a move that infuriated Englishmen and that failed to satisfy Scottish nationalists. What is certain in that this major constitutional change in the United Kingdom is a major step in its unraveling.

As the United Kingdom becomes much less so, the Welsh nationalists, such as the Plaid Cymru and Adfer, will grow. One of their leaders, Gynfor Evans, says: "This country indeed needs independence." For most people, the growth of separatism and independence movements in Britain is little short of incredible.

The lesson for Israel, however, is an important one: if after centuries of quiet acceptance, within the context of a stable, integrated United Kingdom, people of the same religion and general culture can be so divided by ethnic and historical origin, what conceivable hope is there for Arabs and Jews to live together in a land in which they differ in every way and which the Arabs look upon as stolen from them?

All the Rest

Western Europe alone embraces some thirty different un-assimilated ethnic communities. Not universalism but separatism, autonomy, and independence are their dreams.

Belgium: Incredibly, this politically and economically advanced country faces the ravages of division over the question of language. The creation of Belgium in 1830 brought together Dutch-speaking Flemings in the north and French-speaking Walloons in the south. The French dominated the power and the Flemings, now 60 percent of the population, claimed their share of it. Language was the issue, again and again, for language symbolized difference. Crisis bred patchwork solutions, such as the surrealistic one in which the Catholic University of Louvain was partitioned in 1968 into separate Flemish and Walloon branches: the odd-numbered books went to the new French-speaking campus and the even-numbered ones remained.

Bitter street battles took place over language in a country whose national motto is "In Unity There Is Strength." After yet another government fell on the language issue in April 1980, Flemish Christian Social Senator Jan de Meyer said: "The state may appear to exist still, but it is rotten. It will take very little for the Flemings to go off in one direction and the Francophones in the other."

Portugal: In 1978 riot police fought a pitched battle with a gun-firing mob in Ponta Delgada, capital of the Azores. The previous weekend a crowd had physically beaten Portuguese Deputy Prime Minister Antonio Almeida Santos. It was all part of separatist demand for independence for the Azores from Portugal. The islands are 1,000 miles from the mainland and "different," and they are supported by some million Azoreans living in the United States and Canada. A similar independence movement is led by the Front for the Liberation of Madeira, a group demanding freedom for that island some 350 miles from Portugal.

Austria: In November 1972 bilingual signposts in German and Slovene were removed in the Austrian province of Carinthia, which is about 25 percent Slovene, a Yugoslav minority. Yugoslav President Tito warned that he would "not tolerate" Austrian treatment of our "minorities." (Of course, Tito had enough problems with minorities in his own country, as we shall see.) The Slovenes are demanding linguistic "autonomy."

Italy: Conversely, the Austrians bitterly complained about alleged mistreatment of the German minority in the Alto Adige region of Italy, known as the Tyrol to Austrians. The area was severed by diplomatic fiat after World War I. After more than 200 bombings by German-speaking terrorists in the late 1960s, a measure of autonomy was granted, but streets are called *via* by Italians, *Strasse* by Germans, and the situation quietly worsens.

And: The Lapps of Sweden, Greenland's Eskimos, who demonstrate against "Danish imperialism," The Frisians in northeastern Holland—all agitate for "autonomy." And then there is the fascinating problem of nationalism in:

Communist Europe

Yugoslavia: Serbs, Croats, Slovenes, Albanians, Macedonians

With the death of Tito in 1980, most fears focused on whether the Soviets might attack Yugoslavia and pull it back into Moscow's orbit. But the greater question lies in whether the country can keep from falling apart from within. In an effort to cope with rapidly rising nationalism, Tito established a federated system for six constitutent republics and two autonomous republics. For Yugoslavia was not a state but a patchwork of eight major ethnic groups and six other minor ones.

When it was created in 1981 from various South Slav groups, it was an artificial entity. Until World War II it was deeply divided, with the capital of Belgrade favoring the Orthodox Serbs. Most of the conflict arose with the Roman Catholic Croats. World War II added to the bitterness, since many of the Croats favored the Nazis and the Croat fascist Ustachi movement massacred hundreds of thousands of Serbs. The Serbs never forgot, but Croatian nationalists never ceased their striving for national autonomy. Under men like Mika Tripalo and Matica Hrvatska nationalism festered, with Zagreb University seized by Croat students in 1971 and Serbs and Croats trading increasing insults.

Of course, the most dramatic indication of the hatred and longing for separation has been the activities of Croatian nationalists outside of Yugoslavia. Hijacking an airline, seizing a consulate in Chicago, shooting officials in Europe—these are external proofs of the conflict that simmers beneath Yugoslavia's surface.

Yet another problem is Macedonia. In 1878 the Treaty of San Stefano gave Macedonia to Bulgaria. A few months later the Treaty of Berlin took it back and gave it to Serbia. The Bulgarians claim that there is no such thing as a "Macedonia," that the people are racially Bulgarians.

The poorest province in Yugoslavia is Kosovo, inhabited by Albanians who have powerful cultural and family ties with their brethren in neighboring Albania. In 1968 riots shook Kosovo as demands for separation led to violence. This occurred again in 1975, but in March 1980 as Tito lay dying, it was announced that a major trial of fifty Albanian nationalists would be held. The charge was detailed in the Belgrade daily *Politika:* "They distributed hostile banners and pamphlets, spread untruths about Yugoslavia, and advocated irredentist standpoints in connection with our country."

The government has made efforts to defuse the nationalist demands. This means radio and television, books, magazines, and newspapers in eight languages. What the Yugoslavs—and Israelis—cannot understand is that *to satisfy national separatism by catering to it will soothe it for a while, but the very concessions only feed and strengthen the separate identity and appetite, invariably leading to an ultimate explosion.*

Rumanians versus Hungarians

All East European states were virulently nationalistic before they became Communist. All East European states today are Communist and all are still virulently nationalistic. Between the two world wars, Poles, Slovaks, Rumanians, Hungarians, Russians, and Lithuanians hated each other with a passion. After World War II a great international game of musical chairs was played whose major purpose was to push Russia westward.

Thus, Poland lost her eastern territories and 1 million Poles to Russia but received the eastern portion of Germany. Czechoslovakia lost Ruthenia with its Slavs to the Russians but gained parts of Germany. And Rumania lost Bukovina and Bessarabia to Russia (they now form the Moldavian Soviet Socialist Republic) and received some 1.8 million Hungarians along with Transylvania. Indeed, the Hungarians lost another 600,000 to Czechoslovakia and 200,000 to the Soviet Union. Let no one doubt that there are ferment and discontent in Eastern Europe today. Not only are the Soviet satellites sitting on an ethnic explosion, but the most fascinating and dangerous nationalistic time bomb of all ticks away within the huge expanse of territories known as—

The Soviet Union

The Soviet Union is a giant with massive arms of steel and feet of clay. The base on which it stands is rotten and bears within itself the seeds of its own destruction. For there are no fewer than 100 nationalities, religions, and ethnic groups in the USSR, and the ethnic Russians, according to 1980 figures, *officially* have dropped to 52.4 percent of the total population. As the other ethnic groups become the majority of the state, the virus of nationalism that is the Kremlin's secret terror will grow more dangerous. At the moment, the Russians mostly fear the more articulate and broadly "European" minorities—the Ukrainians, Lithuanians, Rumanians, Georgians, Armenians— and, indeed, they should. The specter of Ukrainian nationalism, in particular (the Ukrainians constitute 20 percent of the population), is said to have been one of the factors in the Soviet invasion of Czechoslovakia. An "independent" national communism on the borders of the Ukraine might have endangered the very foundation of the Soviet Union by a massive infection of nationalism. The advanced European minorities look down with contempt on the Russians, and it would not take much to trigger serious dissension.

But it is in Asia that the Russians face an awesome force of separatism. According to 1979 figures, the birthrate of the six Muslim republics in central Asia was *five* times the national average. Not only that, but Western sources have estimated that because of the higher proportions of young people among the Asians, the armed forces may be half Asian and Muslim. And it is known that serious tension already exists.

On May 22, 1978, reliable sources reported that a massive race riot had erupted in Dushanbe, capital of the Central Asian Soviet Repbulic of Tadzhik. At least 13,000 people were involved and the bloody clash was put down by troops from the

201st Motorized Rifle Division. An eyewitness spoke of crowds shouting "Colonialists!" Tadzhk is one of several Muslim Asian republics in the USSR where both religious and nationalist problems persist. The others are Uzbek, Kazakh, Azerbaidzan, Turkmen, and Kirghiz.

At the jubilee session marking the fiftieth anniversary of the Soviet Union, President Breznhev spoke of Soviet achievement in "completely solving the nationality problem in accordance with Lenin's principles." Any hope the Soviets may have of evolving "one Soviet people" from all those whose nationality, language, religion, and culture differ is surely already understood to be a delusion. Indeed, Brezhnev himself admitted as much in his Kremlinesque jargon when he added: "Nationalistic prejudices, exaggerated or distorted national feelings, are extremely tenacious, as they are deeply embedded in the psychology of politically immature people." In far more honest words: There is a serious nationality problem in the Soviet Union. It, along with any Chinese effort to retrieve the "lost Chinese territories" seized by the czars, could drive the Soviets to acts of desperation that might lead to a world war.

There are many other examples of the drive for separatism because of "difference." There is the tribalism of Africa and that of the New World, and the qualitative differences are less than they would seem to be.

In Africa blacks clash violently with whites in southern Africa and then turn on the Asians, who pose an economic threat to them. It was not only mad Idi Amin who expelled his 28,000 Asians. In 1976 the moderate State of Malawi began to expel its 20,000 Asians. It was "statesman" Julius Nyerere of Tanzania (and on his island of Zanzibar, Africans slaughtered their Arab former oppressors). And in the wake of the Soweto riots in South Africa, the *Washington Post* (June 27, 1976) quoted an Asian storekeeper who had been wiped out by rioting and looting: "We got caught in the middle. The blacks took out their fury on our property because we're not black. The police didn't protect us because we're not white. What can we do? It's like that for us all over Africa." *Differences.* White, black, brown. Differences and the need to be separate.

And in Africa it is the tribalism of Nigeria, where a Muslim north crushes a Christian and pagan Biafra; Uganda, where Kakwas clash with Lugbaras; Katanga, which seeks to secede from Zaire (Belgian Congo); Burundi, where Tutsis and Hutus have slaughtered 100,000 of one another; Chad, with fifteen years of civil war between an Arab and Muslim north and a south made up of pagans and Christians; a Somali people that claim huge parts of Ethiopia and Kenya because those areas are inhabited by a majority of Somalis. The tribalism of Africa.

And in the New World, Canada, where the governor-general, Edward Schreyer, in April 1980 asked the Canadian Parliament: "Will Canada still exist as a country at the end of this decade, or will it have been broken up by the terrorism of our past and recent history?"

For Schreyer the thought was terrifying. Not so for the Parti Québecois (P.Q.) of Quebec's Premier René Lévesque. To him, a people with a common language, customs, and culture should naturally form a nation-state. The French of Quebec fear that North America's "Anglo" culture will swamp them. Says poet Fernand Ouellette: "In a milieu of bilingualism there is no coexistence; there is only a continuous aggression of the language of the majority."

And ever since November 15, 1976, when Canada awoke to find that the P.Q. had received a majority mandate in the Quebec Parliament, the French separatists have slowly moved toward that goal. With moral support from France (in 1977 French President Giscard d'Estaing assured Levesque of French support), the separatists have moved to make life more difficult in Quebec for non-Frenchmen. In August 1977 a law known as Bill 101 made French the only official language and radically limited the right of new residents to send their children to English-speaking schools. It was a de facto move toward separatism.

Ever since the British defeated the French under Montcalm in 1759, the French have chafed under British rule. They are Catholic, French-speaking, and French in their ethnicity and life-style. They are different. Two separate nations live in Canada, and the French wish to give *both* their own sovereign independence.

And the United States—not as united as we might think. For thirty years after the war, the United States enjoyed the good life that allows problems to simmer. But they existed, and they have emerged to day in all their fury. More than twenty-five million blacks are "different," very different. In the sixties they broke through resignation and apathy. They burned, looted, killed. It is not over. The hate remains and the blood has been tasted.

And there are the Hispanics: millions of Chicanos in the Southwest and California, Puerto Ricans in the slums of the East and Midwest. The same ingredients of the black mixture exists for them, but more so, for the Hispanics have territorial demands. For the Puerto Ricans there is the cry of "Viva Puerto Rico Libre!" Since 1974 the terrorist F.A.L.N. has claimed responsibility for more than 100 bombings that killed five people. Attacks on U.S. troops in Puerto Rico have taken place. Plans had been made to attack the Democratic National Convention in New York in 1980.

For the Chicanos there is the Southwest, once Spanish, part of Mexico, taken by the United States in the nineteenth century. Absurd? Not to the millions of Chicanos who live there—and who grow more militant.

And there are the American Indians and their International Indian Treaty Council, who told a UN Conference of Discrimination Against the Indigenous Populations of the Americas that the United States is stealing "their resources." And the Eskimos of Alaska, who have joined with those of Canada and Greenland to form the Invit (Eskimo) Circumpolar Assembly. At the first conference in Barrow, Alaska, they declared: "The Invit of Greenland, Alaska, and Canada are one indivisible people with a common language, culture, environment, and concerns."

Blacks, Hispanics, Indians, Eskimos, Orientals—the making of a minority coalition of *forty or fifty million people who are different from the majority, different from each other. Different and unhappy.*

This is the world of many, many worlds. It is a fragmented, separate, and individualistic world in which each group seeks identity, separation, the right to be itself and decide its own destiny.

For the Jews to believe that the Israeli Arab, with every possible difference imaginable, will quietly cede his destiny to the Jewish state is to invite catastrophe. How did the Québecois poet put it? "In a milieu of bilingualism there is no coexistence; there is only a continuous aggression of the language of the majority."

What does the Israeli Arab say about the "aggression" of the language, religion, culture, and destiny of the majority? For Israel there is only one answer: removal of the Arabs from Israel, before the land turns into an ongoing nightmare of mutual communal horror.

There is nothing novel in the concept of removing a hostile minority from a land to which it poses a dangerous, irredentist threat. It has happened before.

Chapter 8

Our Fathers' Children

The remarkable Jewish inability or unwillingness to see the reality of innate Arab hostility toward Zionism and a Jewish state is hardly of recent vintage. From the beginning of the twentieth century, as modern nationalism swept from Europe into the Ottoman Empire, there existed Arab nationalist hostility that grew in intensity and hatred with every Jewish stride toward statehood in the Land of Israel. The problem was that the early Zionists simply did not want to understand the basic fact of nationalism: no people is permanently prepared to live as a minority under another people in a land it considers its own. Our fathers would not see; we refuse to see. We are, indeed, their children.

From the very beginning of the modern political Zionist movement, the question of the Arab population of Eretz Yisrael was subject to incredible delusion and unimaginable self-delusion. It was Theodor Herzl, founder of modern political Zionism, who coined the astonishing slogan: "The land without a people for the people without a land." Perhaps as a journalistic turn of a phrase, it was a *bon mot*. But in terms of reality, Herzl was very, very wrong. That there existed a people—the Jews—without a land was an unmistakable fact. But the land they rightfully called theirs was not empty of people.

The year 1880, from which the beginning of modern Jewish restoration dates, saw some 30,000 Jews in the land. They were of the "old *yishuv*" ("community"), religious Jews living quietly under the Ottoman regime, content to fulfill the *mitzvah* ("com-

175

mandment") of dwelling in the Land of Israel and subsisting for the most part on charity. Alongside them dwelt some 80,000 Arabs.

These latter may have been poor, ignorant, backward, lacking in political awareness, unconscious of a "Palestinian" nationhood, but they were *there*. And no one seemed to notice.

Leo Pinsker, the most significant of the pre–Herzl political Zionists, made no mention of the Arabs as a significant element to be dealt with by the Zionist believers in his book *Auto-Emancipation* (1882). The classic Herzlian work, *Der Judenstaat* (The Jewish state), is also empty of any reference to the problem of Arabs, and as late as June 4, 1921, the official Zionist magazine in Britain, *Palestine,* called the country "a deserted, derelict land."

On the one hand, it was as if Arabs did not exist, or if they did, they really did not matter. On the other hand, there was a naive belief that this backward and primitive people would surely be delighted at the benefits and progress that would be their lot, thanks to the advent of the progressive and talented Jews. As far as an Arab *national movement* was concerned, there was near unanimity that such a creature simply did not exist. Professor A. Yahuda, a delegate to the First Zionist Congress (1897), attempted to persuade Herzl that an Arab *question* did exist, but Herzl was unconvinced. Indeed, the records of the early Zionist Congresses are blissfully empty of any mention of the Arab problem.

In the words of the radical socialist Ber Borochov, "if we plant our culture in the Land of Israel, the *fellahin* ["Arab peasants"] will fully integrate with us. . . . the inhabitants of the Land of Israel have no ground to look upon us with hatred; to the contrary, they recognize that legally the land belongs to us." This amazing statement was made in 1905. It was based on a belief held by many that the Arabs would be culturally integrated, absorbed, and assimilated with the Jews. Michael Halpern suggested hastening the process by intermarriage on a massive scale. The nonsense of Arab "disappearance," culturally or nationally, was to be echoed for years by Zionist leaders, even when it was obvious to all that there was a large and growing Arab movement that was the deadly enemy of Zionism.

As early as 1891, there was already evidence of anti-Zionism on the part of the Arabs of the Land of Israel. In that year several hundred Arab notables from Jerusalem and Jaffa sent a petition to the court at Constantinople asking that the sultan put an end to both Jewish immigration and land purchase. Neither Herzl nor any of the other political Zionists understood the significance of such a move. The Arab was simply a person whose presence was irrelevant to the future of the country. It was the Ottoman Empire, the Turkish "sick man of Europe," that ruled the land and was the partner with whom the Jews had to deal. Either the Turks would agree to a Jewish homeland within the context of their empire, or such a state would come into being as the result of the collapse of the Ottomans and the dismemberment of their territory by the European powers. What would emerge would depend upon how clever the Zionists were in their dealings with the nations. But the term *nation* most emphatically did not apply to the Arabs of the Land of Israel.

One hardly knows what to make of Herzl's naiveté. On the one hand he apparently believed that one bought a homeland in much the same manner as one bought a house or a factory. In a letter to Herzl, the sociologist L. von Gumplowicz asked, "You want to found a state without bloodshed? Where did you ever see that? Without violence and without *guile,* simply by selling and buying shares?" Herzl did, indeed think so, because the Arab question played no part in his grasp of the problem. To him, how could the Arabs, such as they were, conceivably object to a Jewish state in the land they occupied if they became rich through Jewish development? Herzl may sincerely not have meant it, but it was a crude, contemptuous rejection of Arab national pride.

Thus, in a letter to the former mayor of Jerusalem, Yusef Ziah Al-Haldi, Herzl wrote: "Do you believe that the Arab in the land whose house or land is worth three or four thousand francs will be unhappy if his property rises by five or ten times? And that is what will inevitably happen when the Jews arrive. . . ."

And in his book *Altenuland,* Herzl has the Arab Reshid Bey say, concerning the Jewish arrival: "It was a blessing for all of us and first of course for the property owner. . . . Is a person who takes nothing from you but only comes to give to you to be considered a thief in your eyes? The Jews made us wealthy; why shall we complain about them?"

Not all were blind. The Zionist philosopher Ahad Ha'am visited the land in 1891. He came; he saw; he perceived. And that perception led him to write: "We are wrong to believe that the Arabs are savages of the desert . . . who neither observe nor understand what transpires around them. . . . The Arabs, especially the town dwellers, see and understand our work and ambitions. But they feign ignorance since at present they do not see in our activities a danger to their future."

Ahad Ha'am realized, too, that this momentary lack of danger coincided with economic benefits for the Arabs which added to the temporary lack of tension. "But," he added, "when the time comes when the life of our people develops to such an extent that it may encroach in however small a measure upon the Arabs, they will not readily give in. . . ."

But as perceptive as he was, even that one clarion call was not really raised to signal danger. Ishmael, however, was beginning to stir. The winds of nineteenth-century nationalism were late arriving in the Middle East, but the breezes could not forever be blocked.

In 1905 a Christian Arab named Neguib Azoury published a book that may well be regarded as the first cogent expression of the Arab nationalism that Jews insisted was nonexistent. From his exile in Paris, Azoury issued an anti-Turkish, anti-Jewish work called *Le Réveil de la Nation Arabe.* In it he not only called for an Arab state from the Nile to the Euphrates; he also called Zionism a danger to Arab aspirations and declared that "it was clear" that the two nationalist movements could not exist in the same land.

One of the few to be disturbed by rising Arab nationalism and anti-Zionism (Christian Arabs in Jaffa had organized an anti-Jewish gang under Anton Kassar) was the educator Yitzhak Epstein, who during the Seventh Zionist Congress warned, "Let us not anger a sleeping lion. . . . We must solve the question of our relations with the Arabs before a Jewish question arises among them." What did Epstein suggest? Among other things, to raise the Arab standard of living in the fields of education, health, and economy. . . .

Reaction to the warning was typified by Moshe Smilansky, who, in an article in *Ha'Olam,* mocked Epstein and wrote that "he takes the shadow of the mountains for mountains." Smilansky flatly stated that the Arabs of the Land of Israel were not a nation but a social organism divided into tribes and classes.

This early division of opinion typified the two delusions that almost the entire Zionist movement adhered to. On the one hand were those who refused even to contemplate anything as "ridiculous" as an Arab national movement in the land. On the other were those who recognized an Arab problem but insisted that it could be tamed by giving the Arabs social and economic benefits. The first view eventually died, under the sheer weight of Arab bullets and bombs. The second view is still alive and sick in the minds of Jewish leaders in Israel and the Exile.

In 1908 the first organized attack by Arabs against Jews occurred on the night of the Jewish holiday, Purim. The first reaction of fear was put to official rest by the Zionist Establishment, which refused to see any problems. Arthur Ruppin, head of the Palestine office of the World Zionist Movement, in a soothing letter to the president of the movement, David Wolffsohn, wrote: "Instead of being surprised that such incidents occur in Jaffa, we should rather be surprised that relations between Jews and Arabs in the Land of Israel are so calm, despite all the differences."

That year, a revolution deposed the sultan, and a group of "Young Turks" took office, determined to modernize the Turkish Empire. As part of this process they granted the right of political association and expression. To the dismay of the Turks and the astonishment of the Jews, there occurred a veritable explosion of Arab nationalism. An article that appeared in the Hebrew paper *Hatzvi* declared: "From the time the constitution was given, the Arabs in our land began to arouse themselves to a new life. In all the important towns there have been established chapters of the national Arab association, 'Arab Brotherhood.' "

An Arab paper, *Al Atzmai,* appeared in Jaffa and immediately began vicious attacks on Jews. Other Arab papers followed suit. One Arab cartoon in 1911 depicts Joshua Hankin, an early Zionist pioneer, trying to buy land from an Arab and being stabbed by Saladin. The leading anti-Zionist journal was the Haifa newspaper *Al-Karmel,* edited by Najib Natzer, which not only attacked Jewish immigration and land sales but directed its major shafts against the very idea of a Jewish state. The rise of bitter anti-Zionist Arab journalism led a young Jew named David Ben-Gurion to complain, in 1910: "On the one hand they spread libel and false charges against the Hebrew settlement in the Land of Israel in governmental circles. On the other, they sow hatred toward Jews among all the levels of the Arab people."

In January 1911 the Jaffa newspaper *Falastin* warned against the danger of "Zionist imperialism." And when the Arabs succeeded in electing some sixty-five representatives to the new Turkish Parliament—about one-quarter of all the delegates —the Zionists suddenly realized their power. They watched in dismay as the three Arab representatives from Jerusalem, who had been wooed assiduously, joined all the rest in strong anti-Zionist stands. S.D. Levontin, head of the Anglo-Palestine Company office in Jaffa, wrote to Wolffsohn: "We have realized for the first time that the Arab population is not so primitive and that they have cultural powers that should not be denigrated. . . . They have people who understand what freedom means and . . . new political forces are emerging that we must contend with."

The vast majority of Zionist leaders were not impressed. The fact that the Arabs might look upon the land as *their* land was simply too implausible. Three points were constantly raised and reemphasized:

1. The Land of Israel was a barren land, large enough for all the Jews who would come to build their state, as well as the Arab peasants.

2. Arab attacks on Zionism and Jewish settlement were a product of the wealthy landlords' *(effendis)* fear of losing their power.

3. The Arab masses would eagerly welcome the Jews, who would raise their living standards and free them from feudalism.

Almost all Zionists believed this nonsense for years. It does not behoove us to scorn them, however, since nonsense not too dissimilar was spouted even by Begin and other leaders of the Irgun underground, who told the UN commission investigating conditions in Palestine in 1947: "There is no such phenomenon as independent Arab opposition, and all Arab opposition was instigated by the British themselves."

Arab nationalist anti-Zionism began to bear "fruit." In 1909 physical attacks in Jewish settlements in the Galilee led to the formation of Jewish self-defense groups (Bar Biora, Hashomer). Jews were killed by Arab marauders in Yavneel, Beit Gan, and Sajra. Despite the fact that the naive Jews had paid good money for land, the Arabs now discovered the concept of the "dispossessed." Thus, the Jewish settlers of Um Juni or Deganya were accused of dispossessing the Arabs, though they pathetically waved their legal "deed." Arab hatred was now so palpable that in November 1910 even Ruppin suggested building a separate Jewish community in Haifa, "since it is unpleasant for Jews to live together with Arabs, especially in view of the attacks by the anti-Jewish paper *Al-Karmel.*"

The Arab nationalists concentrated on halting Jewish immigration and land purchase. They understood, quite correctly, that the Zionists' eventual aim was a Jewish state and a Jewish majority, and these they swore to fight to the death.

In 1911 some 150 Arab notables sent a telegram to the Parliament in Constantinople, demanding an end to Jewish immigration and land purchase. Natzer founded a group in Haifa for the purpose of boycotting the Jews. "We shall not sell to them, buy from them, or rent them houses," he declared. A similar group called the Ottoman Patriotic Party was founded in Jaffa. The crisis escalated as hundreds of Arabs attacked the Jewish settlement of Merchavya, pillaging and looting food, clothing, and wheat in the fields.

The Zionist leadership now prepared to meet in the Tenth Zionist Congress. Ruppin pleaded that the speakers beware of inflaming the Arabs, "that each speaker weigh every word, and that it would be best if questions concerning the Land of Israel not be discussed at all, except in committees."

Nevertheless, the Tenth Zionist Congress was the first that dealt with the Arab question. Shlomo Kaplansky, the delegate of Poale Zion, the Laborites, expressed his confidence that despite everything, understanding could yet be reached with the "Arab democracy [sic]." Yitzhak Ben Zvi, in later years to become Israel's second president, elaborated on the difference between the Arab Christian intellectuals and property owners (who were hostile) and the general Muslim population who would supposedly be friendly, thanks to Jewish progress and benefits.

This was the Zionist conventional wisdom of the time. Ruppin and Levontin on February 16, 1911, sent the following memorandum to the Zionist Organization's central office in Cologne: "The only source of hatred of Jews . . . is the Christian Establishment, the wealthy Christians and those educated in Jesuit schools. . . ."

For a look at what the "moderate" Muslims thought about Zionism, it is interesting to note the statements made by two Jerusalem rivals for election to the Turkish Parliament. The Nashashibi and Al-Husseini Jerusalem clans were longtime Muslim rivals for power in Jerusalem. Each put up a candidate for Parliament in 1914. Said Rajib Nashashibi: "If elected I will dedicate my efforts, night and day, to eliminate the damage and danger of the Zionists and Zionism." Said his rival, Sa'ad Al-Husseini: "We must, especially, support the *fellah* ["peasant"] . . . to make sure that the Zionist hand does not acquire even one inch of their land."

So much for "moderate Muslims."

This ludicrous attempt to paint the Muslim Arabs as potential allies of Zionism would offer us some minor historical comfort if we at least learned from its delusion. Instead, today, we have reached the absurdity at the opposite end of the pole. We now maintain that it is the Muslims who are the source of anti-Zionist evil, whereas the Christians have now become the source of moderation and coexistence.

Just as early Zionism's delusion was punctured early—the worst inciters against Zionism in the Turkish Parliament were the Muslims—so do today's expert "Arabists" scratch their heads over the "puzzle" of the largest Christian town in Israel, Nazareth, which is the center of PLO agitation under its anti-Zionist Communist mayor, Tewfik Zayad, or George Habash, the extremist (*sic*) in the PLO, who is a Christian.

Ruppin, Levontin, Ben Zvi, and all the rest could build their world of pleasant illusions. Truth suffers fools for a while and then rudely returns them to reality. In the words of Mordechai Eliav, an expert on early Jewish settlements which were then Palestine,: "There is no doubt that Ruppin was convinced that in the days to come the Arabs would be grateful for the economic benefits that the Jewish community had brought them through its dynamic development. But this premise was totally erroneous. . . . No amount of explanation about the growth of benefits could convince them, *for the dispute was political from the outset as the immovable clash between two* national movements [italics added]." ("First Clashes with the Arab National Question," *Bar Ilan University Journal* 1977, p. 297).

Writing in 1913, German Zionist Richard Lichtheim stated: "The Arabs are and will always remain our natural opponents. They do not care a straw for 'the Joint Semitic Spirit.' . . . The Jew for them is a competitor who threatens their predominance in Palestine. . . ."

The nearly two decades that followed were years of bloody violence that included the riots of 1920, 1921, and 1929. During all those years the general Zionist view remained optimistically, wishfully the same: There was no real clash between Jewish and Arab interests. There was room in the country for both people (in a Jewish state, of course), and all that was required was "understanding" and "goodwill." For years nothing could shake this delusion, for the bitter reality was better put out of sight and mind.

Thus, Ben-Gurion, in a 1915 article titled "Facing the Living," wrote: "The Land of Israel is now a half desolate and ruined country—and the Arab minority [*sic!*] element is not capable of resurrecting the land. . . . *we* are building and reviving the land and this is the moral humane basis of our desire and work in the Land of Israel." What Ben-Gurion either could not or would not understand was that the Arab believed that the land was *his* half-desolate or totally so, and that the ability to rebuild it did not, in the Arab's eyes, carry with it any "moral humane right" whatsoever to take it from him.

Again and again the early Zionists attempted to delude themselves with the thought that they were really *benefiting* the Arab, who would sell his political birthright for a mess of socio-economic pottage.

Thus, Achdut Avoda, largest and most influential of the labor groups in the early years (from it eventually came two presidents and three prime ministers), after years of serious Arab rioting, could resolve at its Seventh Convention (1924) that, on the one hand, the convention "sees as an unbreakable foundation . . . the right of the Hebrew people to create a national home in Eretz Yisrael ["the Land of Israel"]." And without blinking an eyelid, the same program could blithely declare its intentions to "create conditions to raise and improve the situation of the working masses, Jewish and Arab. . . . The economic development of the land that will come about with the growth of Jewish immigration and settlement and the faithful influence and help of the Jewish worker's movement will raise the Arab worker from his low state and will prepare him to fill his political and social role. . . ."

One can, of course, imagine the touching impact this blend of socialist *noblesse oblige* and white-man's-burden mentality had on Ishmael. What is more pertinent, however, is the incredible blindness of the early Zionists who had not the slightest understanding of that their efforts on behalf of the Arab would indeed prepare him for his "political and social role," but that role would be very different from the one that the Jewish socialist Kiplings had mapped out for him. What Jewish progress and development would create was a Frankenstein monster, an educated and radical Arab generation that would vow to drive the Jews out of Eretz Yisrael.

Blindness. How else can we explain the 1925 article in *Davar* the Histadrut Labor Federation's official organ? Written by Moshe Beilinson, one of the editors of the paper, it lavishly praised the Jaffa workers council for a successful strike of Arab factory workers. Beilinson wrote: "We know that the Arab people who are not still disunited can and probably will tomorrow be strong and united." The joy that was one presumably supposed to feel over this development was apparent only to those who refused to see that it was precisely Jewish education and organization that would develop an Arab people, strong and united in its determination to wipe out Zionism.

Blindness, yes. But it is apparently a hereditary disease, this political glaucoma, for the children and grandchildren, the present-day generation of Zionists, suffers from the very same case of vision failure. They, too, educate, develop, "raises up" the Arab. They, today, create the PLO leader and follower prepared "to fill *his* political and social role. . . ."

In 1930, after twenty years of bloody Arab rioting, Ben-Gurion could still meet with his inner circle (4 Cheshvan 5680 [1929]) and emerge with a statement that paid lip service to an

Arab national movement and add: "We must explain to him [the Arab] that Zionism does not come to attack the rights of the inhabitants but, quite the opposite, comes to bring its blessing. This explanation can come about only through cooperation in the field of economics and health so that the Arab will feel its results in a practical way."

On of the early proponents of working with the Arabs was a quixotic chap named H.M. Kalvarisky. He considered himself to be both an "expert" on Arabs and an Arabophile. As with most of those who claim, for no logical reason, to have a special liking for a particular people, Kalvarisky really had a snobbish contempt for the Arabs. Thus, he told the Zionist Executive Political Department in 1923 that the Arab was "by nature a materialist and should he realize that no advantage will accrue to him by siding with us, he will naturally turn away from us." There is not the slightest doubt that this contempt lay at the bottom of the majority Zionist view that one could buy the Arab's political soul with economic benefits. It is similarly true that, today, all those who reject the removal of Arabs from the Land of Israel and claim that economic and social "integration" will make them loyal to the Zionist state are just as contemptuous of the Arab.

Every so often a Zionist leader would pronounce a thought of clarity and truth, only to shrink from its implications. Thus, Ben-Gurion, a political chameleon whose changes in thinking revealed not pragmatism as much as confusion and opportunism, called in 1921 for "friendly relations between Jewish workers and the Arab working masses" and suggested a long list of benefits. The Ben-Gurion proposal was based on the old and tried thesis of bad Arab *effendis* and good Arab *fellahin*

Fellow socialist Moshe Shertok (Sharett) differed with the view and wrote to him in September 1921, saying: "Who is more likely to find a response? We, the hated foreigners, or the *muchtar* ["headman"] and the *sheikh* who dwell in the midst of their people and play on such effective instruments as racist and nationalist instincts, language, hallowed tradition, and the force of inertia. . . . *For the sake of self delusion we have made it all sound easy and simple—a handful of* effendis *against the masses of workers* [italics added]."

Nothing changed the minds of those determined not to

change. Ben Zvi insisted that the Arabs of Eretz Yisrael could not even be part of the Arab *general* national movement, let alone a "Palestinian" one, since he had reached the scholarly conclusion that they were really descendants of the Jews who had remained in the land after the Roman conquest and who had later embraced Islam. Clearly, "ex-Jews" would not challenge the right of Jews to the land, reasoned Ben Zvi. It was his opinion that they were not a nation but rather eleven "communities-peoples" and numerous smaller sects. Unfortunately, intellectual dialectics had little impact on the inhabitants of the land, who ungratefully persisted, despite Ben Zvi's research, in regarding themselves as Arabs and "Palestinians."

The socialists continued to cleave, with a religious fervor that would have made the Hasidim of the Mea Sh'arim district envious, to the catechism that social and economic benefits would make the Arab "our friend." In itself that should have been perceived as a ludicrous concept, but the Zionist laborers added yet another astonishing touch to their *pilpulism* Not only were they planning to make the land a *Jewish* homeland, but they also embarked on a desperate struggle to get Jewish employers to hire only Jewish laborers. Clearly, the need to create a solid, employed Jewish working class was vital to creating the infrastructure of a normal Jewish homeland, but just as clearly, it did little to make the Arab worker and peasant love the Zionists.

What was really at work was a process of dual delusion. The Arab would be told that, somehow, Jewish laborers, Jewish immigration, Jewish land purchase, and the ultimate Jewish homeland would not really rob him of any rights. And the Jew, repeating this to himself enough times, would persuade himself that it was true. Thus, the first postwar Zionist Congress (1921) adopted a resolution of "friendship" toward the Arabs, stressing that Eretz Yisrael was the common homeland of two peoples. It never explained how the Balfour promise of a *Jewish* homeland really meant a "common" homeland for Jews and Arabs.

In describing the muddled views of Achdut Avoda in the period between the two world wars, one writer said: "it recognized the existence of an Arab people in Israel but demanded of it that it renounce its rights. It proclaimed the right of the Jewish people to Palestine but recognized the need for coexistence between Jews and Arabs" (Yosef Gorni, "Zionist Socialism and the Arab Question," *Middle Eastern Studies,* 1978).

What to make of this nonsense? Gorni writes: "The key to their subjective approach was the belief that objective necessity would sooner or later create a Jewish majority in Palestine which would solve all the political, ethical and socialist aspects of the problem." Translated into simple, if cynical terms, the policy was: While we are a minority in the land, let us pay lip service to a "common homeland" and "mutual benefits," all the while working to become a majority so that the embarrassing political and ethical question of Arab majority rights will fade away.

Either the Zionist leaders were fools or, more probably, believed the Arabs were. Ben Zvi could tell the Vaad Leumi (Jewish representative committe) in 1922: "Some rights are not dependent on the approval of others. We will employ all possible means of entering the country and since this is historically inevitable the Arabs must understand us. And only when they understand can we arrive at reconciliation with our neighbors." And then the Poale Zion in 1920 could declare that "the interests of the *fellahin* and the masses of Arab workers will not be affected by the Jewish influx. For we wish to build this country not only for ourselves but for all its inhabitants." And finally, a leader of the World Zionist Movement, Nahum Sokolow, could tell the Arabs that the only problem was that of "misunderstanding." The Arabs would have had to be cretins not to give the reply of Arab writer Issat Darwazeh in *Al-Karmel* (1921): "They [the Zionists] keep dinning into our ears the word 'misunderstanding.' Are they trying to tell us that flooding the country with an overwhelming Jewish majority is nothing to frighten the Arab nation in Palestine? . . . Won't Mr. Sokolow tell us which rights the Arabs will *not* be deprived of by Zionist political fulfillment? Let the leaders of the Zionist movement . . . find for their nation some uninhabited country."

Poale Zion spokesman Yosef Aharonovitz, in a 1921 article called "L'Atzmeynu," could somehow write: "The Arab masses, as all uncultured masses, are caught in a net of intrigue . . . by those who spread and arouse among them a passion for vengeance and also by the natural passion in their hearts to plunder and loot. Anyone who tends to see in these intrigues signs of a national or political movement errs and desecrates, by his error, the concept of an ideological movement of any kind. . . . On can speak of all kinds of trends and turnings from various directions but not about an Arab national movement."

Alas, the poor Arab lad insisted that he existed. After the bloody 1921 riots by the "invisible" Arab national movement, the British colonialist government appointed the Haycraft Commission to look into the causes of the Arab riots that took the lives of forty-three Jews. They were hardly an unbiased party, but the fact remains that the anti-Zionist British did not have to fabricate the essential cause of the riots. It was, unfortunately, quite true that the Arab's "main objection to immigration has, however, been political and this obsession, although originating with the more educated Arabs, has filtered through the *khans* and coffee shops into the streets and villages. It can be summed up in the fear that through extreme Jewish immigration Palestine will become a Jewish dominion."

As the Arab national dybbuk refused to be exorcised, the Zionist movement resorted to all kinds of blandishments and devices to "win over" the Arabs. All were based on the time-dishonored Middle Eastern appetite for *baksheesh*—bribes, *money*. Thus, men like Yosef Nahmani became skilled in lavishing entertainment and gifts on local Bedouin sheikhs. Another frequent initiative was to gather Arab signatures on *mazbatas* ("petitions") in support of Zionism. These were obtained for small sums from village heads and were then proudly displayed as external propaganda to show that the Arab population was not unanimously opposed to Zionism. (After the State of Israel came into being and for the first two decades or so, a more sophisticated but essentially similar game was played with the cooperation of the heads of the *hamullas*. That, today, is gone with the shifting sands of time. Thanks to Israeli education, the Arab *today* would stone any official who attempted such a crude approach.)

In any event, these "spontaneous" Arab ads and petitions on behalf of Zionism proved to be a tidy little source of income for the Uncle Ahmeds of their time, but their effectiveness was surely nonexistent. Every Arab knew why another Arab suddenly became "pro-Zionist." The petitions became things of ridicule, and, worse, when a decision was made to end a long-term subsidy, the "pro-Zionist" would turn around and embarrass his Jewish friends by "repenting" and signing an *anti-Zionist* petition.

An even more expensive delusion was the decision to take hard-earned Jewish money and attempt to soothe "the Arab beast" by grassroots benefits. It is estimated that between 1918 and 1921 some £3,000 went for this, and we know that in 1923 Colonel Kisch, head of the Political Department of the Palestine Zionist Executive (PZE), requested £ 8,500 for such activities. To angry (and sober) Zionists who bitterly protested the spending of such large sums (at the time) of money that had originally been raised for colonization, Dr. Chaim Weizmann pathetically replied (June 8, 1920): "It may show little return, but if it only brings a temporary relief to the situation, that is all one wants." Such is the politics of confusion.

The most ambitious delusion was the attempt to create an Arab political movement that, in the words of Kalvarisky, would be a "large Muslim-Arab party favorable to our aspirations." The rankest amateur political realist could have predicted the failure of such an Uncle Ahmed party. What self-respecting Arab would support a political group conceived by Zionists, come into the world with Zionist midwives, and whose entire basis lay in its success in paying out *baksheesh?* Thousands upon thousands of pounds went into Arab pockets, and Dr. Eder of the PZE, commenting on Kalvarisky's "generosity," observed: "He gives out money very readily to people who may be taking the money and laughing at us."

The Zionists went through two Arab political movements, the Muslim National Association and the Palestine Arab National Party, before giving up. In the words of Tel Aviv Mayor Meir Dizengoff in 1923: "The moderates . . . are the *baksheesh* takers who will oppose us if we don't pay them." Samuel Tolkowsky, an Israeli expert on Arabs, gave vent to his "Zionism" by adamantly supporting bribery, because "we must prove to the Arabs that our coming into the country will really be to their advantage and . . . the big majority of the Palestinian Arabs understand by 'advantage,' only material advantage." And Aaron Aharonson: "So far as we know the Arabs, the man among them who will withstand a bribe is still to be born."

What a policy of coexistence! What a way to guarantee

Zionism's peaceful progress! A policy based on mutual contempt of the briber and bribee. . . .

Neither was it successful. Among the most extreme of the Zionist haters was Musa Kazim Al Hussini, president of the Arab Executive. The impossible Kalvarisky met him in 1922 in Lausanne, Switzerland, and at least hinted at the possibility of financial reward if he would moderate his views. According to Kalvarisky, Musa Kazim replied that "his attitude toward us is in our hands." A generous sum of money passed, but within a few months Musa Kazim's behavior reverted to its extreme anti-Zionism. Confronted, he proudly replied: "I am still a patriot and did not sell myself or my people to the Zionists." So much for the lack of hostility of Uncle Ahmed.

Confusion, contradiction, and mass delusion were the characteristics of official Zionist policy vis-à-vis the Arabs from the beginning. Moshe Beilinson gave voice to the prevalent theory within the Achdut Avoda movement in a 1925 article, "On the Controversy Regarding Arab-Jewish Relations." The gist of the theory was that "Palestine" was not generally "of importance" to the Arabs since they had had many other national centers and lands. The Jews, however, had only one land, and it was vital for their physical and spiritual survival. Since the Zionists would thus be taking only a small part of the huge Arab territory, and also guaranteeing a better life for the Arabs in Eretz Yisrael, including equal rights, *surely* the Arabs would eventually realize that Zionism did not really conflict with Arab nationalism.

It was that kind of thinking that could lead Laborite Yosef Sprinzak in 1919 to declare himself "one of the admirers of a Jewish-Arab alliance" and then to insist that "we must receive Palestine without limitation or reservation. . . . There is room for half a million Arabs in a greater Jewish Palestine, but there is not room here for an Arab kingdom." Obviously, the Zionists totally misread the Arab mind. The Arabs were not interested in *a large amount* of the land. They wanted *all* of it, because they believed that it was theirs. Most unreasonable, true. Eminently selfish, beyond a doubt. *But a fact.* And a fact to this day, only more so. Whatever the feeling of the "Palestinian" about the greater "Arab nation" and "homeland," he is first a "Palestinian," and he wants "his" land—*all of it.* The "Palestinians," whether they were a national movement or people in 1880 or

1900 or 1930, certainly believe they are that today. Our refusal to recognize them as such is valid and justified. But that refusal must be accompanied by the realization of the implications. To deny "Palestinian" rights to all or any part of Eretz Yisrael, one must cease deluding himself that somehow and sometime they will accept that. *They never will.* No national group can ever or will ever reconcile itself to the loss of a major part of its land to another people, especially when the latter appears to be weak, isolated, confused, and unsure of its own rights. Let the Jews know that there is no "Palestine" or "Palestinians," but let them not expect the Arabs to accept that.

Ben-Gurion presented his delusion, of Zionism and the Arab national movement not being in conflict because the Arabs had so much land and the poor Jews had only one country, in 1936 to George Antonius. Antonius, a Christian Palestine leader, met with Ben-Gurion three times and in his description of their discussion, the future Israeli prime minister painted a rosy picture in which he sought to portray only a narrow gulf separating himself and Antonius. Just a cursory look at Antonius's replies reveal how shocking was the Zionist leadership's desire to deceive itself. *Antonius saw the very idea of a Jewish state as dangerous to Arab aspirations.* Ben-Gurion heard nothing. He did not want to. We suffer from deafness of the political ear to this day.

There was one small section of the Zionist movement that realized that the Arabs would never accept a Jewish state and that war would be a permanent threat to it. They were not deluded. *Instead, they proposed to give up the idea of a Jewish state.*

This pitiful alternative to Zionist delusions was mainly the Brit Shalom ("Alliance of Peace") group, founded in 1925 by intellectuals of mainly German origin. They included philosopher Martin Buber, Hebrew University President Judah Magnes, Dr. Hugo Bergmann, and others. These people, sensing the essential flaws in the official Zionist argument, called for a binational state, with both Arabs and Jews enjoying absolute equality and parity, regardless of numbers. Bergmann, rising to metaphysics, discovered that by "divine grace," no less the land was intended for *both* peoples. Others, more political, avowed that the noble Jewish gesture of giving up its right to an exclusive homeland in the Land of Israel would move the Arabs to do the same.

Eventually the Brit Shalom intellectuals joined in a group called Ihud and worked with the Marxist Hashomer Hatzair movement in a common League for Jewish-Arab Cooperation and Rapprochement whose goal was a binational state.

Essentially, the difference between the binationalists and the official Zionists was over delusions. Each had its own, and the ultimate common denominator that all refused to see—that all did not *wish* to see—was that the Arabs believed the land was *theirs*—all of it—that as the majority they had the right to it and saw no reason to give up one inch of land or one centimeter of *rights*.

Many blind Zionists; see how they ran! Faced with the unmistakable fact of the existence of the Arab who was a majority in the land, they groped in various directions, saying:

1. The Arab as a distinct entity does not really exist and will ultimately be absorbed by the Jews—so there is no problem.

2. The Arabs do exist and will remain, but they are only a collection of tribes and classes and not a *national* people—so there is no problem.

3. The Arabs are a national people, but if we show them goodwill, learn Arabic, mix with them, and give them economic and social benefits, they will agree to Jewish control of the country—so there is no problem.

4. The Arabs are a national people who will never agree to a Jewish state but will accept a binational state in which both Jews and Arabs will have exactly the same powers and rights, even if the Arabs are a majority—so there is no problem.

5. The Arabs will never accept anything less than their own sovereign state, so partition of that country into separate Arab and Jewish states will give them what they want; they will accept the plan, and all the "Palestinians" who wish to will live within its boundaries and any who choose to remain in the Jewish state will live with the Jews in brotherhood and equality—so there is no problem.

But there is a problem. It is a problem of sons who learned nothing from the errors of their fathers. After one hundred years of Jewish pioneering return; after eighty years of political Zionism; after scores of riots; after four major wars and more than thirty years of a Jewish state, the sons of the fathers, the Jews of Israel, still believe that they can live in peace with the Arabs in a land the Arabs believe is theirs. Time runs out, and we had best, quickly, listen to the Arab voices and believe what they say they plan for us.

Chapter 9

Time Runs Out

The voices of the Israeli Arab revolution are clearly heard in the land, and, as if cursed from heaven, the Jewish leaders of Israel sit, paralyzed. Events within the Arab sector of Israel daily exposed the bankruptcy of Israeli policy toward its Arabs, revealing all the misconceptions, delusions, and error piled upon error. It is a policy woven of many fabrics—contempt for the Arabs, fearful unwillingness to face reality, guilt.

In 1949 correspondent Hal Lehrman, a longtime observer of Arab affairs, visited the new State of Israel and later put down his impressions for *Commentary* magazine (December 1949). In Nazareth he noted that "the Jewish authorities are apparently making a genuine try for the equality promised in their Declaration of Independence . . . keeping the administration as Arab as possible within security limits." Fearful of the threat to that security, the Israelis placed Arabs under a military government. In Nazareth the military governor was Major Elisha Soltz, a kibbutz member of the leftist Mapam Party (today aligned with the Labor Party in a bloc known as the Marach). The Mapam people, at the left, liberal end of the spectrum, are of course passionate advocates of theoretical Arab equality. Lehrman's description of Soltz is a description of general Israeli contempt and ignorance vis-à-vis its Arabs. Wrote Lehrman: "Major Elisha Soltz, who looks and sounds like the *kibbutznik* he is, was troubled only by economic problems. . . . 'If I could find employment for 2,500 breadwinners, the Quakers and I could all pack up and go home.' Major Soltz was not worried about the Communist situation, however. 'Yes, they have good propagandists here, and some influence. *But they are nowhere near a majority.*

195

Their one big advantage was that they had an Arab branch here, underground, which came out as soon as the Arab army left Nazareth.' *But he laughed away the possibility that the Communists could keep growing on Arab discontent.*"

Soltz's attitude was matched by the majority Mapai (Labor) Party, which controlled the Histadrut Labor Federation. Said one local Histadrut hack: "Take away the restrictions on Arab travel. Give us jobs for them. There won't be ten Communists left in Nazareth."

A little more than twenty-five years later, the Arabs of Nazareth had everything the Jewish "head-and-stomach" materialists preached as the prescription for the disappearance of the anti-Zionist Communists. The military government had long since been abolished and the Soltzes of Israel had gone home. Travel restrictions were a thing of the past. There was full employment in Nazareth. And just as the hacks had said, there were not ten Communists left in Nazareth. *There were at least 9,653 of them.*

It was the night of December 9, 1975. "By evening, the automobile horns began to honk. Into the wetness and cold that enveloped Nazareth, rivers of joy poured out. Hoarse throats shouted happily. Emotional eyes cried: We won! Young people clapped each other on the back and kissed. Telephones rang in homes whose lights had not gone out and in stores which had not closed. *Mabruk! Mabruk!* Congratulations! Congratulations! Voices that we will yet hear again" *(Maariv,* December 12, 1975).

Elections in free and equal Nazareth, where Arab heads and stomachs had been filled by deluded Jews for more than a quarter of a century. The Israeli Arabs of the town had just gone to the polls to elect a town council and mayor of the biggest Arab town in Israel. The result was a staggering landslide victory for the Communist Rakah party. Fully 67.3 percent of the voters cast their ballots for the Communist list. More than two-thirds of the voters—9,653 of 14,125—elected a party committed to anti-Zionism, to hatred of Israel. Given the one way to express their desire to be "Palestinians," the Arabs of Nazareth did so—resoundingly.

All this was accomplished despite open and crude efforts at intimidation by the government. Two cabinet ministers were sent on the eve of the election to warn Nazareth against voting Rakah lest it suffer loss of funding. Money was poured into the coffers of the Arab Labor Party puppets. All in vain. The Communists swamped the old *hamulla* chiefs who had slavishly followed the government line in return for political favors.

As usual, the Israeli was "stunned." He could not believe that eleven of the seventeen council seats had been won by Rakah. He could not imagine that the new mayor of Nazareth was Tewfik Zayad. Tewfik Zayad at the time was forty-six years old, a politician and poet. His poetry? To commemorate the first anniversary of the Yom Kippur War, in October 1974, Zayad wrote a poem in praise of the Egyptian crossing of the Suez Canal:

> *The sun was in the midst of the sky*
> *and the black faces fed the soil with their flesh*
> *the heavy half-tracks and the metal eagles*
> *chewed the Bar-Lev Line's insides*
> *. . . and all the eyes wept with joy*
> *. . . the crossing was holy*
> *and holy will be the homeland . . .*

Zayad, already a Knesset member on the Rakah ticket, became a national hero to the Arabs of Israel for his poem and his willingness to incite openly against the state. For, after all, the Arabs did not vote Rakah for its communism, but rather because it was the only successful political group that was anti-Zionist. It was their method of voting against the Jewish state, against the Jewish "occupation" of what was now called "Israel." It was their way of voting for "Palestine," and the only shock that is understandable is that the Jews were shocked by the Rakah win. It was only the venality and corruption of the Nazareth *hamullas* that enabled the Labor Party to perpetuate an illusion of Arab satisfaction with the Jewish state.

The political "boss" of Nazareth for a quarter of a century was Knesset member Seif-E-Din Zuabi. He had been one of the typical "Uncle Ahmeds," a faithful and reliable follower of the government who did its bidding in return for political and economic favors. The Israeli newspaper *Ha'Aretz* (December 12, 1975) called Zuabi "the man who is precious to the authoritites and who for twenty years had behaved as if Nazareth was his own property." He and his large *hamulla* had ensured the illusion of Arab loyalty and Arab acceptance of the Jewish state.

But as the young generation of Arabs rose and, thanks to
Israeli educational, social, and economic progress, threw off the
yoke of the *hamullas*, everything changed. They saw their elders
as Esaus who had sold their national birthright for economic
benefits. The elders would go, the *hamullas* would go—and the
town of Nazareth voted Rakah, voted Zayad, voted Arafat.

Zayad's voice is one of those that leads the Arab struggle
against Israel. It grows in shrillness and in brazenness in direct
proportion to Israel's fear of acting against him. After his poem
praising the Egyptian arm for killing Israeli soldiers, the Dis-
abled Veterans' Organization cabled the Knesset Speaker,
saying, "It is intolerable that the Knesset would contain a man
who hates Israel and who writes words of hatred that pain all
the nation." A special Knesset committee was set up to look into
the matter. It invited Zayad to appear and explain himself. In a
calculated decision Zayad refused to show up. He was proved
correct. The committee announced its findings: the poem was
"not compatible with the oath taken by a Knesset member"
pledging allegiance to the state. The penalty? Nothing. Zayad
laughed.

In his first interview following his smashing victory in Nazareth, Zayad told Israel Radio: "We are not alone, not in the
country and not in the world." It was a warning to the Jews not
to move against him. It was a gamble that worked because of
Jewish fear. Nothing Zayad said in terms of hatred, incitement,
and sedition moved Israel to take action against him, and so he
became an Arab national hero.

On March 6, 1976, Zayad told a wildly cheering crowd of
1,200 in Nazareth to fight against government expropriation of
land in the Galilee: "The government throws stones at us so it
is time to throw stones at it—and it should keep in mind that it
lives in a glass house. . . . They wish us to get out—we say to
them: We stay and you will go." Knesset member Yigal Cohen
demanded that the attorney take action. No action was taken
against Tewfik Zayad.

On May Day, 1976, Zayad addressed a crowd of 4,000
Nazareth Arabs. As he spoke, the few Israeli flags were lowered.
Said Zayad: "From now on there will be no communities and
religious groups but only a single Arab minority, part of the

Palestinian nation." And because of this, "the Arabs of Israel will not remain neutral over events in the West Bank. For the Arabs of Israel are Palestinians and the Arabs of the West Bank are our people, our flesh and blood." He concluded by calling on the Arabs to escalate the struggle in the Galilee "and not to spare as many sacrifices as are necessary. If they will take our lands we will lie, by the thousands, under their bulldozers." His call to defy the government was met by wild cries of "The Galilee will return to the Arabs." "The Galilee is Arab, *you* leave." "We will give our spirit and blood for the Galilee." No action was taken against Zayad for incitement.

On May 1, 1978, Zayad had this to tell a crowd of 3,000 in Nazareth's main square: "The war policy of the Maarach [Labor coalition] caused it to lose the elections—but Yasir Arafat is still alive and in existence. The Likud has risen to power—it too will fall. *But Arafat will remain, and Arafat means that the Palestinian people lives and exists!"* He concluded by saying: "That which was taken by force will be returned by force." No action was taken against him for sedition.

In June 1980 a meeting of mayors and local council chairmen met to protest the attack on the two PLO mayors of Sechem and Ramallah (*Jerusalem Post*). Against a background of cries of "We are all Fatah" and "We are waiting for Arafat," Zayad said, in part: "The government is a bunch of criminals and animals." "People under occupation have the right to oppose the conqueror with any means they choose." "The Palestinian flag will soon be hoisted all over the country."

Ra'anan Cohen, head of the Labor Party's Arab Department and one of the leading exponents of "head-and-stomach" bribery, was furious. He called Zayad's words "very clearly, subversion of the very existence of the state." Perhaps; *undoubtedly.* But no action was taken against the Arab.

In the face of this utter failure of both the Labor and Menachem Begin government to act—a failure clearly born of fear of Arab rioting and world opinion—it is little wonder that the ordinary Israeli Arabs also grow bolder. Thus, on a visit to the Israeli Arab village of Tayba, a *Maariv* reporter (March 1, 1978) recorded the following open comments by young Arabs: "Yasin, who calls himself Abed al-Naser, says that there must rise a Palestinian state under Yasir Arafat. And what is to be done with the Jews? 'The Jews,' he says, 'have to return to Europe, from where they came. Those who remain will live in neighborhoods as they once lived, in Germany.' One of the youngsters cries out from the side: 'The Jews into the sea!' "

And so Moshe Sharon, Begin's former adviser on Arab affairs, complained that in certain Arab villages, expressions of joy were heard after the massacre of more than thirty Jews by terrorists on the coastal road. Said Sharon: "Unlike past terrorist massacres when a wave of letters, telegrams, and statements of condemnation of the terror actions were received by the prime minister's office, this time—after the coastal massacre—only three telegrams were received." It might be added that after the murder of six Jews in Hebron in 1980, not one Arab body sent a message of condolence.

The Rakah Communist Party, at the moment, is the leading organized anti-Zionist group. Well organized and financed by Moscow, it already controls many local village councils. Because of this, well over half the members of the chairmen of Arab local councils—always considered the most moderate and pliable of the Arab institutions—met on January 20, 1979, and declared their support of the PLO. The resolution welcomed the struggle of the West Bank Arabs "against the occupation, annexation, and colonialist settlements" and expressed their solidarity with "the struggle of the Palestinian people under the leadership of the PLO to establish its independent state."

The takeover of village after village by Rakah shows that time is running out for Israel in its struggle to avert an Arab uprising. Said Knesset member Amnon Linn, a member of Begin's own Likud bloc (January 1979): "The radicalization of Arab students and Galilee local councils heads is far more serious now than it was during the tenure of Maarach governments."

Boldness bred success for Rakah, and success bred more boldness. After the Land Day Rebellion, Israeli Arabs watched with pride and delight as Rakah presented the Knesset a motion of no confidence in the government. Rakah Arab member Tewfik Toubi, an older colleague of Zayad's, rose to thunder: "Why is the government of murderers not here? Why do the cowards kill and then run away from the call of the blood they shed . . . ? Where is the archmurderer . . . ?"

Time runs out. Twenty years ago—*fifteen* years ago—Toubi would never have dared say such a thing. It is a different Arab Israeli world today. It is a world of groups that challenge Rakah as not being *sufficiently* radical. Groups such as Bnei Hakfar with their Progressive National Movement and the leftist, nationalist Abna-el-Balad are strong challenges to Rakah for the minds and souls of Israeli Arab youth and intellectuals.

That segment is already radicalized, and nothing Israel can possibly do will change the stark fact. Back in February 1978 a group of fifty-six Israeli Arab intellectuals from Nazareth and large villages of the Triangle issued a public statement demanding official recognition of the "Palestinian Arabs living in Israel" along with full political rights. In addition, they demanded the return of all Arab property and declared their recognition of the PLO as the sole legitimate representative of the "Palestinian" people. It is a new era.

Alongside the rapid growth of secular nationalism is a startling return to and growth of Muslim fundamentalism, at least as nationalistic and bitterly anti-Israel. There is little doubt that the rise to power of Khomeini in Iran gave tremendous impetus to the religious insurgence among Arab Israelis. In a January 1979 symposium on Islam among the Arabs of Eretz Yisrael, Moshe Sharon pointed out that "Islam is the outstanding expression among the Arabs of Eretz Yisrael of their national entity." He pointed to a spontaneous religious revival among Israeli Arabs as a form of national identity. This included a rash of new mosques and a large number of young Arabs sprouting beards and traditional clothing (à la the Muslim Brotherhood) and seeking to study in the Muslim College in Hebron.

But religious or secular, bearded or beardless, town or village, the Israeli Arab dreams of his own sovereign Arab Palestine. And in the meantime he shapes his political struggle by stages.

Zayad gave one of the most significant Arab speeches on May Day 1976, when he demanded that the State of Israel implement the full equality for Arabs that is pledged by the Declaration of Independence. Specifically, he demanded that in proportion to their (then) population, the Arabs be allotted eighteen Knesset seats and three cabinet ministries, as well as a proportionate number of senior posts in the various ministries. Warned Zayad: "If the Israeli Arabs do not obtain equality of rights within the state of Israel, they shall become citizens of another state."

It is rather frightening for those who have studiously refused, until now, to look at the fundamental contradiction between a Jewish state and one in which the Arabs actually demand political representation that begins to move toward eventual Arab democratic control. There is an intense measure of hypocrisy in the manner in which we fall over ourselves in fulsome praise of the Israeli democracy that allows Rakah to rave against the state when it has *five members.* Zayad and other Arabs are now demanding their *proportionate share,* and that is quite another thing for all the liberal proponents of democracy. The call for greater Arab representation will be heard, however, with increasing intensity whether we like it or not, and as their population grows, they will sit in the Knesset without our largess.

And as they grow in population, the Israeli Arabs will push ever more stridently for return of all their families and fellow Arabs who fled during the 1948 War of Independence—this, and the return of their property which is now in Jewish hands. They will rely on United Nations resolutions giving those "refugees" the right to choose between compensation or return. No matter that the Arabs themselves contemptuously rejected the United Nation's original partition scheme in 1947. Arab cynicism and duplicity are legendary, and when aided by a United Nations of political prostitutes and professional Israel haters, contradictions bother no one. Again, Israel will be faced with the specter of more Arabs entering the land as part of the Israeli Arab program to destroy the Jewish state from within.

The population growth within the Galilee and the Triangle will quicken the irredentist call for Arab sovereignty over those areas, first through "autonomy" and then through outright annexation to the "Palestine" that will be called for in Judea-Samaria. Justifications for this are already endlessly repeated. We are a majority, say the Arabs of those areas, and we wish to control our own destiny. We wish to live our own cultural and ethnic life. This area is Arab by virtue of its population, and we demand an autonomy that gives us the right to procure that which our identity demands. Again, the United Nations will be called down to justify such demands. Under the world organization's 1947 proposal, much of the Galilee and the Triangle (plus many other cities) were supposed to be part of the Arab state. The Arab mind has no patience with the logic of the fact that *they* rejected the plan and went to war in hope of destroying the Jewish state. The fact that in the war that they began, they lost both the battle and the moral right to talk about the UN plan they rejected is totally irrelevant to the Arabs. It is interesting to note that in 1949, less than a year after their defeat, an Arab official of the Communist Party in Nazareth was asked by Hal Lehrman why the party in Nazareth was called the Arab Liberation League and not the Israel Communist Party, as elsewhere. His reply was: "Nazareth is Arab. Partition said so. It should be part of an Arab state." Nothing has changed. The demand for autonomy will grow into a roar, aided, ironically enough, by the awesome blunder of Menachim Begin's "autonomy plan."

Not only did the Begin plan bury the hope of annexing the liberated lands, it also—in the words of Moshe Sharon—"is likely to bring down disaster upon us. I have no doubt that this is the kernel of a Palestinian state which Israel is in effect helping to create." But even worse, from Israel's point of view, is the dynamic effect autonomy in the territories would have on the Arabs of Galilee and the Triangle. Even before Begin produced his incredible autonomy scheme for Judea-Samaria, there was talk of autonomy for the Galilee. Now, when the territories have been offered autonomy, the effect on the Israeli Arabs in the Galilee and Triangle will be explosive. Worst of all is the fact that the two major Arab concentrations in Israel border on the "autonomy in the Galilee and the Triangle but for linkage to the autonomy of their brethren in Judea-Samaria.

From that it is only one short step to the demand for the *separation* of the Galilee and the Triangle from Israel, and their becoming part of the Palestinian state upon which they border and to which they are tied by race, history, language, and religion. Sharon himself told *Maariv* (February 2, 1979) that he saw "the dangerous likelihood of the formation of a legal Arab party that will demand that the Arab autonomy. In such a case, the Israeli Arabs will demand a return to the partition of 1947."

A similar warning was given by Knesset member Amnon Linn
on December 9, 1975, when he charged that elements among the
Israeli Arabs planned to revolt and demand annexation of areas
of Israel to any new Palestinian state.

Of course, Israel will not agree, and bloody will be the battles and terrible the bombs and bullets. Rebellion will raise its
head in the midst of Israel, and the nightly television news will
show pictures of Israeli soldiers shooting Arabs in the Galilee. It
will be dangerous to travel through the area, let alone live there,
and all the while the Arab population growth will mean more
Arab legislators in the Knesset and another step toward a "democratically" created "Palestine."

Too late, the Israeli government realizes the danger and
frantically attempts to prevent the Arabization of the Galilee by
"Judaizing" it, filling it with Jews to offset Arab population
growth. Of course, even at this late critical stage of national
emergency, there are Jews whose liberal instinct clashes with
their Jewishness and their sense of national self-preservation.
And so President Yitzhak Navon absurdly tells Galilee settlers
that the term "Jewish settlement" is preferable to "Judaizing,"
lest the latter be seen as either racist or implying driving the
Arabs out. But whether one calls the child by its real name,
"Judaizing," or plays games of self-deception and conjures up
"Jewish settlement" or even the innocuous "development of the
Galilee," the fact remains that the Israelis are desperately attempting to raise the Jewish population in the area that is the
focus of Arab nationalism and irredentism. It is a policy that is
far too little and far too late.

When Moshe Rivlin, head of the Israeli Jewish National Fund
and a longtime Labor Party official, cries: "If we fail, G-d forbid, to . . . change the Jewish-Arab population ratio in the
Galilee to a minimum of fifty-fifty, Israel will soon face a grave
danger," one can understand his fears. But in reality, the danger
of the Arabs does not end even if we can somehow manage to
keep a precarious equality of population in the Galilee. The fact
that the Roman Catholics in Northern Ireland are a minority in
no way prevents them from demanding annexation to Eire, the
Irish Republic. A huge, growing, hostile Arab population of 40
to 50 percent is enough to turn the Galilee into a perpetual
bloody scene of confrontation. Furthermore, there is no possible

way that, eventually, Israel will find enough Jews to settle in the Galilee to offset the incredible Arab birthrate there.

Nevertheless, the thought of a solidly Arab-populated Galilee turns strong Zionists weak, and as early as 1966 Prime Minister Levi Eshkol proposed a plan to settle Jews in upper and central Galilee. Because of the Six-Day War the plan was shelved; only in the aftermath of the Yom Kippur War and the rise of the Arab revolt did the government revive and embellish it. The key to settling the large numbers of Jews and building farms, villages, and urban centers is expropriation of lands.

Unfortunately, the government's courage does not match its appreciation of the danger. And so, in the face of the bitter Arab resistance (*they* understood quite well the purpose of the plan) which culminated in the bloody Land Day Rebellion, the government, in fear, backtracked and plucked the vitals out of the program. Instead of an honest presentation of the problem— *Arab population and irredentism, a threat to the Galilee as part of Israel* —the government issued an "information-background" bulletin, built on an apology and defensiveness that was not lost on the Arabs: "It has always been the government's policy to encourage and foster the dispersal of the country's population and to move toward an evening-out of the population-density pattern. . . . *Certainly it is not a measure directed against any particular population group* [*sic*]. . . ."

Shades of early Zionist contempt for the Arabs! All the fraud and lies and self-delusion revived! If the project was so good for the Arabs, why the uproar? Why the riots? Why the rebellion?

Because, despite the subconscious feelings of the liberals and leftists, *the Arabs were not fools.* Such absurd Israeli government explanations might satisfy wealthy UJA givers and heads of the Liberal American Jewish Establishment; they did not deceive the Arabs.

And so, the Rakah Arabic-language newspaper *Al-Ittihad*, on June 6, 1975, wrote: "We became aware of the existence of this conspiracy about a year ago because of the renewed talk about the 'Judaizing of Galilee.' . . . We will not remain silent in face of this sinister, racist plan. . . . This is indeed a question of life."

Voices. If one wishes to understand why the Jews of Israel

retreat and face catastrophe while the Arab star ascends, listen to the two voices; listen to the contrast. One, the Arab voice, is shrill, loud, brazen, confident. The other, the Jewish voice, is defensive, apologetic, guilt-ridden. Between two such adversaries there is no contest. The Arabs have a definite goal, and their programs are unabashedly aimed at it. The Jews, beset by contradictions, set up schizophrenic plans that go rushing off madly in opposite directions. The results are obvious.

If Israel would be honest and state the problem truthfully and starkly, world Jewry would understand. But if, on the one hand, it denies a problem and then takes "anti-liberal" actions to solve it, what is anyone to think?

There are Jews who understand the desperate nature of the problem and the need to deal with it boldly. It was this understanding that led General Avigdor Ben-Gal to characterize the Arabs of the Galilee as "a cancer." His reprimand by Begin's minister of defense, Ezer Weizman, was only further evidence of the fearful lack of direction and firmness in Israel today.

Perhaps the clearest and boldest perception of the problem was that of Yisrael Koenig, representative of the Interior Ministry in the north. In a secret memorandum sent to Prime Minister Rabin in 1976, Koenig warned that an Arab majority in the Galilee would threaten Israeli sovereignty in the region. As an example of the problem, Koenig pointed out that in 1974 a mere 759 Jews were added to the Galilee population as against 9,035 Arabs! He called for the following actions to be taken: to settle Jews in heavily populated Arab areas; to limit the number of Arab university students and encourage them to study outside the country, then make it difficult for them to return; to cut sharply national insurance payments to Arabs; and to limit employment opportunities for them.

Koenig's plan, as good as it was, was unfortunately not nearly the necessary answer. But it was drafted with knowledge of the guilt-ridden lack of a sense of national self-preservation that gripped Israeli Jews and that prevented an even more vigorous and effective plan from being adopted. In the end, even Koenig and his plan were the targets of the disoriented, confused liberals. Thus, the *Jerusalem Post* (September 9, 1976) called it "a scheme tainted with nationalist fanaticism." Mapam Knesset member Aharon Efrat called for Koenig to be fired. Tourism

Minister Moshe Kol called it "a damaging document." *Yediot Aharonot* writer Yehoshua Ben-Porat lamented the Koenig report violated all that the State of Israel promised "in the Declaration of Independence and pledges daily . . . equal rights for all its citizens—including the Arab minority." He then proceeded to display the contradiction and confusion that must be the lot of all guilt-ridden liberals as he proclaimed the right of all Jews to settled anywhere in Israel "as long as they do not violate the rights of the minority. . . ."

But, of course, that is precisely Ben-Porat's confusion. The Declaration of Independence, if it grants equal rights, grants the right of the minority to become a *majority.* Is that what Ben-Porat defends? Will he, like some modern Voltaire, stand and shout to the howling Arab mob that cries for the end of a Zionist state: I will differ with you over this but will defend to the death your right to become a majority? How difficult it is to be a liberal and a Zionist.

And Aharon Meged, one of the intellectual self-haters in Israel, in a thundering article, bewailed the policy of "Judaizing" and then proclaimed that "the path that Koenig suggests contradicts Zionism and its path!" Indeed. Political Zionism was born with a book called *The Jewish State;* it was embodied in a Declaration of Independence that creates a *Jewish* majority. But Judaizing the Galilee is anti-Zionist! Koenig's efforts to save the country's Jewish and Zionist character is anti-Zionist! Meged is not a Zionist. In his own self-hatred, he is an intellectual pseudo-Samson whose death wish is accompanied by a desire not to go alone.

It took a gentile reporter, William E. Farrell of the *New York Times,* to put his finger on the only relevant question. Writing on September 22, 1976, he stated: "The report has also once again brought into focus a crucial question—still to be answered—that has vexed Israel since its founding: can an Arab minority participate fully and democratically in a state that Prime Minister Yitzhak Rabin recently described as predicated on 'the ingathering of the Jewish people's exiles' and 'living the life of a Jewish state'?"

But, of course, the question has been answered in the reality of the ultimate contradiction between the two concepts. A Jewish state can exist in peace only with a large Jewish majority.

It cannot grant the right to a minority to take its home away peacefully. It is a contradiction that the Arabs are determined to resolve in their own favor, and democracy is joined by demography to plunge Israel down the road to catastrophe.

And as the political clock ticks on, the hands moving toward the era of political and violent confrontation, the Arabs inside Israel in many different ways chip away at the political, economic, and social stability and health of the Jewish state.

The angry Arab shout over the expropriation of land is in reality a tactic to cover the incredible amount of state land stolen by Arabs over the years, thanks to Israeli fear of provoking incidents. Not only have literally hundreds of thousands of dunams of state land been stolen through Arab squatting, but the illegal building of Arab houses, which tends to eternalize the theft as well as cut off and surround Jewish villages, has reached the epidemic stage. The thefts are in the Negev, in the Galilee, and increasingly in the center of the country, including the heart of the cities.

The huge wholesale theft of lands created *political facts.* The Arab squats on state lands; the Jews do nothing; the Arab works it, builds houses on it, and then claims it as his own. Indeed, for every dunam of Jewish settlement in the liberated lands, thousands of dunams go into de facto Arab illegal settlements inside Israel (as well as in the liberated lands). The situation has gotten so desperate in the Negev that Agricultural Minister Ariel Sharon told the Knesset Foreign Affairs Committee (July 30, 1980) that it will be necessary to set up five new settlements east and west of Beersheba, between the Gaza Strip and Hebron Hills, to prevent Bedouin encroachment on state lands *which could create terrorist continuity between the present Arab-inhabited areas of Judea and Gaza.* Using a map, Sharon showed how Bedouin tribes from the Beersheba area had fanned out alarmingly to the north, west, and east.

The Markovitz Committee, set up to report on the problem of stolen state lands, reported in June 1980 that the stealing of lands had become a plague. The major problem was the Bedouin growth. Thanks to Israeli health facilities and agricultural progress, not only were there more Bedonins but infinitely more Bedouin flocks. As to the Bedouins themselves, in 1948 there were between 12,000 and 15,000 of them in the Negev.

Today more than 40,000 live there! This tripling of the population in thirty years, thanks to a growth rate that today reaches a world record of 7 *percent,* means an inevitable explosion in the years to come. As far as Bedouin flocks, whereas in 1948 there were some 30,000 Bedouin animals, by 1978 there were nearly *half a million.* Not only did they steal the land and then make it de facto "Arab," but because of their irresponsible overgrazing they destroyed it from an agricultural and ecological standpoint.

● The Arabs have grown bolder thanks to the incredible apathy and timidity of the government. In September 1979 a Nature Reserve patrolman, Asahel Lev, discovered a large flock of Bedouin animals illegally grazing on state land. When he left his jeep to warn the Bedouins, he was attacked by seven of them, armed with knives, who shouted *"Itbach-al-Yahud"* ("Slaughter the Jew"). He fled.

● In December 1979 Knesset member and Dimona mayor Jacques Amir tabled an urgent motion for discussion of Bedouin harassment of the Jewish settlement of Nevatim in the Negev. According to Amir, the settlers—Jews from India—"have suffered heavy property losses from the Bedouins, who do not hesitate to use force." The Jewish residents told of Bedouin flocks eating away at their fields and trees. On the tombstones of the settlement's graveyard could be seen goats' droppings. The police never arrested one Bedouin.

● Members of the settlement Bitha, near the Negev town of Ofakim, were so frustrated over two years of Bedouin encroachment on their lands that in March 1978 they exploded and burned a Bedouin tent. Four Jews were arrested.

● Between 1976 and 1978 nearly the entire Sinai Bedouin tribe of Al-Haiwat moved into the southern Negev along with 5,000 animals. They gradually became residents of Israel, aside from seizing and destroying land.

● On March 4, 1978, Alon Galilee, head of the Nature Reserve's Green Patrol unit, claimed that Bedouins had taken over land within the Israeli army firing range area. More than 10,000 head of livestock were in the area. The same problem was also noted in army range areas in the Galilee. The army was not only forced to limit and postpone important training, but as Galilee pointed out, the Bedouins had access to classified military information. In addition, thefts of army weapons and ammunition had become an epidemic.

●   That hostile political elements realize the importance of establishing Arab "facts" on as much land as possible was emphasized in March 1978 by Yitzhak Bardimon, head of the Interior Ministry's southern district, who said that Bedouins were being incited "by enemies of the state" to try to gain control of government land. He also pointed out that the sudden"wild building was an effort to establish facts."

The Bedouin theft of land, which, in the words of Ariel Sharon, is "a result of Jewish weakness," is only one side of the coin. *The fact is that the lands on which they grazed when the state came into being in 1948 are for the main part not theirs either.* The Bedouins, wanderers and nomads, never owned land. They would move from one part of the country to another with their flocks. Present efforts on their part to claim "ownership" are transparent efforts to legitimize their theft.

Thus, at a press conference in Beersheba on March 28, 1978, Negev Bedouins were unable to produce any legal titles *(kushanim)* to the land they claimed. This sheds more than a little necessary light on the controversy surrounding the efforts of the Israeli government to take over desperately needed land for the new post–Camp David air bases.

Israel, a country with 3.1 million Jews on barely 8,000 square miles, desperately needs every inch of *its* land. Agricultural land for Jews is scarce, water supplies precious. The Negev, covering more than half of pre-1967 Israel, clearly is a region that Jews see as their future. For decades, however, Israel preferred not to make this clear to the Bedouins, thus allowing them to stake their claim to most stretches of land. Suddenly, Israel must pay the price.

The disastrous Camp David accords not only called for Israel's giving up the Sinai with its oil, but also the vital Israeli air bases. It was agreed that new bases be built in the Negev. The question was where. Experts carefully surveyed the possible sites, and it was decided that to replace the base at Ohira, to be given up in 1982, a new one would be built in the Negev on land of Tel Malhata. The thirty years of Jewish unwillingness to grapple with the issue of the Bedouins now came back to haunt them. Riots, protests, threats—and suddenly the Bedouins were laying claim in the Negev alone to 600,000 dunams (150,000 acres) of land. Nuri-El-Urbi, secretary of the Committee for Bedouin rights in the Negev, vowed on July 7, 1980, that the Arabs "will not budge from their lands . . . . They can cut the Bedouin into pieces and we still will not leave the lands."

Naturally, the Arabs receive support from the professional Jewish self-hater. A fascinating document was a petition circulated by the extreme leftist Sheli Knesset Party which called the proposal to expropriate the Negev lands at Tel Malhata (with impressive compensation to the Bedouin squatter) "a blatant violation of the fundamental principle of equality." It was suggested that the petition be sent to non-Zionists and non-Jews to increase pressure on Israel. Among the "suggested signers" were Ramsey Clark, Jerry Brown, Teddy Kennedy, Leonard Bernstein, Jane Fonda, Woody Allen, Saul Bellow, Arthur Herzberg, Nahum Goldman, and Joachim Prinz. . . .

The Galilee is yet another area of Arab land grabbing and establishment of facts. In February 1979 the Interior Ministry claimed that in the past twenty years no fewer than 40,000 dunams (10,000 acres) of Galilee land had been taken over by Arabs in Military Areas 9 and 117 alone. On July 21, 1976, Knesset member Yehuda Ben Meir warned that not only was land being grabbed but more than 1,600 illegal buildings had gone up on state land. He said that one reason was to cut Jewish contiguity for political reasons described the method as one of *chap* ("grab"): "They put up two or three houses on a hill. If there is no reaction they begin to build more houses on a hill. Gradually, the area becomes a village, as occurred with the village of Danun in the western Galilee. Today there are 1,700 people living there, and no one dreams of moving them out."

Despite Ariel Sharon's warning on September 7, 1977, that "Arab squatters [in the Galilee] must be prevented from their continued campaign to seize state dunams," the process continues. Jewish Agency official Amos Harpaz reported on December 26, 1979, that just in recent months 800 more dunams (200 acres) had been seized by Arabs in Military Area 9. "They plowed and sowed the land and now claim title by right of undisputed possession."

To the threats of "democracy" and "demography" was

now added that of "geography." But despite the awesome political implication, in September 1976 the Ministry of Interior announced a "retroactive" legalizing of the illegal houses. And on
February 16, 1978, the Jewish Telegraphic Agency was able to
report the following: "The Israel Lands Administration has
changed its tactics with regard to illegal houses built by Arab
villagers in Galilee on State-owned land without obtaining government permits. Instead of bull dozing them, it is leasing the
land to the Arabs, who readily admit they are getting 'a real
bargain.'

"A case in point is the village of Iskal in lower Galilee, with
a population of 5,000. Over the years the local residents built
some 300 houses without permits, leading to repeated conflicts
with the Lands Administration. In three instances, the government sent in bulldozers to raze the houses. But that only increased the bitterness. Recently, the Lands Administration
reached an agreement with the village council. It legalized the
buildings retroactively and leased the land to the villagers at
1970 rates, which are relatively cheap.

"Ahmad Abdul Hahman Assad, a building contractor, will
have to pay the Lands Administration IL 50,000 for the land on
which he built his house 13 years ago. Assad is pleased with the
deal 'When I built this place it was illegal. Now I am paying for
it,' he said. He will also receive permits to build additional
houses on the leased land for his children.

"The Mayor of Iskal, a known sympathizer with the Rakah
Communist Party, feels the villagers have won a victory. 'What
we did was actually an illegal settlement,' he said. 'We simply
forced the government into the agreement.' The Lands Administration has leased about 25 percent of the land to the village
council for public purposes. A new mosque is under construction and a new road is being built at government expense
amounting to IL 1.2 million.

"News of the 'bargain' traveled fast in Galilee. Yaacov
Vaknin, director of the Lands Administration, will meet this
weekend with representatives of other Arab and Druze villages
in Galilee to work out similar deals."

That the startling decision to give the Arabs their illegal
houses and the state land was a victory for them can hardly be
doubted. The Arabs were more convinced than ever that time
was on their side.

The sensitive area of the Triangle that divides Samaria from the populous Jezreel Valley and the coastal plain is the scene of both illegal Arab "immigration" and the seizure of state land.

As in the case of Jerusalem, where the figures are in the thousands, hundreds of Arabs from the liberated lands just across the "Green Line" have illegally settled in the Triangle. Many "disappeared" into the numerous Israeli Arab villages there, but others simply squat on state land. They work in nearby Jewish cities and towns—Natanya, Hadera, Kra Saba—and gradually become part of the growing permanent Arab population in Israel. They, too, "create facts."

The land seizure is heartbreaking. Wadi Ara, the Triangle, is a strategically sensitive area. In the midst of more than 40,000 Arabs in the immediate area stands the *one* lonely Jewish settlement in the region, Mei Ami. It was originally set high up on a hill with large areas of empty land about it. No longer. The hostile Arabs of the region have seen to that, says thirty-year-old Uri Bejarno, the treasurer of Mei Ami. "They have taken over. They settle every parcel. They build, plant—and then force the planners to recognize accomplished facts."

It is estimated that the Arabs have built some 600 illegal houses in the region. They are rapidly swallowing up all the available land in the Triangle so that Jewish settlement will be impossible to establish—one more step toward "autonomy" for the Arab Triangle.

And they have moved into the very heart of Israel. In October 1977 Agriculture Minister Sharon declared that Israel was in the midst of a process of "10,000 Arabs taking over state lands between Ashkelon and Hadera and building houses there." When Sharon says Hadera, he is talking of the very heart of the country, an area far north of the Negev. The Bedouins have already reached there.

One finds them everywhere in the heartland of the coastal and central region. On the outskirts of Rehovot, Ramle, Givat Brenner, Mazkeret Batya, Nes Tziyona, and on, northward. They find land, private or more likely state land, and set up tents or primitive houses. They and their hundreds and thousands of animals have acquired "land." Yitzhak Nir, of Moshav Mazkeret Batya, near Rehovot, says: "They are sitting on state and private land. They use large quantities of water for their

flock; they wander freely around a high-security military facility." Near the Moledet quarter of Holon, hundreds of Bedouins
have settled on the sand dunes, their human and animal feces
littering the area.

Alon Galilee of the Green Patrols is worried. Three whole
tribes of Bedouins have crossed over from Sinai to live in Israel.
Thousands of others have crossed from the liberated lands into
the area of the state proper. Galilee now calls this "the invasion"
into the heart of Israel. It is not only that the Bedouin herds are
destroying the land, having eaten up entire gardens, parks, and
lawns all over the southern part of Holon, which borders on Tel
Aviv. Galilee warns that "lack of awareness of how serious the
situation has become is resulting in the loss of actual Jewish
control over vast stretches of land for which fierce battles once
took place. The open country has become largely Arab."

Indeed, the questions of geography and demography are
choking Israel. Arabs from Ramallah in 1978 built twenty-seven
illegal Arab buildings on state land inside Jerusalem's northern
border. This followed the contemptuous defiance in September
1976 by Arab landowners of a military government ruling for-
bidding new buildings without a permit. The Arabs are surrounding Jerusalem with a noose of illegal buildings that prevents Jewish expansion.

But what is happening in Jaffa is the clearest indication of
the catastrophe toward which Israel races.

Jaffa is today part of the city of Tel Aviv. In the War of
Independence of 1948, some 70,000 Arabs fled in panic, leaving
a few thousand frightened and humble brethren behind. Today,
the Arab of Jaffa is neither frightened nor humble. Under the
leadership of four separate *hamullas,* the Jaffa Arabs have taken
over entire areas of the city, seizing state-owned land and building houses and stores on it. Jews are terrified, and many are
leaving the area.

In the area known as Jaffa Daled is a large fenced-in area of
forty-five dunams (11 acres) known as "The Grove of Abu-
Sayaf." Abu-Sayaf is one of our four Arab clans that has seized
land in Jaffa (the others are the clans of Dacha, Shnir, and
K'chil). In a letter of complaint to the Ministry of Housing, at
the beginning of 1980, the director of the Halamish Company,
Mr. Aharon Farber, wrote: "The area is held illegally by an

Arab *hamulla*. . . . that is now building dozens of illegal houses, factories, and stores. The residences are then rented to Arabs from the territories." The police are aware that the area is the center of crime of all kinds and that neighbors complain regularly. On a visit to the site, *Ha'Aretz* reporter Ilan Shchori was forcibly prevented from entry by two Arabs. Says Miriam Levi, a Jewish resident of the neighborhood: "We live in constant fear. There is a nearby playground for children and the Arab hoodlums hit them and chase them away. After 7:00 P.M. we are afraid to leave the house. It is difficult to believe that we live in Jaffa. . . ."

What makes the problem politically explosive is the fact that the Abu-Sayafs claim the property was theirs before 1948 and that they have merely retaken it. This effort to return Jaffa to the pre-state situation is a clear and present danger to the state. Nor is Jaffa an isolated case.

In Jaffa Gimel, near the border of Bay Yam, is an area belonging to the Israel Lands Administration. It has been planned by the state that the twenty-dunam (five-acre) area shall be used to build 250 housing units, a public park, and public services. But the Dacha Arab *hamulla* has decided otherwise.

They have taken over the land (it is now known as "The Dacha Orchard") and built numerous dwellings in which live Arabs of the territories. They also claim title to the land since before the days of the state. This seizure of land by Arabs is a forerunner and precedent on the part of a hundred thousand others for the return of "their land" all over the country. And the authorities? "Everyone complains but the authorities do not lift a finger"—the words of Shula Elyakim, who lives opposite "The Dacha Orchard."

And as the Arabs turn the clock back to 1947 in terms of geography, so, too, with demography. Ilan Shchor wrote in *Ha'Aretz* (May 9, 1980): "A new phenomenon has appeared in the last months in the region of Kedem Street in Givat Ha'Aliya in Jaffa. Scores of Jewish residents have sold their apartments to Arab families and are leaving the area. The region has changed character and become an Arab ghetto, and an unseen hand has even changed the street signs from Hebrew to Arabic. The apartments are sold over and beyond their real value. Members of the Alfandari family . . . relate that they received an offer from a Jaffa Arab one and a half times greater than the market price. . . . The Alfandari family did not ask questions, took the money, and moved. . . . . The apartments are bought by Israeli Arabs *but immediately rented to Gaza Arabs, some of whom dwelt here before 1948.* In a period of three months, on Kedem Street, no fewer than twenty-two Jewish apartments were sold to Arabs."

The return of pre-1948 Jaffa Arabs and their families not only illegally adds to the Arab population of Israel but adds an element that will serve as a catastrophic precedent, opening the door to loud demands of other—hundreds of thousands of other —Arabs who fled for a similar "right to return." From the government there is only silence.

The Alfandaris may not have asked questions, but at least one query is pertinent to yet another sickness within Israel. *Where do the Arabs get so much money?* It is estimated that Arabs have tens of millions of dollars in cash stored away. According to tax officials, "Illegal capital is growing in the Arab sector and is evidenced by the building of luxury villas in rows of villages, the purchase of new cars, travel abroad, and the acquisition of various luxury items" *(Yediot Aharonot,* January 22, 1979). Where does this money come from when the vast majority of Israeli Jews struggle desperately to "finish the month"?

The answer is: They do not pay taxes. They pay nothing or only an absurd percentage of what they should.

For the State of Israel, faced with a desperate need for funds to solve the economic and social problems of its needy Jews, the Arabs of the state—who pay so little in taxes—are an intolerable burden. They receive billions in national funds for welfare and services.

In a memorandum sent to Finance Minister Simha Ehrlich in early 1979, Knesset member Meir Cohen wrote: "The Arab sector in the country never paid and does not pay taxes. . . in relation to its economic capacity and income. Traveling on the new road between Kiryat Ata and Nazareth, one sees that in the villages on the side, where ten years ago stood huts, there have now grown villas, more luxurious than those of Savion. . . ."

The following is taken from an article that appeared in *Ha'Aretz* (March 16, 1976): "The Arabs make up 15 percent of the state's inhabitants, but pay only 1.5 percent of its taxes. According to Finance Ministry people, this is ludicrous and in no way mirrors the conditions of the majority of Arabs *whose income today is much larger than* [that of] *the Jewish residents of development towns.*"

"Most of those who owe taxes receive national insurance, but the National Insurance Institute will not allow the Finance Ministry to take what is owed to it by garnishing the benefits. . . .

"The tax people know of entire villages where, except for workers in regular jobs, no one pays taxes, despite the fact that the living standards in those villages rose enormously."

And this startling item *(Yediot Aharonot,* June 13, 1976): "The heads of the Likud faction in Knesset dealt last weekend with the question of Arab citizens who have stopped paying taxes. From the discussion it was learned that since March many Arab citizens have stopped paying taxes in the villages of Tayba, Tira, Kfar Kassem, Jaljilia, and others. . . ."

The question is: What causes the government to overlook the massive tax evasion? What causes it to refuse to levy penalties on Arab property, something it does swiftly in the case of Jewish offenders? What causes the municipality to do nothing when a resident of Jaffa says concerning the Arabs: "Every night there are screams, drugs, police. It is impossible to live here any longer"? What stops it from acting against the Maronite Arabs around Ohev Yisrael ("Lover of Israel"!) Street when they freely build illegal buildings and say: "Our priest [*sic*] gave us permits to build"? What allows the Jewish authorities of the new, non-*Galut*, non-ghetto Israeli brand to watch calmly as whole areas are taken over by Arabs and populated with illegal residents of the territories—with all the political dynamite that this portends?

The answer: "In the Tel Aviv-Jaffa municipality they know of the massive illegal takeover . . . but because of fear of confrontation with the Arab residents the municipality avoids concrete steps" *(Ha'Aretz,* May 9, 1980).

"In the Arab sector levies are not made on property in the event of tax delinquency for fear of violent reactions in the Arab villages and because of hostile public opinion. . . ." *(Yediot Aharonot,* May 9, 1980).

The growth of the Arab population, its dispersal

throughout the country, and its sense of growing power have given birth to a new boldness that manifests itself in yet another area that cripples the state: a sharp rise in crime. The police in Tel Aviv, in May 1980, estimated that fully 25 percent of all the Gush Dan (the area including Tel Aviv–Jaffa, Bat Yam, Ramat Gan, and other major cities) crime was committed by Arabs. In addition, they declared, there is an inordinate percentage of Arab involvement in *sexual* crimes.

And although it is clear that Arab crime has individual or clan gains as its underlying motive, at the same time it cannot be doubted that the fact that the Jews are the victims is a definite consideration.

Green Patrols head Galilee specifically pinpointed Bedouins as a major factor in the rise in crime in the country. The head of the Mazkeret Batya council told *Maariv* (August 13, 1976): "They [the Bedouins] and the Arab workers from the territories steal agricultural produce and expensive equipment. At times it appears to me that an organized gang works here that specializes in dismantling water pipes and irrigation parts and smuggling them into the West Bank."

Other examples include the arrest near Afula (July 10, 1980) of Bedouins of the tribe of Arab e-Shibli for stealing army ammunition and agricultural equipment from Jewish settlements. Among the items stolen were mortar shells. A watchman at the Ahuzam Moshav shot a member of a gang (July 30, 1980) from the West Bank who specialized in fruit stealing, a plague in the country today.

Indeed, the Arabs have created wholesale theft and smuggling gangs, stealing millions of dollars' worth of equipment and selling it in the territories and Arab countries. They also play a large role in the alarming rise in drug traffic. (In Jaffa, Jerusalem, and Haifa, Arab drug peddling is notorious.)

Clearly, this is not to say that there would be no crime in Israel without Arabs. There certainly is a sadly large amount of crime committed by Jews. But the amount added by Arabs is sizable and badly injures the economy and people of Israel. The worst is the amount of crime that is strictly based on the fact that the victims are Jewish. Such crimes include arson, especially in Jewish National Fund forests in the Galilee and north. In July 1978 fires destroyed tens of thousands of trees. Jews of Moshav

Yodfat specifically charged Arab shepherds with starting fires, and a resident of the Arab village of Kfar Kabul was arrested on October 27, 1977, for setting fires in the JNF forests near Haifa and Kibbutz Ginegar.

Jewish property is a political target for the Arabs. Jewish residents of the "mixed" Jerusalem neighborhood of Abu-Tor organized in July 1980 to protect themselves from what they called the third rash of vandalism to Jewish-owned cars in a year. They bitterly complained of lack of police response and insisted that they were certain the attacks were "politically motivated."

Attacks on the physical persons of Jews grow in proportion to Arab boldness and arrogance, which in turn feed upon the lack of Jewish response to the attacks. Instances of neither Arab attacks nor Jewish refusal to respond are lacking.

On July 24, 1979, a group of Jewish teenagers was attacked by twenty Arabs in the Bitzaron neighborhood of Tel Aviv. Cursing and shoving Arab workers stabbed sixteen-year-old Yaakov Abrian, who barely survived. According to *Maariv* (July 27, 1980): "Two of the neighborhood residents, Rafi Hadi and Sholom Azulai, complained: 'Our young children are afraid to go out and play. During the day the Arabs chase them away. At night they are afraid they will attack them and rape the girls. Not long ago a sixteen-year-old girl was attacked. She went into shock and the family wants to leave the neighborhood.

" 'The Arabs work in almost all the large and small factories in the area and most remain to sleep at night without permission. They walk about cursing the Jews and playing loud Arabic music on the radio so as to disturb and anger us.' "

Israel, 1980. The state of Jewish pride.

It is in every city where Arabs have begun to appear. In Ramat Gan, on Memorial Day, 1980, as Jewish worker Yona Ben Yona heard the siren in memory of the victims of the Holocaust, he paused and stood at attention. Three Arab workers began to laugh, one shouting: "Why do you stand up for the dogs?" Then they attacked him.

But the worst is in Jerusalem—Jerusalem of gold; Jerusalem of 120,000 Arabs; Jerusalem of Teddy Kollek.

Kollek, the mayor of Jerusalem thanks to Arab votes, is the primary symbol of the stubborn refusal to see the Arab danger.

In *Yediot Aharonot* (April 11, 1980) Kollek replied to the question of whether tension had grown in Jerusalem recently by saying: "There is no greater tension, and one of our outstanding achievements is that, practically, there is no outstanding tension." The very next page carried a story headlined: "Residents of Jewish Quarter: Attacks on Us in the Old City Have Increased." The story discussed attacks on a group of yeshiva students near the Arab school Umriya; the stoning of a five-year-old Jewish girl; the near trampling of a father and three sons by an Arab on a horse. In the words of Tziporah Levin, a resident of the Old City Jewish quarter: "To our sorrow, this has become the norm." Why do they not complain to the police at the Kishla Old City police station? Yet another lesson: "In the Kishla sit mostly Arab police who are not prepared even to listen to complaints of Jews attacked by Arabs."

Yet another incomprehensible bit of Israeli policy: the creation of Arab police in the dangerous Old City, Arab police whose most natural basic instincts are Arabic. They are supposed to ensure that Arabs will not harm Jews. The case of a twenty-one-year-old American immigrant who was on leave from the army in Jerusalem tells one of many such stories. Walking back from the Western Wall, he was attacked by an Arab who was joined by ten others. Breaking away, he found an army patrol, and they in turn called the police. Two Arab policemen came—and shook hands with the Arab attackers. By the time all had arrived at the Kishla police station, the Arabs had arrested the soldier on a countercomplaint. Other Jews have told of beatings by Arab policemen within the station.

In June 1976 several cases of Jews being slashed were reported. Writer (and today Knesset member) Moshe Shamir wrote in *Maariv* (June 11, 1976): "We have read about small incidents of violence, about a stabbing. We have not read about the daily actions of hoodlums, of breaking into Jewish yards, petty thefts, vandalism. . . . Israeli weakness yields Arab boldness."

Arab attacks injure people, damage property, cost millions, and instill fear and tension in Jewish lives in the reborn Jewish state.

The chairman of the Jerusalem municipality's Committee on Security, Shmuel Pressburger, angrily resigned in May 1980.

In a statement to a local paper, *Kal Ha'Ir* (May 9), he said: "The shaky security situation in Jerusalem recently stems from the improper policies of the security authorities, and Teddy Kollek has a not insignificant influence in this. They try to build reciprocal relations . . . but lack of [Jewish] response does not prove *tolerance*, but rather it proves *weakness*. . . .

"I know places where Arab residents attack Jews every day —East Talpiot, for example—but these incidents are not publicized. . . . "

What is especially not publicized are the Arab sexual attacks; thus, the number of Bedouin rapes of women in Eilat, tourist beach areas, and the Negev (the rape-murder of a woman soldier, Vered Wiener, by a Bedouin was especially horrifying). In Jerusalem, women residents of the Diaspora Yeshiva on Mount Zion have suffered for more than a decade from Arab sexual attacks.

The Arab sexual perversions result in cases such as the one in which five Arab laborers were accused of paying Jewish children from Tel Giborim and then practicing sodomy on them. The children ranged in age from eight to ten years *(Yediot Aharonot,* January 22, 1976). There is little doubt that the sexual crimes committed by Arabs against Jewish women are derived from both the usual sickness and what one might call the "Eldridge Cleaver" phenomenon (as expressed in *Soul on Ice*) of wishing to attack and degrade the enemy. The more the Arabs multiply and reach Jewish areas, the greater will be the number of general crimes, and sexual ones in particular, committed against the Jews.

The degrading phenomenon of Jewish prostitutes catering to Arab clients in the citrus groves of the coastal plain and in cheap hotels and backyards of Tel Aviv is all too well known. The Arabs constitute a sizable number of the clients of Jewish prostitutes in cities such as Jaffa, Haifa, and Acre; Arab pimps direct them. The social destruction and the moral humiliation need not be elaborated upon.

Nor can one escape the growth in social intercourse between Jewish women and Arab men that escalates yearly, thanks to both the breakdown in Jewish tradition and the increasing contact between Jews and Arabs, because of the universal presence of Arab laborers, the government's integration plans, and the growth of the Arab university student population. The amount of intermarriage in Israel is on the rise, but even more startling is the number of Arabs who live with Jewish women.

On the one hand are the predominantly Sephardic women from *moshavim* or poor urban neighborhoods who are easy prey for Arabs who promise them a "better life." The twenty-four-year-old Holon Jewess who was involved in scores of burglaries with her Arab boyfriend from the village of Baka Al-Gharbiya is just one example.

On the other hand are the predominantly Ashkenazic women from middle- and upper-class families who—for all the unhealthy reasons seen among such women in the United States during the civil rights and radical eras—find an outlet for rebellion and personal confusion in relationships with Arabs. These contacts are made mostly at the universities. Both the Jewish women and the foreign Jewish students are easy targets for the Jew-hating Arab student. In a series of articles on the problem, the *Jerusalem Post* wrote (February 23, 1979): "A lecturer well versed in the atmosphere of Arab student life on the campus added a blunt comment: 'I wouldn't say it for all the mixed couples on campus, but in some of the cases, it is very much a matter of the best way of — the Jewish State is to — a Jewish girl and broadcast the fact as widely as possible." The Arabs clearly understand the importance of humiliation of Jews and the place that sexual relations with Jewish women have in that humiliation. For the foreign Jewish woman student, the contact is often made on the basis of deliberate deception. The handsome Israeli she met as "Moshe" later turns out to be "Musa," but by the time she finds out she is deeply involved. None of this is helped by policies such as at Ben-Gurion University in Beersheba, where dormitories are totally mixed, male-female and Arab-Jewish.

The government is playing no small role in breaking down the social barriers between Jews and Arabs. It will avail Israel nothing politically, but will lead to a disintegration of Jewish separatism and Zionism, and to growing sexual relations and intermarriage. Thus, the Education Ministry in a press release (July 27, 1979) concerning government-sponsored summer camps stated: "There also are camps which contain both Arab and Jewish students." One may favor such a thing on the grounds that nothing will succeed better in knocking down social barriers between Jews and Arabs. That is, of course, true. And nothing will better lead to intermarriage. Again, let it be clear that this will in no way solve the Arab political demand for a "Palestine" instead of an Israel, any more than massive Jewish assimilation in Western and Central Europe solved the problem of anti-Semitism. All that will happen is that in the frantic efforts of the government to solve the problem of the coming explosion, they will wreck Jewish uniqueness and weaken the desire or understanding of the Sabra for a specifically *Jewish* state. This and nothing else will be the result of tragic governmental policies such as the one described in the *Jerusalem Post* (October 20, 1977): "Israeli Jewish schoolchildren will be taken to Arab towns and villages this year on study tours and exchange programs, Eliahu Mansour of the Education Ministry's Arabic-language division told the *Jerusalem Post* yesterday. He said that the scheme would also bring Israeli Arab children into Jewish homes." Not the slightest progress will, of course, be made in persuading Arabs to accept happily their second-class status in a Jewish state. But the breakdown in Jewish uniqueness will persuade large sections of Jewish Israelis that the concept of a *"Jewish"* state is hardly worth dying for, expecially since they have such fond memories of the mixed camp and school, of visits and food in the Arab village. Especially when their girl friends —or wives—are Arabs.

Being told that there is no basic difference between Jews and Arabs is the surest way to convince the Jew that if he can be given peace, there is no difference between an "Israel" and a "Palestine." And as long as the Arabs remain in Israel and they and their threat grow, the Israelis will frantically search for a solution. This disintegration and ideological destruction will be their only bewildered answer.

And finally, there is the staggering economic burden of these barely taxpaying Arabs, both those in the state and those in the liberated areas. Many billions of Israeli pounds are spent yearly on services of all kinds in the Arab sector. They include national insurance, welfare, schools, health facilities, highways, electricity, police, sanitation—all the many services of a welfare state. One need only see the amounts of national-insurance money collected by Israel's Arabs for child benefits to be staggered by the drain on the state's coffers.

At a time when both inflation and recession shake the economic structure of Israel; when young couples cannot purchase or rent a decent apartment; when the defense budget along with the budgets of all other departments must be cut; when subsidies for basic foodstuffs are slashed; when economic collapse sends the Israeli Black Panthers into the street to threaten social and communal clashes; when thousands of young Israelis leave and many more think of leaving for other countries—who can afford the enormous economic burden of the Arabs?

Economy, demography, geography, democracy—all combine to push Israel closer and closer to the abyss. What is the solution?

There are those who understand the danger of Arab growth and who call for more Jewish babies. Indeed, there should be more, but the Jews do not want them. There are those who urge us to teach Arab women to have fewer babies. Indeed, we should do that, but the Arabs see their babies as a national weapon against the Jews, which they are. There are those who call for mass *aliya,* immigration, to Israel. Indeed, is there anyone among us who will object to the Jews of the United States, Canada, Britain, France, Australia, or anywhere else leaving all that they have and coming to Israel? But they do not come; the only meaningful *aliya* in the last fifteen years has been from the Soviet Union, and today those Jews prefer the West to the Jewish state. By all means let us attempt to have more Jewish babies, fewer Arab ones, and more Jewish immigration. But those are all faint hopes, and we will be doing well if we can succeed in not having the balance of population increase in favor of the enemy in the years to come.

The Arabs of Israel grow in numbers, in education, in hatred of the Jewish state, and in confidence that time is on their side. Time is running out for a state whose spokesmen follow in a long tradition of Zionist leaders who either could not or would not understand that a Jewish state is an impossibility with a large and exploding Arab population. All the "peace" in the world on the part of Egypt or Syria will not save Israel from the cancer raging within. It is not Arab armies from without that are the problem, but the quietly—and soon loudly—ticking bomb inside the Jewish state itself. There is an insoluble contradiction between the right of Arabs to become a majority and the Jewish state. Every day the Arabs of Israel move closer to that majority. And we sit, stricken dumb.

Is there, then, no answer? Is there, then, no hope?

Of course there is an answer. Of course there is hope. If all that has been written prior to this is depressing and painful, it is only because the reality is, indeed, depressing and painful. But escape from reality does not make reality disappear or less painful. It becomes worse and more dangerous, and our very national life becomes threatened. It is necessary, therefore, to force the Jew to look at the painful reality and depressing truth so that the enormity of the danger becomes frighteningly apparent and he will rush to save himself. Can he? Is there hope? Of course: *If* we have the courage to be *Jewish* and sane. *If* we can throw off the needless and false burden of guilt and the gentilized, twisted concepts that are so wrongly called "morality" but constitute the worst kind of immorality. *If* we can free ourselves from the false shepherds, the leaders of Israel who have driven their Jewish flocks to the pastures of the shadow of death.

Our answer, our hope, is to remove the Arabs of Eretz Ysrael from the land.

Chapter 10.

Separation—Only Separation

A double miracle occurred in 1948. The Almighty saved the Jews of the new State of Israel from the Arabs—and from themselves.

The greatest blessing to befall the Jews as their state came into being was the wild, panic-stricken, apparently illogical, irrational flight of the Arabs from the territory of the fledgling state. Against all reason and contrary to their own interests, more than 500,000 Arabs fled, ridding the State of Israel of a huge minority that would have destroyed it from within. The blessing was a particularly difficult one for the G-d of Israel to shower upon His people, since, as so often in the past, they went to extraordinary lengths to attempt to reject it.

Had the Arabs remained, fully 40 percent of the new nation would have been Arab. The pitiful economic machinery of the state could not possibly have absorbed a million refugees in a decade. Between a quarter and a third of the Knesset would have been immediately Arab. A fifth column and social tensions of massive proportions would have developed. Many, many Jews who eventually did come to live in Israel would not have, in view of the bombings and civil strife that would have resulted. It was a divine blessing, an unexpected gift that even a child could understand and be grateful for.

But the Jews of Israel? Consider. The mixed Arab-Jewish city of Haifa fell to the Haganah, the Jewish defense force, on April 22, 1948. Panic seized the Arabs; the first exodus began. The Jews pleaded with them to stay, offering to continue the equal binational municipal council. The Arabs would not listen.

227

The exodus became a wild and irrational flight. Haifa Jews faced the joyful prospect of a Jewish city, free of tension and communal war. Their reaction was recorded on April 26, 1948, by the British chief of police of Haifa, A. J. Bridmead: "Every effort is being made by the Jews to persuade the Arab populace to stay and carry on with their normal lives. . . ." It had become a race between two irrational groups, each working against its own interests. The question was: Who would win by losing?

On April 28 the Jews made a determined effort to prove that they were madder than their enemies. The Workers' Council printed thousands of fliers to be distributed to the fleeing Arabs which read, in part: "Do not destroy your own homes with your own hands and do not bring unnecessary tragedy upon yourselves by unnecessary evacuation and self-imposed burdens. By moving out you will be overtaken by poverty and humiliation. But in this city, yours and ours, Haifa, the gates are open for work, for life, and for peace, for you and your families."

No amount of Jewish suicidal tendencies could help them. Haifa's Arabs were determined to destroy themselves, and they fled with no one in pursuit. Marie Syrkin, writing in *Commentary* magazine (January 1966), described the incredible scene: " . . . 60,000 Haifa Arabs began to flock wildly toward the port, seeking to escape by any craft available. Families crouched for days on the docks. . . . This was a headlong stampede in which people seem to have jumped suddenly from a dinner table, from bed, or from their work, driven by an impulse to flee."

In town after town, the glorious, irrational Arab flight occurred. Tiberias's 6,000 Arabs stunned the 2,000 Jews on April 18 by suddenly fleeing. The Jewish community council issued a statement declaring: "We did not dispossess them; they themselves chose this course. But the day will come when the Arabs will return to their homes and property in this town. In the meantime, let no citizen touch their property."

Hal Lehrman attests to this general Jewish attitude: "In the beginning, no one could conceive of a new Israel without a large Arab population. Even when they were already in full flight, the eventual return of most of the Arabs was taken for granted." Indeed, every official Israeli information sheet and all the Zionist writers go out of their way to emphasize that the

Arab flight was neither caused by nor desired by the Jews. An inexplicable people.

In 1978 Israel was rocked by a bitter debate over a film called *Hirbet Hiza,* which depicted the expulsion of Arabs from their village in 1948. The debate raged over whether such a thing could actually have happened. One side said it did happen; the other vigorously denied it or said that if it had occurred, "it was unrepresentative, not typical." The underlying assumption of both camps was that such an expulsion was "immoral." It is that kind of perverted "immorality" that has bought Israel to the brink of catastrophe. If there is any room for the wringing of hands, it is over the fact that the Jews did *not* understand the need for *Hirbet Hiza.* They, by their misplaced mercy, have brought potential cruelty and tragedy down on Israel and its Jews.

The G-d of Israel continued to compel His foolish children to accept miracles. In Safad no fewer than 14,000 Arabs faced 1,500 Jews, mostly elderly religious Jews. One night the Arabs were there and the next morning they were gone.

All kinds of reasons for the flight of the Arabs are given by the very secular Jews, who in their own brand of irrationality wished them to remain: the Arab leaders ordered it; the British instigated it; the Irgun "massacre" at Dir Yassin panicked them; they left to make it easier for the Arab armies to sweep through. There were a hundred different "explanations," but not one explains the real, irrational panic that swept areas in which Arabs controlled the countryside and in which there was no fighting. It is hard for the secularist to recognize a miracle, since in running from it his back is usually to it.

By May 15, 1948—the end of the British Mandate and the proclamation of the Jewish state—some 200,000 Arabs had left. Jaffa added 70,000 who joined the panicky flight, and the city of Tel Aviv was thus saved from the perpetual nightmare of having more than 80,000 bitter enemies on its doorstep. In the next few months another 300,000 joined the rest.

A miracle had indeed taken place; the majority of the Arabs had fled. A golden opportunity was at hand to clear the country of its enemies and save it from the tragedy of today. After all, what more natural thing than to rid the land of people who massacred Jews throughout the twenties and thirties and who had vowed to wipe the Jewish state off the map as soon as it was born? What would any other people have done under the same circumstances? We need not look very far for the answer.

The German Minorities in Europe

The European states of Poland and Czechoslovakia are classic examples of those that harbored in their midst a dangerous minority that brought them misery and grief. In both cases the minority was German, and both Poland and Czechoslovakia, having barely survived the catastrophe that their German minorities had brought them, at the first opportunity solved any potential future problems by firmly expelling them.

The Poles had been a people without a state for well over a century. Their land having been divided among Russia, Austria, and Prussia, they finally attained independence again after World War I. A sizable group of Germans remained in the new Polish state, especially in its western provinces of Pomorze, Poznania, and Upper Silesia. Almost from the start, despite formal protestations of loyalty, the German minority did not change its true attitude toward the Polish state. There were many cases of spying in which the leaders of the German minority were often involved. In 1926 a spy ring was discovered in Upper Silesia, closely connected with the Volksbund, the leading German Silesian organization. Ten prominent members of the organization were sentenced to imprisonment for treason.

The Polish-German nonaggression pact of 1934 did not bring about any change in this attitude. Quite the opposite. Hitler was using his German ethnics for his dream of a "German Reich." The agents of the German government in Poznan, Pomorze, and Silesia offered secret credits on very favorable terms to German farmers, traders, and artisans in return for a promise to work for the return of the lands to the Reich. Things came to such a pitch in 1936 that the Polish government closed thirty branches of the Deutsche Vereinigung. In the following year the subversive activities of the organization Rat der Deutschen in Polen became so obvious that its president, Gero von Gersdorff, was arrested. In the same year the conspiracy of the National-Sozialistische Deutsche Arbeiter-Partei in Silesia was discovered. Its members swore loyalty to Adolf Hitler personally. In this trial 109 Germans were prosecuted, the majority being found guilty of treasonable activities and sentenced to varying terms of imprisonment. The existence of a German fifth column in Poland was the direct result of the Nazi doctrine. This doctrine refuted the idea that Germans living abroad owed any loyalty to the states of which they were citizens and stressed the exclusive importance of the blood link with the German nation.

The consequences of such a doctrine were obvious enough: every German abroad, conscious of his nationality, was an agent of the German Reich, of a Reich preparing for war. Poland was a victim of the work of the German fifth column.

Hitler was immeasurably aided by the German minority in Poland and used it as an excuse to attack the Polish state. Not only were the Poles accused of mistreating the German minority, but the war was touched off by German demands for the annexation of Polish Pomerania, the "Polish Corridor," in order to obtain territorial continuity between Germany and East Prussia.

With the speedy Nazi conquest of Poland, the western provinces were incorporated into the German Reich on October 26, 1939, as part of the German policy of annexing land on its borders that contained sizable numbers of ethnic Germans. (Other areas were Austria, through the *Anschluss,* the Sudetenland, Memel, and Danzig, as well as certain contiguous lands that were not in any way German [such as the rest of Poland and Czechoslovakia]). Hitler planned to remove all non-Germans from those areas over a period of ten to twenty years and replace them with Germans. This led to the second part of the plan, the resettlement in this "Greater Germany" of all the ethnic Germans then living outside the Third Reich. Agreements to this effect were made with the various states involved to resettle Germans from Latvia, Estonia, the South Tyrol, East Galicia, Volhynia, Rumania, Croatia, Bulgaria, and Hungary. Between 1938 and 1941 the German Reich increased its German population from ten million to nearly twenty-two million. Millions of Germans were settled in what had been Polish territory.

At the end of the war the Poles counted their dead in the millions (not including its Jews), and the rape of the country by the Germans would never be forgotten. When the Soviets informed the Poles that they intended to annex a huge chunk of eastern Poland up to the Curzon Line (and, to ensure tranquility for itself, expel some three million Poles westward), the Polish government demanded compensation. Stalin agreed that eastern Germany up to the Oder–Neisse River line would be given to Poland. The Yalta Conference gave its approval to the *fait accompli.*

The Poles, having learned to their eternal grief what a hostile minority meant, determined that the German population in Poland would go. Never again would they allow the state to be subverted from within. They were joined by the Czechs, who had a similar problem and determined upon a similar solution.

Three million Germans found themselves citizens of the new Republic of Czechoslovakia after the defeat of the Germans and Austro-Hungarians in World War I. They lived in an area that came to be known as the Sudentenland. When the area had been part of the Austro-Hungarian Empire, the Germans had looked with disdain and contempt on the supposedly inferior Slavic Czechs. All manner of political, economic, social, and cultural discrimination was practiced against them. The blow to German pride, therefore, when they found themselves a minority in a Czech Republic, was shattering. Many Sudeten Germans made no effort to conceal the fact that they were first and foremost Germans. In the Czech Parliament, when a speaker challenged their desire to belong to the Reich, Josef Mayer interpolated that the Sudetens would go to Germany "in the night and barefooted."

The rise of Hitler brought a tremendous upsurge of Sudeten German nationalism, and demands for autonomy along with all kinds of stories of persecution laid the ground work for Hitler's plans to annex the area and eventually seize all Czechoslovakia. The presence of the Germans in the Sudetenland gave Hitler his excuse. And so, in reference to Germans in Austria and Czechoslovakia., Hitler said on February 20, 1938: "Over ten million Germans live in two of the states adjoining our frontier," and that it was Germany's duty to "protect" them.

The German Nationalist Party in the Sudetenland, under Konrad Henlein, was an eager fifth column. On April 24, 1938, in a speech in Carlsbad, Henlein demanded "autonomy" for the German border regions. The Czechs, instead of acting forcefully, negotiated, giving both Hitler and the Sudetens greater

boldness. Brazen protests and riots against the Czech government took place. On September 16 Henlein demanded *annexation*
of the Sudetenland by the Reich. This was followed by Munich,
the separation of the Sudetenland from Czechoslovakia, and the
eventual collapse of the Czech Republic.

After the terrible war, with humiliation and destruction the
cost of its German minorities, the Czechs, too, understood the
lesson. There would never again be a large number of Germans
in the country to dream of separation and to give anyone an
excuse to destroy the country.

With or without anyone's permission, the Poles and Czechs
were determined to get rid of their Germans. At Potsdam, however, in August 1945, Truman, Attlee, and Stalin informally
agreed (adding Hungary, too) and thus provided an interna-
tionally legal basis for the expulsions. The "Big Three" agreed
as follows:

XIII. ORDERLY TRANSFERS OF GERMAN POPULATIONS

The Conference reached the following agreement on
the removal of Germans from Poland, Czechoslovakia and
Hungary:

The Three Governments, having considered the question in all its aspects, recognize that the transfer to Germany of German population or elements thereof, remaining in
Poland, Czechoslovakia and Hungary, will have to be undertaken. They agree that any transfers that take place
should be effected in an orderly and humane manner.

The Poles and Czechs, with the memories of German
atrocities fresh in their minds, were interested in rapid expulsion, "orderly and humane" or not. Large-scale expulsions
had begun before the Potsdam Conference had ever convened,
and millions were given twenty-four hours to leave. Billions of
dollars in property was left behind. Not a penny of compensation was offered. The refugee arrived destitute and in misery.
Time magazine (October 22, 1945) wrote: "It is a tale of
horror. . . ." In the West Pope Pius protested; an American
Committee Against Mass Expulsion was formed; General W.
Bedell Smith called it "repugnant and unacceptable." The Poles
and Czechs could not have cared less.

Neither Pius nor the committee nor Smith was a Czech, or

a Pole, or a European who had harbored a snake in his house and been bitten for his pains. An inscription on the gate of the Czech Internment Center at Budweis read: "An eye for any eye and a tooth for a tooth." The same *Time* magazine article admitted: "But the Poles and Czechs who expel them will be thinking of the past and of the future. The German minorities in eastern Europe were not harmless, either as guests or, later, as masters."

Hungary, which also received "approval" at Potsdam, immediately expelled some 260,000 of its Germans. Rumania, Yugoslavia, and the Soviet Union did not bother even to raise the question—they simply acted. By 1950 the following number of Germans had been removed by their host countries:

Oder-Neisse Territories	6,817,000
Sudetenland	2,921,400
Eastern Europe (Poland, Hungary, Rumania, Yugoslavia, Memel-Danzig)	1,865,000

This total of 11,603,400 does not include the German ethnics within the Soviet Union whose fate was not fully clear.

In pre–World War II Europe, a huge German population had brought misery to the countries in which they resided as a minority. They would never do so again.

The period between World War I and II in Eastern and Central Europe had seen the curse of the national minority groups. Each felt a far greater loyalty to its communal, ethnic people across the border than to its host country. Every area in which they lived in sizable numbers became a hotbed of irredentist calls for "autonomy" and separation. At least in the case of the Germans, the nations of the region determined to eliminate the problem.

It is interesting to note, however, that in February 1946 Hungary and Czechoslovakia eliminated the mutual minority problem that had plagued them for decades. They agreed on a voluntary exchange of their respective minorities, transferring 31,000 Magyars to Hungary and 33,000 Slovaks to Czechoslovakia.

When two people are heirs to wide and fundamental differences—ethnic, religious, linguistic, and cultural—and when those differences have led to decades of hate, hostility, and war, the most drastic solution is sometimes the most obvious and most easily accepted. In order to save both peoples the inescapable and permanent killings and suffering which are the fruits of the conflicting claims to the land, governments sometimes realize that the only solution is—once and for all—permanent separation. Sometimes this is done, as with the Germans, unilaterally; rarer are the instances of governmental agreement and cooperation. But there are outstanding instances in modern times in which logical, hard-headed governments understood that the existence of a large, hostile minority within its borders was a guarantee of future disaster and misery. Acting on that assumption, the enemy minority, the potential time bomb, was defused through removal.

Turkey, Greece, Bulgaria

By the beginning of the twentieth century, the Balkans and Asia Minor were raging pits of nationalist intrigue. The Ottoman Empire was in an advanced state of decay and disintegration. In 1821, the Greeks had already succeeded in liberating part of the peninsula and had set up an independent state. Other nationalities followed, setting up their own independent states —Rumania, Serbia, Montenegro, and, in 1878, Bulgaria. But other nationalities still seethed under the Ottoman yoke; *parts* of the nationalities that had won their independence were still living as minorities within other national states, and the new nations still had claims not only against the ottomans but against *each other*.

Bulgaria was born thanks to its Great Power protector, Czarist Russia, which sent the Ottomans to a crashing defeat. The Turks were forced to sign the Treaty of San Stefano (1878), which called for a "Greater Bulgaria" extending from the Black Sea on the east to the Aegean on the south and as far west as Saloniki. This area took in not only Turkish territory and population but that claimed by Greeks and Serbs. When the Congress of Berlin (1878) forced the Bulgars to give back much of the territory, that now became in their minds "Unredeemed Bulgaria," including the whole of Macedonia and most of Thrace. The inevitable occurred.

When the Balkan states in secret alliance defeated Turkey in the First Balkan War (1912), all of European Turkey was conquered except for the area around Constantinople (Istanbul). The victorious powers immediately began to quarrel over the spoils, and in the Second Balkan War (1913) Bulgaria was humiliatingly defeated. It vowed vengeance and the "redemption" of land and people.

As a result of the two wars and the Treaties of Bucharest and Constantinople, massive emigrations took place. More than 100,000 Turks fled the Balkans; 15,000 Bulgarians fled Macedonia for Bulgaria; 10,000 Greeks left the area of Macedonia ceded to the Serbs and Bulgars; 10,000 Greeks fled western Thrace, then occupied by Bulgaria. These fled on their own, but under the Treaty of Constantinople (1913) 48,570 Muslims emigrated from western Thrace to Turkey and 46,764 Bulgarians left Turkey's eastern Thrace for western Thrace.

The Turkish-Bulgarian emigrations, although spontaneous, were nevertheless recognized by Turkey and Bulgaria in a protocol annexed to their 1913 peace treaty. For the first time the idea of an *exchange of populations* was formulated. It actually confirmed a *fait accompli,* but both states realized the ultimate wisdom of being rid of dangerous minorities.

The Balkan–Asia Minor caldron bubbled on. The Young Turks of the Ottoman Empire came to the very correct conclusion that any of its territory inhabited by a strong national group guaranteed rebellion and separation. The Turks chose to solve the problem by giving the minorities the choice of being "Turkified" or eradicated. The Armenians suffered the most, with some two million massacred and many others expelled. But there was a general determination by the Turks to make the empire a homogeneous Turkish estate. In 1914, 115,000 Greeks were expelled from eastern Thrace to Greece; 150,000 Greeks were sent from the Turkish coast of western Anatolia to Greece; and Turkey accepted 115,000 Muslims from Greece in exchange. Turkish propaganda calling upon Muslims living in other Balkan countries to come "home" to Muslim Turkey brought 135,000 more refugees.

Meanwhile, the Bulgarians, seething with irredentist vengenance, joined the Central Powers in World War I to regain land and people—and once again lost. By 1919, after the war, 139,000 Bulgarians lived in land held by Greece. Greek Premier Venizelos understood that no permanent peace with Bulgaria could ever be achieved as long as a sizable Bulgarian population remained in land looked upon as "unredeemed" Bulgarian territory.

It was therefore agreed by the Convention of Neuilly (1919) that for the sake of peace and stability, there would be reciprocal emigration of the Greek minority in Bulgaria and the Bulgarian minority in Greece. The treaty spared oceans of blood.

But the Greek-Turkish hatred raged on. During World War I some 600,000 Greeks and 300,000 Muslims had been separated. Turkey was now a defeated power, and Greece in 1920 initiated the Greco-Turkish War by occupying Smyrna and western Asian Minor. The Turks, however, under Ataturk, decisively defeated the Greeks in 1922, and the Greek army retreated from the area. In rapid succession, within a few months, almost the entire Greek population of western Asia Minor, Pontus, Eastern Thrace, and much of Constantinople—*one million people*—fled to Greece.

To halt the apparently endless wars, the Turks and Greeks met and concluded the Lausanne Convention in 1923, on *"compulsory population exchange."* It was a triumph of good sense. Under it the flight of the Greeks was formalized, and under the auspices of a League of Nations international commission, the remaining 150,000 Greeks in Turkey (except for Constantinople) were forcibly repatriated. The convention provided for the compulsory transfer of most of Greece's Muslims—400,000 people—to Turkey. The same international commission continued its work in this and other population exchanges. *By the time it had completed its work in 1932, more than four million people in the Balkans and Turkey had been involved in deportations, flights, and forced exchanges. But no wars.*

In much the same manner, the very last Greek-Turkish problem, on Cyprus, was finally resolved. Decades of bitter hostility, communal riots, wars—there was, again, apparently no end to it. And then came the Turkish invasion and the flight of Turks north and Greeks south. The hostility remains, but the opponents are separated by a border. Today there is hate, and that is sad. *But there is no bloodshed.*

India and Pakistan

As Indian nationalism, led by men like Gandhi and Nehru, inexorably pushed Britain out of the subcontinent, the nation that was India, nearly 400 million people, was divided into scores of languages, religions, and sects. But, in particular, it was the broad category of Hindus versus Muslims that made the original British decision to grant the country independence impossible. In 1942 the British had proposed freedom for India with a pledge by the new country "for the protection of social and religious minorities."

The Muslims adamantly refused to rely on this promise. They made up only some 22 percent of the total population and did not trust the 68 percent Hindu majority. The reason? *Difference; major and fundamental difference.* Under Muhammad Ali Jinnah, they won the battle to partition the subcontinent into a Hindu "India" and a Muslim "Pakistan." But that clear understanding of the impossibility of living together in one state did not solve the problem of the minorities who would be living in a smaller version of an unpartitioned state. The nineteen million Hindus and Sikhs who would now become minority citizens in a fiercely nationalist Islamic Pakistan began nervously to consider the resentment that the Muslims, mostly poor farmers, had borne against the Hindu merchants and storekeepers.

In turn, Choudharry Rahmat Ali, founder of the Pakistan national movement, wrote: "To leave our minorities in Hindu lands is . . . to forget the tragic fate that overwhelmed our minorities which—in more favorable times— . . . we left in Sicily, Italy, France, Portugal, Spain, Austria, and Hungary. Where are they now?"

The reality was not long in coming: massacres and communal riots. In the Punjab, where Muslims made up 57 percent of the total population. In Lahore and Amritsar, mobs, knives, and fires swept the cities. By June 23, 1947, at least 3,200 people had been killed in the Punjab alone. The Hindus and Sikhs began to flee. By July a quarter of a million Hindus had fled to India. Panic spread to other parts of the subcontinent.

Hindus began to flee in terror from East Bengal. By 1948, 100,000 had run from Pakistan's capital of Karachi—the fear of minority status, the fear of being strangers, the desire for sanctuary among their own people. The most horrible kind of murder and looting took place. It has been estimated that 200,000 people were killed in the Punjab alone. To quote one observer, "There was a positive lust for blood. . . . Casualties resulted not merely from chance encounters but from systematic butchery and hunting down of victims."

People fled in every possible way: trucks, trains that were jammed beyond belief. Thousands died along the way. Nothing could stop the flight. Hindus and Muslims knew that only among their own people would they find safety. The largest single refugee column in history began arriving in October from Pakistan, more than 800,000 Hindus and Sikhs on foot, forming a forty-five-mile-long procession. A month later a column of 600,000 Muslims marched in the opposite direction.

Official figures list 6 million Muslims as having fled India for West Pakistan and 4.5 million Hindu refugees from the latter. In addition, a total of some 8 million Hindus and Muslims moved between India and East Pakistan, a staggering exchange of population of 18 million people! Their flight saved them from the horrors of communal savage strife. The existence in one land of people with deep hatred for one another, a history of mutual wars and killing, different in every way, could have led only to never-ending strife. Had the instinct of the people not driven them to flee, eventually they would have been expelled on an agreement reached between the two governments for compulsory exchange of populations.

But the Jews did not do what common sense and Jewishness cried out for. Given the opportunity to complete that which the Almighty had begun for them, the Jews of Israel failed to realize the vision and, in their failure of nerve and understanding, planted the seeds for the tragedy of today—and tomorrow.

The pity is that there was beginning to be an understanding of the opportunity and need. During the second half of the War of Independence, after May 1948, the magnificent "luck" of the flight of Arabs from Haifa, Jaffa, and West Jerusalem was correctly translated by Israelis into the difference between a "Jewish" state with 40 percent of its population composed of rapidly breeding Arabs versus a state with few or no hostile Arabs. And so, there were instances when that understanding gave birth to the good sense of self-preservation. The Arabs of Ramle and Lydda, two large and hostile towns, were expelled after their brief resistance had caused heavy Jewish casualties. Had they remained as an Arab concentration between Tel Aviv and Jerusalem, Israel's demographic and strategic situation would have been infinitely worse.

There remained now the largest and most dangerous concentration of Arabs, those of the Galilee. And it appears that the
Israelis gave serious thought to the expulsion of those Arabs,
too. But they faltered.

The all-Arab city of Nazareth is the capital of Arab Galilee
and the heart of the Arab opposition to Israel. Its mayor, Tewfik
Zayad, is the chief hater of Zionism in the country and the
potential leader of the dangerous Israeli Arab minority. It is
Nazareth that is the political and intellectual center for the Arabs. It is Nazareth that is the largest Arab town in Israel. It is
there that the Land Day Rebellion of 1976 was hatched. Without a Nazareth and its numbers, leaders, and intellectuals, the
Arab threat to Israel from within would be far less. And it was
Nazareth that in 1948 was the key to the expulsion of Arabs
from all the Galilee.

The truth is that Israel, today, would be free of the Arabs
of both Nazareth and the Galilee if not for the actions of a Canadian Jew who now resides in Canada with his Sabra wife, Yael.
The name of the Canadian is Ben Dunkelman. He, and all others who believe the Arabs should remain, caused Israel im-
measurable damage. In his own words he claims to have saved
the Arabs of Israel.

By July 1948 the Jews of Israel, after bloody fighting, succeeded in turning the tide. Arabs had fled in panic from Jaffa,
Lydda, Ramle, Haifa, and other cities, and the Jewish armies,
which until just a few weeks earlier had been fighting to save the
Jewish state and its Jews from the "massacre" promised by the
Arab League director, were on the move. Now, the Galilee, the
heart of the Arab resistance, was beginning to collapse.
Dunkelman was the head of the Seventh Army Corps, the unit
that captured Nazareth.

Three years ago, he decided to capitalize on his experience
and published a book ghostwritten by Peretz Kidron, entitled
Dual Allegiance, which appeared in both English and Hebrew.
From it we learn the startling fact that Dunkelman received orders to evacuate the entire Arab population of Nazareth and
refused. It was this that "saved" Nazareth, prevented a general
Arab flight from the Galilee, and left Israel with a ticking time
bomb known as the Israeli Arab minority. Here is the actual
account as written by Kidron at Dunkelman's direction:

"Two days after the second truce came into effect, we were

withdrawn from Nazareth. Avraham Yaffe, who had commanded the 13th battalion in the assault on the city, now reported to me with orders from Moshe Carmel to take over from me as its military governor. I complied with the order, but only after Avraham had given me his word of honour that he would do nothing to harm or displace the Arab population. My demand may sound strange, but I had good reason to feel concerned on this subject.

"Only a few hours previously, Haim Laskov had come to me with astounding orders: Nazareth's civilian population was to be 'evacuated': I was shocked and horrified. I told him I would do nothing of the sort—in view of our promises to safeguard the city's people, such a move would be both superfluous and harmful. I reminded him that scarcely a day earlier, he and I, as representatives of the Israeli army, had signed the surrender document, in which we solemnly pledged to do nothing to harm the city or its population. When Haim saw that I refused to obey the order, he left.

"A scarce twelve hours later, Avraham Yaffe came to tell me he was relieving me of my post as military governor and I felt sure this order had been given because of my defiance of the 'evacuation' order. But although I was withdrawn from Nazareth, it seems that my disobedience did have some effect. It seems to have given the high command time for second thoughts, which led them to the conclusion that it would, indeed, be wrong to expel the inhabitants of Nazareth. To the best of my knowledge, there was never any more talk of the 'evacuation' plan, and the city's Arab citizens have lived there ever since."

The tragedy, of course, is that the Arabs would have slaughtered every Jew they found had *they* won. At the same time, they would gladly have accepted any Jewish terms that kept them alive, once they realized they were defeated. It was the disastrous, perverted "humanity" of Dunkelman, who later left Israel, that saved the Arabs and that today threatens Israel from within.

The Arabs of the Galilee remained, as did clusters of thousands in Jaffa, Haifa, Ramle, Lydda, and among the Bedouins. Not only did Israel not remove them, but it increasingly began to accept back numbers of Arabs who had fled. Some 70,000 were allowed back under a "family reunification plan." Thousands of others illegally infiltrated and were allowed to remain. The Rhodes Agreement brought some 30,000 Arabs of the Triangle into Israel. They were the Arabs who remained to become the nucleus from which grew the present ticking time bomb. They remained to be the thorns in our eyes and the thistles in our sides of our time. They remained to grow in quantity, in brazenness, in danger to the existence of a Jewish state.

They remained, but more than 700,000 Jews from Arab lands came to Israel. There was the opportunity for a multiple blessing: Jews to Zion, Arabs to their own lands. Hundreds of thousands of Jews coming home to their brethren from lands where they had lived for centuries but which were not theirs. Hundreds of thousands of Arabs leaving a land that was not theirs and finding a home among *their* brethren.

In 1948 Jews lived in almost every Arab land in the Middle East and North Africa: Morocco, 300,000 Jews; Tunisia, 25,000; Algeria, 150,000; Libya, 40,000; Egypt, 75,000; Syria, 45,000; Iraq, 145,000; Yemen, 55,000; Lebanon, 20,000; Aden, 5,000. Of these, the overwhelming majority left the land of their birth, where their families had lived as minorities in official Muslim states without equal rights, and came home to their own people.

They left behind a fortune in property, today worth billions of dollars, for which the Arabs never gave them a penny in compensation. The Jews from Greater Arabia came home, but the Israelis did not complete the transfer of the Arabs from the Jewish state. Had they done so, there would have been an exchange of population that would have brought both Jews and Arabs back to their own people. It was a golden opportunity, *lost*.

And in great measure, the failure to realize the opportunity of 1948 led to the catastrophic blunder of 1967, when the G-d of Israel gave His people a second opportunity—this time to drive out their enemies from all of western Eretz Yisrael. Once again Israel failed—this time, utterly, miserably.

The Six-Day War of 1967—what a divine, golden opportunity! What a disastrous failure to seize it!

They poured across the ancient lands—theirs. The children of Israel. The soldiers, children of a generation that went to the gas chambers, a thing the Gentile had come to equate with the

Jews. Now they burst across the ground from which, just days earlier, the Arabs had boasted of the coming slaughter. The trap, the iron noose, which the Arabs had built around the Jewish state in May 1967 was shattered. "The trap is broken, and we have escaped!" (Psalms 124).

Across the land—*theirs*—they poured. *Judea,* and its hills! *Bethlehem,* where David was born and where for two millennia Rachel stood weeping for the sons and daughters who now returned. *Hebron,* where the fathers and mothers of the nation lived and are buried. *Samaria,* with *Shechem* and *Bet El* and *Shilo* and *Jericho* and *Gilgal* and the ten tribes and Elijah and Hosea and—history. *Gaza,* where Samson smashed the Philistines. . . . And now, the children had returned, incredibly, swiftly, mightily, to free the land from the trespassers, to redeem the stolen homeland.

What an opportunity! The Messiah knocked and history smiled and they touched fingers with their ancestors. *Now, now* was the opportunity to rid the land of those who a bare forty-eight hours earlier had danced in an orgy of Jew hatred, vowing to do unto Jewish men what they had done—partly—in the decades past and to inflict on Jewish women the horrors of which they were so capable. *Now, now* was the moment whose time had come. *Now.*

How the Arabs expected to be slaughtered! How they knew what *they* would have done if the roles were reversed! In Hebron white flags flew from every window as the inhabitants shook in terror, remembering 1929. The sixty-seven murdered Jews rested heavily on their heads as they waited for Jewish vengeance. . . .

Eight years later an Arab resident of the territories, Muadi Abu-Minsha, told an Israeli reporter: "I could not bear the crushing defeat we suffered. I even feared a mass slaughter. But thank G-d, the Israeli soldiers did not slaughter us. . . ."

No, the Israeli soldiers did not slaughter them—and how they expected it! And how they would have fallen and kissed the soldiers' boots had they been told: "You know what you deserve. You know what you did and what we should do to you. You know what you would have done in our place. But we are not you: we are Jews, and we give you a chance to live. You have forty-eight hours to take all that you can and cross the Jordan. *Out!*"

They would have kissed Jewish feet and fled.

Israel would have been free of them, and the ugly world that just days earlier had waited in expectation and *anticipation* of Jewish tragedy would have remained silent, so thunderstruck was it at the miracle of the Six-Day War! And Israel would have been free of the cancer, the terrible specter of 800,000 more Jew haters. And Jews could have settled the length and breath of the land, and we could have brought the redemption so much closer. . . .

But no, the gentilized and the Hellenists—whose terror of man is an article of faith replacing awe and faith in G-d—fled from greatness. It was the same fear of world reaction that saw orders given not to shell the Old City lest Christian and Muslim holy places be damaged. Jewish soldiers had to pick their way through the narrow streets and alleyways. Dozens were killed by sniper fire—*all needlessly,* all murdered by Arab bullets and Jewish timidity.

The Arabs were neither killed nor driven from Hebron. Defense Minister Moshe Dayan, one of the architects of Jewish disaster, raced to the city to assure the Muslim *Khadi* ("priest") that the Cave of the Machpela would remain in Muslim hands. The cave in which are buried Abraham and Sarah, Isaac and Rebecca, Jacob and Leah, and which had been barred for centuries to Jews, now would continue to be a Muslim site. Hebron would remain Arab, thanks to Dayan.

It was the policy of a man who opposed attacking the Golan Heights for fear that the Soviet allies of Syria would intervene. It was the fear of a man who not only refused to expel the Arabs, but forcibly returned those who had already fled! The Arab village of Kalkilya, which touches Kfar Saba, was for years one of the most vicious nests of terrorists. Regularly, the vipers would slither from Kalkilya to murder Jews. For years, Jews watched with gritted teeth and waited for the day . . .

In 1967 it came. The populace fled in panic. Thousands abandoned their village and swarmed eastward to the Jordan. Dayan ordered paratroopers to catch them and bring them back —lest the world think that Israel was preparing a new wave of refugees. Heaven forbid!

The miracle came and was rejected. The gold was turned by reverse alchemy into dross. Rather then being free of 800,000 enemies, the Jews allowed them to remain—them and their endless number of children. They drain us of our money, kill our children, steal our land. In 1967 Muadi Abu-Minsha feared a slaughter. In 1975 he said: "Israel has no choice. . . . I think the whole world recognizes the justice of the Palestinians. . . . Arafat's plan is a good one and I think Israel should adopt it."

History will never forgive Israel its failure of nerve and fear of world opinion. The nation as a whole is already paying the price.

Why did Israel—why does she to this day—steadfastly refuse to allow the Arabs who fled in 1948 to return? Because she understood that each is a foreign body opposed to the Jewish state and committed to a "Palestinian" people and country. Israel knew that the Arabs who would return were a fifth column both in the sense of their potential to act violently against the Jewish state and in their very numbers that could some day tilt the population scale in favor of an Arab majority. The idea of allowing these people to return was unthinkable.

There is not the slightest logical, moral, or rational reason to allow the same thing to occur through the Arabs we did not have the good sense or courage to remove. The keeping of Arabs in Lebanon lest they destroy Israel from within and the refusal to move others now in Israel to Lebanon, despite the same danger, is utter madness. There is no moral obligation to allow one's home to be taken from him merely because the one who seeks it is already in the house. There is nothing unjust in removing those who would rob you of your own land before they can accomplish their desire.

The question is not how *can* we remove the Arabs, but rather how can we *not*? To do nothing is the simplest and most simplistic policy. It will certainly spare this government, and perhaps the next, both the agony of having to take the bold and excruciating step and the price of not taking it. The deluge, the flood, will not come tomorrow. But come it certainly will, and sooner than we think. This generation already feels the first searing heat that will become the terrible flood of fire. No, the question is: *How can we possibly sit and not rid ourselves of the Arabs who seek to destroy us from within?*

What inexplicable loss of national preservation, will, and sanity makes the Jews of Israel hesitate to save themselves? We know that the Arab believes that we are thieves who stole his

land. We know that he murdered Jews in the land from the beginning of the Zionist revival and attempted to destroy the Jewish state at birth. We know that under the best of circumstances
he is a defeated enemy who suffered a humiliating disaster that
turned him from a majority in the land into a minority in a
Jewish state ruled by the *Jewish people* and whose character and
destiny are stated de jure as being *Jewish*. We know that the
Arab differs from us in every possible way—ethnically, religious-
ly, culturally, linguistically—and that everything about the Jewish state is foreign to him. We know that he grows explosively in
quantity (even as Jews do not), and that in the face of his huge
population growth and the pitiful Jewish birthrate, *aliya* figures,
and abortions, he will be a powerful and dangerous minority
tomorrow, aiming—under the democratic rights of the state—to
be a majority in the future. We know that he is educated and
ever more radical, and that his students and intellectuals openly
call for support of the PLO and a "Palestine" state rather than
Israel.

We know how many Arab Knesset members will be democratically elected and how, together with the Jewish left, they
will be a force in the land. We know the Arab call for "proper"
representation in the Knesset and cabinet. We know that whole
regions of Israel have an Arab majority today and that there are
cries for "autonomy," cries that escalate as they border on areas
of the liberated lands that have been promised "autonomy." We
know that calls have been made, and will grow louder, for annexing those parts of Israel to a "Palestine" entity that will
emerge alongside them. We know that this is merely a prelude
to demands to implement the UN Partition Plan 1947 and to call
for the return of the refugees who fled in 1948. We know that we
dare not give up an inch of Jewish land of either the state or the
liberated lands, for this would only bring the enemy closer to the
heartland and the event for which he waits—the destruction of
Israel. We know that with the growth of a large enough minority, Israel will be turned into another Northern Ireland and
Cyprus with regular bombings, demonstrations, riots, killings.
We know that there will be no escape from worldwide condemnation and sanctions. We know the economic and social disintegration to which the Arab contributes.

We know the vast amounts of funds spent on the Arab sec-

tor at a time when the economic burden on the state is a staggering one and Jewish social and economic problems worsen for
lack of money. We know the vast amounts of state land taken by
the Arab and the thousands of illegal buildings he has put up.
We know the corrupting influence of cheap Arab labor and the
ever-growing reliance on the Arab worker whose strikes can par-
alyze whole sections of the economy. We know the ugliness of
intermarriage, prostitution, and sexual contacts between the
Arab and Jewish women.

We know the support the Arab has in the form of the Arab
states and universal world opinion. We know how he senses Israeli weakness, division, and retreat. We know the confidence he
has that time is on his side and the boldness that he displays. We
remember the horrible rape of Jewish women and the brutal
mutilation of Jewish men when he was the majority. We know
the sheer hate he feels for the Jews and the state and what he
would do if ever, G-d forbid, he would have the opportunity.

All this Israel knows, and yet she fails to leap to her feet and
rid herself of the danger to her very existence. The most basic
sense of self-preservation calls for a policy of making life as difficult as possible for the Arabs to induce them to leave. Israel,
however, for more than thirty years, has done precisely the opposite. Israel has made every possible effort to make life in Eretz
Yisrael better and better for the Arabs. The Arab of Israel receives national insurance and welfare; Israel subsidizes his
babies and encourages him to have more; he is not forced to do
any national service whatsoever and so can make money from
the ages of eighteen to twenty-one while the Jew must serve in
the army. He pays little or nothing in taxes while the Jew groans
under the burden. He squats on government land and builds
houses illegally, and the authorities look the other way. Is it any
wonder that he prefers to remain and plot to destroy Israel from
within?

The liberated lands of 1967 are the classic example. Not
only did the Israeli government, and Dayan in particular, throw
away the golden opportunity of ridding Eretz Yisrael of the Arabs of Judea-Samaria-Gaza, but they announced a policy that
guaranteed that they would happily remain. An "open-bridge"
policy was implemented, allowing Arab farmers of the area to
ship their products to Jordan and other Arab countries. This not

only saved the Arab farmers from ruin but opened the door to an era of affluence they had never known. Immediately after the war a huge agricultural surplus existed which had always been shipped to Jordan and the Persian Gulf. The entire rural populace of Judea-Samaria depended on this. Had the surplus spoiled, it would have been an economic disaster for the Arab farmers and a less-than-subtle signal that life under the occupation would be very difficult.

But the Israelis, incredibly, saved Judea-Samaria Arabs from economic collapse. Joel Marcus, dovish writer for the liberal paper *Ha'Aretz,* painted an idyllic picture of all this in the Jewish Agency's publication *Midstream* (June–July 1968): "Thanks to this trade . . . the West Bank was saved from economic collapse. Since the war, over $40 million worth of goods have passed over the Jordan in both directions. Everywhere in the West Bank trucks can be seen loading the harvest; when they get to the Allenby bridge, they change their Israeli license plates for Jordanian ones and continue on to Amman where their cargo is sold to its traditional customers."

The government has made the Arabs of Judea-Samaria-Gaza richer than they ever dreamed they could be. Large sums of money have been poured into these areas, and the best of Israeli technology has trained and advanced the Arabs there. And so, Israel was delighted to learn on April 4, 1976, that "agricultural production in the administered territories [*sic*] has grown at a faster rate than anywhere since 1968!" The speaker was Reuven Eiland, director general of the Ministry of Agriculture. He gladdened Jewish hearts by announcing that in eight years the average per capita income of Judea-Samaria farmers grew from $133 to $666 (a jump of 500 percent!) and that this income was 4.5 times higher than the average Egyptian farmer's. He added that "apart from receiving professional help from Israel, they also get credit, loans, and export incentives."

Workers from the territories poured into Israel to work for cheap wages, eliminating Jewish jobs, creating a steady pool of cheap "dirty labor" that destroyed the Jewish work ethic, and making Israel dependent on them. They did not pay taxes, and the territories became boom areas with houses built right and left, appliances filling homes that now had electricity, toilets, and things never imagined before the Israelis came.

And the Arabs were allowed an incredible amount of local autonomy and freedom. In Marcus's words, "Was there ever an occupation under which people could move so freely . . . and not encounter a single armed soldier?" Marcus's bliss was shared by Peace Now sympathizer Shlomo Avineri, former director-general of the Foreign Ministry. Writing in *Commentary* magazine (June 1970), he exclaimed: "The kind of military administration set up by Israel . . . was a brilliant improvisation. . . . The general idea was that the less the military administration meddled in the daily affairs of the population, the better, and the result is that today Arab municipal self-government on the West Bank and in Gaza remains intact and Jordanian and Egyptian laws are still the law of the land."

Of course, the real result of this "brilliant improvisation" was that Israel's failure to declare sovereignty over what it told the world was Jewish territory merely convinced one and all that the Jews were indeed "occupiers" and thieves. And the low profile of the Jews and their leaving in place Arab laws and municipal self-rule were convincing proof to the local Arabs that the Israeli's presence was only temporary. It was this disastrous policy that kept the Arabs from leaving, that blocked Jewish sovereignty, and that eventually led to the riots, killings, and rebellion of today.

The architect of the disastrous policy was Moshe Dayan, whose contributions to Israeli tragedy will yet be fully outlined in the history that will be written of our times. Dayan is a man with an extraordinary ability to adopt contradictory positions. In a 1968 newspaper interview on the occasion of Israel's Independence Day, Dayan gave the following insight into his views on the territories—and himself. After calling for ensuring that contact with the Arab countries not be cut off, he continued: "We Jews must not interfere too much in their domestic affairs, such as their educational system, their law courts, the way they elect their leaders, and representatives, their newspapers, etc. We must let them live their own lives. If these two conditions are met, I don't think that the Arabs of the West Bank would mind if Jews were to live in Hebron. . . . All in all, in terms of the Arabs' readiness to live side by side with us, I believe that the prospects are better today than they have ever been before." No commentary is necessary at all.

The results of the enlightened and "brilliant improvisation" can be seen in the years of riots, rebellion, hatred, and murder of Jews. The massacre of six Jews in Hebron, the stoning of soldiers, the bombing of buses—all these occurred because of the policy. Israel's liberal policy went so far as to allow elections for mayors in Judea-Samaria in April 1976. The results were a sweeping victory for PLO supporters in almost every municipality. "The Israelis are shocked—they didn't expect such results," crowed Ramallah's Karim Khalaf.

Rioting and uprising became so bad that the foreign minister of Israel on January 23, 1979, warned the Arabs of Judea-Samaria and Israel that if they allowed themselves to be "carried away by the mood of fanatical Islam," they would "pay very dearly for it." Strange words from Mr. Begin's foreign minister, whose name was Moshe Dayan. . . .

Bankruptcy—an Israeli policy that is worse than total failure. It is a heartbreaking tragedy. An opportunity was granted Israel in 1967 to rid itself of all the Arabs of the territories, who even a child could understand would be a bone in Israel's throat. Dayan, the government, Israel—in fear of world opinion—rejected it. Israel today pays the price.

A policy of liberalism that allows the Arabs a life of material gain and freedom guarantees their remaining in the land and attempting to destroy Israel from within. *They must leave the country for their own lands—that must be Israeli policy.* As part of that policy, life must be made very difficult for them. That is the way to encourage emigration and spare Israel tragedy.

I urge the adoption of a program to deal with the Arab problem in Eretz Yisrael, with its basis the real rational and Jewish relationship of citizen, nation, and state.

I urge the adoption of the following program to clarify the character of the nation, the state, and its citizens and the position of its noncitizens; and to prepare the framework for the transfer of Arabs from the Land of Israel (the state and the territories liberated in 1967):

The land, the state, exists to serve the people. Only tyrants say the opposite. In the beginning there was the family, tribe, clan, people. They have a common origin, history, heritage, destiny. The land has a definite, specific function. It exists to serve the people as a vessel to hold them and to allow them to live their unique way of life, to achieve their national purpose and heritage. The state is a tool to serve that purpose and to enable the people to achieve their fulfillment. Neither state nor land has a will or authority of its own. The identity and character of the land and state are decided upon and granted by the people. The land and state do not command, they obey; they do not order, they serve; they exist only for the purpose of the people whose name is attached to them.

The people are the masters and proprietors of the land, and as such they are the citizens of it. Those who are not members of the family, tribe, clan, people, nation, clearly have no ownership, proprietorship, or legal ties to the land. They cannot be citizens since they are not members of the people, the nation. Strangers can, of course, become part of the people and nation through the process and discipline of Judaism and *halakah*. But that is the only way they can become citizens of the state.

What rationality is there to claim that a piece of land has the will, authority, and power to convey to those who live on it citizenship, regardless of who they are? It is human beings who define the land, not the land that defines the human beings. One does not become an "Israeli" because one lives in the land. For the land itself is defined by the will, ownership, and title to it of the people of Israel. One can be an "Israeli" when belonging to the people of Israel, when joining the nation, the people, not simply by living on the piece of land that is the mere servant and vessel of the people.

And so, the right of non-Jews to live in the Land of Israel is a thing to be decided upon by the owners of the land, its citizens —the Jews, under the Jewish concept of *resident stranger (ger toshav)*. Residence or removal of noncitizens is decided by the owners of the land according to that concept and what is good and right for the people and nation whose land and state it is. With this as a basis, let it be declared that:

1. *The identity between the state and the nation shall be the sole basis of citizenship in the State of Israel. The State of Israel belongs to and exists only for the Jewish nation and is therefore the Jewish state, the home in which the Jewish nation lives. It is therefore only membership in the Jewish nation which gives citizenship in the Jewish state. All members of*

the Jewish nation—without exception and whoever they may be—are entitled to automatic citizenship in the Jewish state, and no one who is not a member of the Jewish nation can acquire such citizenship. Membership in the Jewish nation and people can be acquired through the process and discipline of Judaism and halakah. *Non-Jews can live in the land without citizenship and political rights, up to a number whose maximum is limited by the security consideration of the state and Jewish people. No state, no matter what the attitude of the noncitizens, can allow unlimited numbers of them to live in the country. The resident permits of all resident strangers shall be good for one year and shall be reviewed at the end of every year.*

2. *Every Arab resident of Eretz Yisrael shall be offered a voluntary transfer to an Arab or, if possible, a non-Arab land. Those who accept shall be given full compensation for property, plus a cash bonus, as well as first priority for visas for the West (with occupational training if necessary). Fair compensation for property shall be fixed by an impartial body with payments to be made in regular, reasonable installments. The body shall include members of the Jewish and Arab communities. Payments to Arabs for their property shall be made with consideration for the debts owed those Jewish communities. Arab oil states shall be asked to contribute the money they received for the property expropriated without compensation from the Jews who were expelled from Arab lands. This offer of compensation and bonus shall be good for two months so as to enable all Arabs in the land to consider it carefully. After that, step 3 of the program will take effect.*

3. *Arabs who decline the offer shall be asked to make a pledge of their loyalty to the Jewish state in which they accept the Land of Israel as the home of the Jewish people and recognize total Jewish sovereignty over it, as well as the absolute and exclusive right of the Jewish people to it. Those who do so shall remain as residents and noncitizens of Israel with no national sovereignty and no political and voting rights, since they are not members of the Jewish nation. They shall have individual rights to live their own*

cultural, economic, religious, social, and communal lives, without those government benefits available only to citizens. The state shall limit the number of noncitizens in accordance with security considerations.

4. *Those who refuse to accept noncitizen status shall be compensated for property, but not given a bonus, and shall be transferred only to Arab—not Western—lands. The transfer shall be effected peacefully, if possible, but if the Arab still refuses, then forcibly and without compensation. The Arabs who are transferred shall be taken to the Lebanese or Jordanian borders or to the area separating Israel and Egypt.*

5. *Remaining Arabs who have pledged loyalty to the Jewish state, but who shall subsequently be found guilty of national or security offenses, and all those who knowingly aid such people shall not be imprisoned but shall be deported without compensation.*

6. *The world Jewish community shall be thoroughly informed on the problem and especially on the consequences of failing to carry it out. World Jewry shall be asked to mount an emergency campaign to finance the emigration program.*

7. *In the meantime, there shall be a campaign to persuade the Arabs to leave voluntarily. Arabs shall be required to serve for three years in a work corps beginning at the age of eighteen, and for one month every year thereafter. No Arab shall be allowed to study in a university without a declaration of loyalty to the Jewish state.*

8. *Taxes shall be collected fully from the Arabs of Israel, unlike the present policy which allows a vast amount of tax evasion. Similarly, a firm and vigorous policy will prevent land seizure and illegal building by Arabs.*

9. *National insurance payments shall be limited to Jews only*

10. *There shall be created, within the context of national army service, labor battalions for Jews, which will train them in*

physical, manual labor and occupational vocations. A cam-
paign to hire Jewish workers shall be given top priority.

The question of the poor and deprived in Israel is one
that is loaded with potential for explosion. The desperate
problem of young couples unable to find decent housing because of the staggering costs; the pitiful state of education;
the lack of schools and centers to impart values and training;
the escalating costs of food and all basic items—all add up to
a social problem that could erupt into riots and civil war.
The *shchunot* ("neighborhoods") are centers of conflict between rich and poor, Sephardim and Ashkenazim. Money is
needed for housing, jobs, basic needs. There simply has not
been enough money until now.

The transfer of the huge bulk of Arabs from the country
will enable the government each year to transfer many
billions in funds previously spent on the Arab sector to the
impoverished Jewish classes. The left bemoans the fact that
there is not enough money for both the poor and the new
settlements. Nonsense! The monies that are today spent on
Arab national insurance, welfare, schools, health facilities,
roads, sanitation, and all the other services can be made
available for Jewish needs. Removal of the Arabs will be a
giant step toward removal of both enemy and poverty.

There are many benefits. The Arab property—homes,
fields, and villages—that will be bought by the government
can be made available to young couples under a population-
dispersal program, which will be a boon to the country
strategically, socially, and economically.

The exodus of the Arabs will put an end to the wholesale seizure of state land, which would then become available for settlements of all kinds.

The exodus of Arab workers, far from being a permanent blow to the economy, will prove a blessing. Because of
the availability of plentiful and cheap Arab labor, Jews
began to shun manual, physical labor. The result was a sick,
unhealthy society in which Jews used and then came to depend on Arabs to do the vital but unsavory tasks without
which no society can exist. Not only did the Arabs create a
crisis in terms of a dangerous Jewish disdain of physical la-

bor, but as a result Jews stopped working, and this created a critical shortage of Jewish labor. This, in turn, made Arab labor no longer a luxury but a necessity. The reliance on Arab labor is both a national disgrace and a danger. In addition, the hiring of Arab children and women to work for slave wages and in outrageous conditions not only takes jobs from Jews who cannot work for such low wages, but is a moral shame and outrage that corrupts the Jewish character.

In addition, of course, there is the stark fact of growing physical strength on the part of Arabs who do hard manual labor while Jews grow soft. This has led to the attacks on Jews in cities of "mixed" population. And the very fact that factories hire Arabs brings them into the cities, where the incidence of crime and sexual attacks soars.

All this will, of necessity, be changed. When there are no Arab workers, the Jews will be *forced* to work. When there is no choice, Jewish employers will be *forced* to pay decent wages. When there is a national work shortage, the government will be *forced* to adopt an emergency policy of Jewish labor. "Work battalions" will be created within the army or other national service. Every young soldier will be given intensive training in occupational vocations and experience in basic manual labor. No student will be able to graduate high school or enter a university without having spent part of each year giving national service in the form of manual labor.

The removal of the Arabs from the land will throw open the territories as a challenge to world Jewry, especially the young. The opportunity to settle everywhere in the biblical portions of Israel and, thus, truly meet Jewish historic destiny can be presented to them as it has never been until now.

Opponents of Arab emigration call such plans "incitement to revolution." But the truth is that the very existence of the State of Israel already assures that. It is the presence of Jews and Jewish institutions in East Jerusalem, the government's plans to "Judaize" the Galilee, the very existence of Tel Aviv and an "Israel" in place of a "Palestine," that incite and assure Arab hatred and dreams of revenge.

The idea of transferring Arabs out of Eretz Yisrael is not

new. Joseph Weitz of the Jewish National Fund saw the Arab problem clearly and wrote: "It should be clear that there is no room for both peoples to live in the country . . . and in that case there is no alternative to moving the Arabs to the neighboring countries, moving them all, except, perhaps, those living in Bethlehem, Nazareth, and the Old City of Jerusalem. . . ." (Joseph Weitz, *Diaries and Letters to the Children,* Tel Aviv, 1965, p. 181).

Weitz was a strong proponent of the Judaizing of the Galilee and was influenced by veteran Joseph Nahmani of the Jewish National Fund. Nahmani's understanding of the problem is seen in the memorandum sent to Prime Minister Ben-Gurion in January 1953 concerning the problem of the Arabs in the Galilee: "The very existence of a unified Arab group in this part of the country is an invitation to the Arab states to press their claims to the area. . . . When the time comes, it will play the part played by the Germans in Czechoslovakia at the beginning of World War II. . . ."

An angry Professor Ephraim Urbach told a symposium on the Arabs in 1968: "I read an interview with the author Haim Hazaz [one of Israel's most pretigious writers], in which he simplistically suggested solving the problem of the Arabs as follows: the war cost us three billion pounds—let's take three billion more pounds and give them to the Arabs and tell them to get out" *(Midstream,* April 1968). Urbach is a well-known dove. He did not find Hazaz's views, in his words, "edifying." Perhaps not, but Urbach has no answer at all.

In 1937 the British Royal Commission under Lord Peel proposed as a possible solution to the Jewish-Arab conflict the partition of Palestine into a Jewish and an Arab state. As part of this plan the transfer of some 200,000 Arabs from the proposed Jewish state to the Arab one was proposed. A great debate arose in the Zionist movement over this, and especially in the largest of the groups, the Laborite Mapai. Two of the central figures in the party, who were also among the leading figures in the Zionist movement, came out strongly for the transfer. Berl Katzenelson, ideologician and spokesman, declared: "The question of the transfer of population has aroused controversy: Is it permitted or forbidden? My conscience in this is perfectly clear. A distant neighbor is better than a close enemy. They will not lose by their transfer and we certainly will not. In the last analysis, this is a political reform settlement for the benefit of both sides. For a long time I have felt that this is the best of the solutions, and during the times of trouble I understand even more strongly that one of these days this thing *must* come about. I did not, however, imagine that the transfer 'outside of Eretz Yisrael' would mean to the area of Shechem. I believed and still believe that they will yet move to Syria or Iraq . . ." (1937).

The other proponent of removal of the Arabs from the proposed Jewish state was the future first prime minister of Israel. On July 29, 1937, David Ben-Gurion said: "If it is possible to move Arabs from village to village to village within the boundaries of the British mandate—it is difficult to find any political or moral reason not to transfer the same Arabs from an area under Jewish rule to one that will be under Arab rule. . . . Even under the maximum moral scruples it is impossible to object to a transfer that guarantees the transferees both satisfactory material conditions and maximum national security. For the Arabs who will be settled in an Arab state, this transfer will be a full and total satisfaction of their national aspirations."

Some of the best-known early Zionist spokesmen discussed the transfer of Arabs. Arthur Ruppin, in May 1911, suggested that the Zionists buy land near Aleppo and Homs in northern Syria for the resettlement of Palestinian Arabs. Both Leo Motzkin and Nahum Sokolow, later to become president of the World Zionist Organization, considered the idea of transfer. The most consistent and persistent advocate of the concept was the Anglo-Jewish writer Israel Zangwill, who sought a state for the Palestine Arabs in Arabia.

There is the beginning of an awakening. In 1972, when I first raised the issue in public in a speech at Haifa University, universal reaction was hotly negative. Prime Minister Golda Meir publicly charged that I had offended the sensibilities of the Arabs, and editorials and columnists vilified me. One of the most bitter attacks was by nationalist "hawk" Moshe Shamir. In 1973 charges of incitement were filed against me when the Jewish Defense League of Israel (Kach) launched a campaign among the Arabs of Israel offering to aid those who wished to emigrate. Not only did Arabs from all over Israel and the territories respond, but an Israeli Arab from the Galilee village of

Fasuta, Emanuel Khoury, worked full-time in the region and gathered many names. The lesson to be learned from this is that a sizable number of Arabs would be eager to leave the country for some *Western* state. This should hardly surprise anyone, for are there not many Israeli Jews who happily do the same?

In the years that followed, difficult years for myself and the Kach movement, persistence and determination in the face of arrests and vilification were rewarded. Not only is there a dramatic change in the attitude of the general public vis-à-vis the need to transfer the Arabs, but various personalities have begun to speak out on the subject. To be sure, they have not yet the courage or understanding to call for a compulsory transfer of all Arabs who will not accept conditions of noncitizen residency, and they still speak of "voluntary emigration," but they are beginning to move in the right direction. They are proof of the power of small but determined catalysts.

And so in January 1979 Meir Har-Zion, one of the best-known heroes of the Israeli army, wrote concerning the Arabs: "I do not say we should put them on trucks or kill them. . . . We must create a situation in which for them, it is not worth living here, but rather in Jordan or Saudi or any other Arab state."

Har-Zion was applauded by Israeli's most famous songwriter, Naomi Shemer ("Jerusalem of Gold"), in an article in the Labor newspaper *Davar* (February 9, 1979): "Arab emigration from Israel, if done with mutual respect and positive agreement . . . can be the correct answer."

And during a debate in the Knesset on Arab terrorism in the territories, Likud Knesset member Amnon Linn said (May 18, 1976): "We should begin mass expulsion of entire communities that participated in demonstrations and riots—and transfer them across the border. This is said for women, men, and children."

They are still a minority of public voices and have not yet understood the totality of what must be done or lack the courage to say so. But they have come a long way. Above all, many Israelis, particularly in the Sephardic communities, do understand and will support a policy of Arab transfer under voluntary or compulsory conditions.

In the meantime, life for the Arabs of Israel must cease to be one of avoiding obligations while enjoying material well-being and waiting for demography to put an end to Israel. Life must be made difficult for them as part of a definite campaign to induce them to leave the country.

There must be an end, first of all, to the wholesale evasion of taxes and land laws. There should be set up an efficient governmental office, working with the Border Patrol, to track down every piece of state land that has been the target of squatters. All illegal buildings must be demolished and stiff fines and prison terms levied, but with the possibility of their being waived in return for a promise to emigrate. All state lands that were leased to Arabs under the government's change of policy in the late seventies should have their leases terminated. The "Judaizing" of the Galilee and Triangle should be openly admitted—with all its good and sufficient reasons—and expropriation of land with compensation vigorously executed. The large number of Bedouins and Arabs from Judea-Samaria-Gaza who have illegally entered Israel must be heavily fined and then deported.

In addition, a special tax department working with the police must see that every Arab pays his fair share of taxes—income, value-added, and others. Stiff fines and levies on property should be the punishments, and justice should be swift and sure.

The Arab youth must prepare to serve for three years in a work corps at the age of eighteen, and for a period of a month each year after that, just as his Jewish counterpart serves in the armed forces and national service. The freedom of the Arab from such service enables him to work and save money during the long periods that the Israeli Jew must sacrifice while in national service. This consideration of no national service, little or no taxes, and land seizure is intolerable, and, of course, it goes far to defeat any incentive for the Arab to leave. This must change, as must the present system of university education for the Arab, regardless of his views. The process whereby Jews allow their universities to be production lines and training grounds for the intellectual leaders of the PLO cannot continue. Any Arab who wishes to study at a university will have to pledge his acceptance and support of the Land of Israel as the exclusive and permanent home—of the *Jewish* people. If he is not willing, he has no place in a Jewish university. The governmental funds that now go to scholarships for Arab students should be shifted to the Jewish Agency, which will give the money to deserving, needy Jews.

Stiff punishments should be exacted on all employers who hire Arab workers for less than the official or going wage. Similar heavy fines and jail sentences should be meted out for hiring young children and for keeping workers in unhealthy and dangerous working conditions. Morally such things are indefensible, and from an economic standpoint they encourage the hiring of Arabs because of the lower expense to the employer. These employers should be encouraged in every way to hire Jews.

And finally, national insurance, which among other things subsidizes the high Arab birthrate, must be transferred to the Jewish Agency, which as a nongovernmental organ will give benefits only to Jews. The process of encouraging the huge Arab birthrate that is designed to put an end to the Jewish state smacks of irrationality.

The goal of a fair and humane transfer of Arabs from Eretz Yisrael, with full compensation and as part of an exchange of populations, will be immeasurably advanced through the ending of conditions that only encourage Israeli Arabs to remain and comfortably wait for their "Palestine" state to replace "Israel." Life must be made difficult and uncomfortable so that emigration will ultimately be the better of the Arab's choices.

The program of Arab transfer will be the target of unprecedented hate and vilification from both inside and outside Israel. Even so, the great obstacle to its success does not lie in the reaction of the Gentiles, but in the anticipated fanatical extremism of its Jewish opponents.

There is a loud and influential contingent of Israeli Jews who would sooner see Israel come to an end as a Jewish state than transfer the Arabs out of the country. They will be joined by large numbers of American Jewish liberals and the Jewish Establishment. These will be driven both by their gentilized, liberal concepts and by fear of the repercussions of such a move for *them* as a minority in the Exile.

Their presence is already noted in their shrill attack on the Jewish settlements and demands for retreat from large sections of the liberated lands. They are essentially non-Zionists, despite their vigorous denials. Their basic tendencies are toward universalism, not nationalism, and their very ties to Jewishness are tempered with guilt as the contradictions between the particularism and separatism of Judaism conflict with nonbarrier universalism and nonsectarian brotherhood. These contradictions have been sorely tested in the past decade over the Arab issue, in any event. The question of transferring Arabs out of the land will drive them to a frenzied condemnation of Israeli policy. Their danger is their influence on large numbers of simple, good American and Western Jews.

The simplistic and demagogic use of labels such as "immoral," "inhumane," "un-Jewish," and "Nazi-like" is likely to find a troubled, sympathetic ear with the ordinary, decent Jew. Thus, we will pay for all the years of deceit and delusions. For all those decades Jewish and Israeli leaders refused to tell the truth about the remedy of the Arab problem in the Land of Israel. They preferred to avoid it and to lie to world Jewry. It is not surprising that any sudden policy that calls for transfer of the Arabs will meet with astonishment and guilt. It is imperative that there begins, *today*, a campaign among world Jewry to explain the full extent of the Arab hatred and danger. The complete truth must be told to the masses of good Jews both to justify the need to remove the Arabs and to expose the dangers of the liberal Establishment bloc.

The Jewish opposition from within—that is the obstacle to successful transfer of Arabs and the saving of the Jewish state. There is no gentile problem, only the Jewish one of self-destruction.

The problem in the Jew who stupidly equates the transfer of Arabs with Hitler's genocide of the Jews, as if we were advocating gas chambers or the killing of the Arabs in any form! As if the separation of Jews and Arabs will not *save* Arab and Jewish lives both! As if it is not precisely the policy of the perverted moralists that will lead eventually to the horrible bloodbath the Jewish realists see all too well!

How outrageously dishonest is the equation. How they cheapen and demean the terrible historical uniqueness and horror of the Holocaust, those intellectual dwarfs who equate it with any event they cannot abide! Did the Jews of Germany say that the land was really theirs, stolen from them by the Germans, and that they would work until the day they became the majority and take the land and make it "Judea"? If they did, the Jews of Hitler's time can be equated with the Arabs. Did the Jews of Europe massacre Germans, rape their women, burn their settlements, and vow to drive them into the sea? If they did, Europe's Jews and Israel's Arabs are the same.

And if they did—if Germany's Jews killed Germans and sought to take their state from them—Germans would have been justified in removing them from Germany and saving their country. But if, as really happened, the Jews sought, not to destroy Germany, not to separate from Germany, not to be independent of Germany, but to be good, loyal, fervent, assimilated Germans, then what the Germans did was horrible, and what the Jews who equate the murderous Arabs with the murdered Jews do *is obscene*. With no apologies, no defensiveness, no hesitation, the Jew rejects with contempt the gentilized Hebrews and the neo-Hellenists. He knows the Jewish response to threats to destroy people and state: "If one comes to slay you, slay him first" (Sanhedrin, 72d). "Do not be overly righteous" (Ecclesiastes 7). "Said Rabbi Shimon ben Lakish: He who becomes merciful unto the cruel is destined to be cruel unto the merciful."

How cruel are the overly righteous, the carriers of perverted morality, the unthinking, *the gentilized*. How many Jewish women and children will die because of the mercy of the overly righteous to the cruel? The foolish children, the twisted adults, all calling in the name of "humanity" for the destruction of the Jewish state—*they* will be the problem, nothing else.

But there are questions: How can we persuade the Arabs to leave? The answer is: We do not come to the Arabs to request, argue, or persuade. The government that comes to power will remember the past and the hopes of the Arabs to repeat it. It will not request. The Arab will be given the choice of accepting noncitizenship and the difficult new conditions that status will entail, of leaving willingly with compensation, or of leaving unwillingly without compensation. He has no other options, and the election of a strong, iron-handed government whose reputation and determination to implement this program at all cost are known to the Arab will keep resistance to a minimum.

There will be a small percentage who will agree to the conditions of the noncitizen resident stranger. They will be mostly elderly people. They will remain. The majority, however, will accept reality. Knowing that eventually they will have to leave in any event, the largest group will accept the compensation, bonus, and hoped-for visa to the West. They will leave willingly.

Ideally, the Western nations will be convinced that it is both the most humane thing *and in their own interests* to accept Arabs in their countries.

A decade ago the United States took in more than a quarter of a million refugees from Cuba. It was more than a display of generosity. Having moved to the brink of nuclear war during the Kennedy-Khrushchev confrontation, Washington saw in the growing tension and antigovernment agitation within Cuba a danger that the United States would become involved yet again in a showdown with the Soviets. This time there was not a chance that the Russians would back away, and America was no longer prepared to go to war for principles. The decision was made to take in large numbers of anti-Castro Cubans who might rise up against the government. *It was a political decision intended to defuse a potential time bomb.*

The same lesson should be taught the Western powers in regard to the Middle East. The Israeli government must make strenuous efforts to convince them that it they truly seek peace and tranquillity in the region so as to ensure stability and the orderly flow of oil, the problem of the Arabs within Israel must be solved.

There will be no peace in the region, no matter what agreements are reached with outside Arab governments, if the Arabs remain within the Land of Israel. They must inevitably rise up, forcing the Arab states to come to their aid. Any and all agreements reached between Israel and her neighbors will be worthless as the region explodes in war. Oil boycotts will be declared as the anger of the Arab world is directed against the West, and the shaky thrones of the pro-Western, feudal Arab monarchs will come crashing down, with all that that implies for the West.

There will be no peace as long as the Arab-Jewish problem festers in Eretz Yisrael, and it is to the vital interests of the Western nations to agree to accept Arab emigrants from Eretz Yisrael. The United States, though theoretically bound by quotas, makes much immigrant policy on an ad hoc basis. In the past quarter-century more than a million refugees from Cuba, Hungary, the Soviet Union, and other countries have been allowed into the United States under the attorney general's "parole" power. Congress has also made exceptions to the law in response to particularly critical events as they have occurred.

The Arabs of Eretz Yisrael are intelligent and good work-ers, and there is need in the West for those willing to do the important but unsavory jobs that go begging for lack of local hands. In addition, the shortage of skilled workers in particular sections of the economy is acute, and a careful survey by Israel of the peculiar needs of each Western country could lead to a training program for Arabs tailored to specific skills in demand in the West.

There will be those who will refuse to leave willingly. They will be the worst of haters and the most dangerous of the Arabs, those whose transfer is most urgent. Their removal from the country must be accomplished quickly and without hesitation. These Arabs will be transported to the Lebanese or the Hashemite Kingdom of Jordan, which joins all the rest in work-ing toward the elimination of Israel.

"But what will the world say!"

That is the question that makes Jews tremble. What will the world say? They will condemn Israel universally. And to-day, of course, they love her. . . .

Dear Jew, look about you; listen. The voices you hear and the hate-filled faces you see are those that prove the wisdom of the rabbis who, millennia ago, pronounced: "It is law; know— Essau hates Jacob." The coat of Jew hatred is of many colors, woven in jealousy, produced in deeply ingrained primeval emo-tions, now stretching from Mexico to Korea. It is a magical coat. It expands to hold people of all colors and creeds; First, Second, Third and Twelfth Worlds; Communists and Nazis; Soviets and Chinese; Vietnamese and Cambodians; Ayotollah Muslims and Vatican Christians. It is an ecumenical miracle, bringing the worst of enemies together under the unifying banner of Jew ha-tred.

Let those who fear the gentile world's anger and condemna-tion know that even without this program Israel faces, in the years to come, international hatred, viciousness, and threat such as no nation, not even South Africa, has encountered. *There is nothing Israel can do about this; for the demands of the world are essential-ly nothing less than the disappearance of Israel. Nothing that Israel does or does not do affects this hatred.* It is a pathological hate that has its roots in the existence of the Jew. If the nations feel that they can, they will move against Israel, no matter how "kind" the Jewish state is to her Arabs. If they understand Israel's fierce determination to use *all* its deadly weapons against whatever enemy dares to come against her, they will limit themselves to raving.

Israel took in the Jews from the Arab lands; it will give them Arabs from the one Jewish land: an exchange of populations; separation for peace.

In the end, let the Jew forever bear in mind two things. *The first is that Israel has no choice.* To sit and allow the Arabs to grow and destroy Israel from within is unthinkable. Let the Jew never forget the utter and complete hatred of the Arabs for Israel and their determination to destroy her. It may take years, decades, centuries—the Arab will wait. He will use every possible means, but he is obsessed. It was always so, from the beginning of Zionism. It is so today. It will be so tomorrow. Remember the voices: *"Today I am in the minority. The state is democratic. Who says that in the year 2,000 we Arabs will still be the minority? . . . Today, I accept the fact that this is a Jewish state with an Arab minority. But when we are the majority I will not accept the fact of a Jewish state with an Arab majority"* (the teacher Na'ama Saud at the Israeli village of Araba).

Is the Jew prepared to sacrifice his only state on the altar of the democracy the Arabs will use to destroy Israel?

And another voice, that of one of the most famous Arab scholars in his classic 1938 work *The Arab Awakening.* Thus wrote "Palestinian" George Antonius: "The logic of facts is inexorable. It shows that no room can be made in Palestine for a second nation except by dislodging or exterminating the nation in possession."

That is what the Arabs believe and have in mind for us. Never. There is no room for a second nation in Eretz Yisrael. The Arabs must leave. We have no choice, for it is either they or the Jews. *It will not be the Jews.*

On the day following the Land Day Rebellion in 1976, *Maariv* reporter Menachem Talmi (April 2, 1976) reported a conversation between two Jews whose cars had been halted near the Arab village of Kfar Kassem by an Arab roadblock. One of the men said that the only way to deal with the Arabs was with force. The other replied that with such an attitude "we will never reach understanding and settlement with the Arabs."

It is instructive to listen to the reply of the first Jew: "Don't worry, my friend, they have no desire at all to reach understanding and settlement with you. What they want is to see you swimming in the sea. They say it openly, but we don't want to hear.

"There were two villages here in the Triangle, Miski and Tira. All the gangs used to come from there to attack the Sharon plain. We wiped Miski off the map but spared Tira. I have no idea why. The members of Kibbutz Ramat Hakovesh, who ate dung because of them as far back as 1936 and later in the War of Independence, pleaded that they should be expelled after they were captured. But no one listened to them. Now the Arabs there 'thank us.' They throw stones at and burn police cars."

This is a simple Jew who understands that there will be no "understanding and settlement," that only the transfer of the Arabs out of the country will save us heartbreak. That it is either they or we. That it cannot and will not be the Jews.

And the second reply to frightened Jews. What has happened to you? Have you forgotten who the Jewish people are? Have you not the slightest idea of the historical destiny and immutability of the State of Israel? Have you become so gentilized that you so utterly forget the G-d of Israel?

Conclusion: But There Is a G-d in Israel

The analysis and proposed transfer of Arabs from Israel that I have set down are not personal views. They are certainly not *political* ones. This is the *Jewish* outlook, based on *halakah* the law as postulated in the Torah.

The removal of all Arabs who refuse to accept the exclusive, unquestioned Jewish sovereignty over Eretz Yisrael is not only logical and normal for any Jew with a modicum of an instinct for self-preservation; it is also the Jewish *halakic obligation*. It is important that we know this in order to realize what true "Jewishness" really dictates and in order to instill in ourselves the faith and assurance that if we do this, all the nations in the world will be incapable of harming Israel.

The Torah viewpoint on the status of non-Jews in Eretz Yisrael is part of a total viewpoint on the very nature of the Jewish people and of the Land of Israel. Of necessity, it opens up the questions: What is a Jew? Why the Land of Israel? What is the relationship of Jew to Gentiles? In the eyes of Judaism, Jewish nationalism, as such, is meaningless. What, after all, is the logic behind a separate nation, flag, parliament, defense system? Why set up barriers between people? What nonsense is the national anthem that glorifies one people that is, in essence, no different from another? Nationalism is, at best, foolish. At worst, it leads to hatred, to division, to war. There is no special meaning to the Jewish people if it is merely one *more* of the myriad of nations. In that case, the fate of the Jew is like the fate of the Moabite or Canaanite or Finn or Turk. The Jewish people can then exist, evolve, and die out. Its disappearance from the world scene is then as possible, and as probable, as that of all the other ancients who were Jewish contemporaries in biblical times and are long since gone.

But the Jewish people is *not* merely one more nation.

267

"Though I put an end to all the nations among whom thou art scattered, but I will never put an end to thee" (Jeremiah 30:11). Israel is indestructible. It is unique, it is holy, it is the Chosen of the L-rd; it has a reason for being. Its national uniqueness is built on an idea, on an ideology, that it alone has. That is, indeed, reason to be different. The Jew is selected and obligated to be a religio-nation, commanded to obey the laws and follow the path of Torah. Through sacred covenants, first with each of the three Patriarchs, Abraham, Isaac, and Jacob, and then with *the entire nation* standing at Mount Sinai and listening to the voice of the Almighty, the Jewish people was born: "Now therefore, if you will surely obey My voice and observe My covenant, then you shall be unique unto Me above all the nations, for all the earth is Mine. And you shall be unto Me a kingdom of priests and a holy nation" (Exodus 19:5–6).

The covenant. The Jewish people took upon itself the yoke of the L-rd, acknowledging Him as G-d and observing His laws. The Almighty chose them as His unique people, pledging that they would be indestructible and would live in peace and prosperity in their own land, Eretz Yisrael.

Eretz Yisrael. "Unto they seed have I given this land from the river of Egypt unto the great river, the River Euphrates" (Genesis: 15:18).

The land was given as a reward, as a blessing. But it is more, much more, than that. The people of Israel have more than a *right* to the land; they have an *obligation*. "For you shall pass over the Jordan to go in to possess the Land which the L-rd your G-d gives you, and you shall possess it and dwell therein" (Deuteronomy 11:31).

A unique people given, uniquely, a *particular* land. Unlike all the other faiths that are not limited to one special country, the Jew is given a particular land and commanded to live there. And for a reason, as Moses explains: "Behold, I have taught you statutes and judgments, even as the L-rd, my G-d, commanded me, *that you shall do so in the Land whither you go to possess it*" (Deuteronomy 4:5).

It is impossible to create a holy, unique people that dwells as a minority within lands that belong to others. The majority culture *must* infiltrate, influence, corrupt, woo, tempt, pervert. The Jew is commanded to create for himself a holy nation, and that can only be done free of others, separate, different, apart. That is why the unique Jewish nation, chosen for holiness and a unique destiny, was given a land for itself: so that it might create a unique, holy society that would be a light unto the nations who would see its example and model.

Such a state is reserved to the nation to which it was given for its particular goal and destiny. It was *taken* from nations—the Canaanites—in order that the Jew fulfill his obligatory destiny.

The L-rd, Creator and Proprietor of the world—all the lands are his. He took that which was His from the Canaanites and gave it to His Chosen People Israel. "And He gave them the lands of the nations and they inherited the lands of the people, so that they would observe His statutes and guard His laws . . . " (Psalms 105:44–45). The right of the Jewish people to the land is not based on human favors or historical residence. It is a title granted by the Builder and Owner. Clearly, it was not taken from one set of nations in order that others share it with the Jews. The land was given to serve the Jewish people so that they have a distinct, separate place in which to fulfill their obligation. There can be no others who freely live there, let alone share sovereignty and ownership. To allow such a thing is to invite both military attack and spiritual assimilation, and thus to destroy and put an end to that unique Torah society for which the Land of Israel was given to the Jews.

This is so for all non-Jews. Any grant to them of citizenship that implies ownership and a right to shape the destiny and character of the state destroys the uniqueness and entire purpose of giving the land to Israel. It invites spiritual assimilation and eventually demands for political autonomy.

How much more so for the non-Jewish residents of the land who lived there before the L-rd gave it to the Jews. Those residents refuse to recognize such a fact. They believe the land to be theirs and will dream of the day when they will regain it. To allow them to remain as proprietors, or even freely living with restrictions, is to ensure not only the general spiritual assimilation that is threatened by any large number of non-Jews, but also the threat of revanchist political and military attack.

So basic and important is this concept that as the Jews prepared to cross the Jordan into the Land of Israel, as the waters rose to enormous heights and the Children of Israel rapidly crossed to the other side, as they were in the middle of the now-dry riverbed, suddenly Joshua paused and spoke to them. What was so vital that could not wait until they had crossed safely to the other side? What had to be said now, in the middle of the Jordan, as the waters piled higher and higher?

"While still in the Jordan, Joshua said to them: Know why you are crossing the Jordan! In order that you drive out the inhabitants of the Land from before you as it is written" (Numbers 33:52). "And you shall drive out all the inhabitants of the land from before you." "If you do this—it shall be good. If not —the waters shall come and inundate me and you" (Talmud, Sota 34a).

Nothing was more urgent than this message, for allowing the nations of the Land of Israel to remain there freely was to invite physical and spiritual threats, military or political efforts on the part of bitter, angry revanchist people to regain the land, spiritual and cultural assimilation, and disintegration of the uniqueness of the special society that the Jew was commanded to build.

And as the Torah clearly commanded: "And you shall drive out all the inhabitants of the land from before you. . . . But if you will not drive out the inhabitants of the land from before you, then it shall come to pass that those which you let remain of them, shall be thorns in your eyes and thistles in your sides and shall torment you in the land wherein you dwell. And it shall be that I will do to you as I thought to do to them" (Numbers 33:52–56).

The biblical commentators are explicit: "And you shall drive out the inhabitants and then you shall inherit it, you will be able to exist in it. And if you do not, you will not be able to exist in it" (Rashi—Rabbi Shlomo Yitzchaki).

"When you shall eliminate the inhabitants of the land, then you shall be privileged to inherit the land and pass it down to your children. But if you do not eliminate them, even though you will conquer the land you will not be privileged to hand it down to your children" (Sforno—Rabbi Ovadiah ben Yaakov).

". . . The verse speaks of others aside from the seven Canaanite nations. . . . Not only will they hold that part of the land that you did not possess, but even concerning that part which you did possess and settle in—they will distress you and say: Rise and get out . . . " (Ohr Ha'Chayim—Rabbi Chaim ben Atar).

And so, the Talmud tells us: "Joshua sent three messages to the inhabitants [of Canaan]. He who wishes to evacuate— let him evacuate; who wishes to make peace—let him make peace; to make war—let him make war" (Va-Yikra Rabah 17).

The choices are given. Either leave, or prepare for war—or make peace. The choice of "making peace" is explained by the rabbis as involving three things. To begin with, the non-Jew must agree to adopt the seven basic Noahide laws, which include prohibitions against idolatry, blasphemy, immorality, bloodshed, robbery, eating flesh cut from a living animal, and a positive action—adherence to social laws. Once he has done this, he has the status of a resident stranger *(ger toshav)* who is allowed to live in Eretz Yisrael (Talmud, Avoda Zara 64b), *if he also accepts the conditions of tribute and servitude.* (It should be noted that the use of the word *ger,* ["stranger"] in the Torah refers invariably not to the non-Jewish stranger, but to the convert to Judaism.)

Biblical commentator Rabbi David Kimchi (Radak) explains (Joshua 9:7): "If they uproot idolatry and accept the seven Noahide laws, they must also pay tribute and serve Israel and be subjects under them, as it is written (Deuteronomy 20:11): 'They will be tribute and shall serve you.' "

Maimonides (Hilchot Mlachim 6:11) declares: "If they make peace and accept the seven Noahide laws we do not kill them for they are tributary. If they agreed to pay tribute but do not accept servitude or accepted servitude but not tribute we do not acquiesce until they have accepted both. And servitude means that they shall be humble and low and not raise their head in Israel. Rather they shall be subjects under us and not be appointed to any position over Jews ever."

Far better than foolish humans did the Almighty understand the dangers inherent in allowing a people that believed the land belonged to it to be given free and unfettered residence, let alone ownership, proprietorship, citizenship. What more natural thing than to ask to regain what it believed to be rightly its own land? And this over and above the need to create a *unique* and distinctly separate Torah culture that will shape the Jewish people into a holy nation. That "uniqueness" can be guaranteed only by the non-Jew's having no sovereignty, ownership, or citizenship in the state that could allow him to shape its destiny and character. And so, concerning any non-Jew, Maimonides says: " 'Thou shalt not place over thyself a stranger who is not of your brethren' (Deuteronomy 17:15). Not only a king, but the prohibition is for any authority in Israel. Not an officer in the armed forces . . . not even a public official in charge of the distribution of water to the fields. And there is no need to mention that a judge or chieftain shall only be from the people of Israel. . . . Any authority that you appoint shall only be from the midst of thy people" (Hilchot Mlachim 1:4).

The purpose is clear. The non-Jew has no share in the Land of Israel. He has no ownership, citizenship, or destiny in it. The non-Jew who wishes to live in Israel must accept basic human obligations. Then he may live in Israel as a *resident stranger,* but never as a citizen with any proprietary interest or with any political say, never as one who can hold any public office that will give him dominion over a Jew or a share in the authority of the country. Accepting these conditions, he admits that the land is not his, and therefore he may live in Israel quietly, separately observing his own private life, with all religious, economic, social, and cultural rights. Refusing this, he cannot remain.

This is Torah. This is *Jewishness.* Not the dishonest pseudo-"Judaism" chanted by the liberal secularists who pick and choose what "Judaism" finds favor in their eyes and who reject what their own gentilized concepts find unacceptable. They weigh "Judaism" on the scales of their own intellectual arrogance—an arrogance, incidentally, of intense ignorance.

And if this is not only the right of Jews but their obligation, what do we fear? Why do the Jews tremble and quake before the threat of the nations? Is there no longer a G-d in Israel? Have we so lost our bearings that we do not understand the ordained historical role of the State of Israel, a role that ensures that it can never be destroyed and that no further exile from it is possible? Why is it that we do not comprehend that *it is precisely our refusal to deal with the Arabs according to halakic obligation that will bring down on our heads terrible sufferings, whereas our courage in removing them will be one of the major factors in the hurrying of the final redemption?*

More than 2,500 years ago, a giant of a Philistine named

Goliath strolled out to the ranks of Israel and mocked them: "I have humiliated the armies of Israel this day—give me a man that we may fight together." No one moved. The giant was too powerful, and it was madness, suicide, to confront him. Instead, they sat in shame and fear, as every morning and every evening —for forty days—the Philistine taunted and humiliated them.

And then came young David; untrained in war, a shepherd, come to bring food to his brothers serving in the army. And as he stood there, Goliath emerged. David listened in fury. David waited eagerly—who would leap up to smash the Philistine? David watched in disbelief as no one moved. All feared the power of the Gentile.

David's wrathful words sound across the ages, as an eternal guidepost: "Who is this uncircumcised Philistine that he should humiliate the armies of *the living G-d?*

David, instinctively, understood that the humiliation of Israel was, simultaneously, the humiliation of the *G-d of Israel.* He realized that the brazen readiness to attack and mock the Jews stemmed from a total lack of fear and awe of the G-d of Israel. For the Philistine there was no G-d of Israel; at best he was impotent; in truth He did not exist as a divine power.

This contempt for the G-d of Israel as manifested by the humiliation of the Jews is *Hillul Hashem, the desecration of the name of the L-rd.* Rejection of Jewish rights and power, the contemptuous refusal to recognize Jewish sovereignty, threats against the Jew and his land, all are signs of disregard and contempt for the G-d of the Jews. "The degradation of Israel is the desecration of the name of the L-rd" (Rashi, Ezekiel 39:7).

All this David understood, and he understood, too, that *Hillul Hashem* dare not be countenanced: it must be erased. There is no room for fear, because the entire reason for Jewish being is *Kiddush Hashem, to sanctify the name of the L-rd* and thus persuade the world to follow Him.

And so, young David went out to face the giant Philistine, veteran warrior and professional soldier, "whose height was six cubits and a span . . . a helmet of copper upon his head . . . armed with a coat of mail . . . and the staff of his spear was like a weaver's beam, and his spear's head weighed six hundred shekels of iron. . . ." And David spoke to him before he killed him, saying: "Thou comest to me with a sword and a

spear and a shield; but I come to thee in the name of the L-rd
of Hosts, the G-d of the armies of Israel, whom thou hast humiliated.

"This day will the L-rd deliver thee into my hand, and I
will smite thee and take thy head from thee . . . *that all the earth
may know that there is a G-d in Israel.*"

And David slew him and took his head from him and the
earth—*and the Jews*—knew that there was a G-d in Israel.

What is wrong with us? Who blinded us and blocked from
our memories the existence and power of the G-d of Israel? Did
a Jewish people exist for 2,000 years without state, government,
or army, wandering the earth interminably from land to land,
suffering pogroms and Holocaust and surviving powerful em-
pires that disappeared into history, just by coincidence? Did a
Jewish people return to its land from the far corners of the earth
to set up its own sovereign state—exactly as promised in the
Bible—through mere natural means? What other nation ever
did such a thing? Where are the Philistines of Goliath today?
Where is imperial Rome with its Latin and its gods? Who de-
feats armies in six days, and on the seventh they rest?

Who if not an Israel because there is a G-d in it! The Land
of Israel is His divine Land, the State of Israel is His divine
hand. History is not a series of random events, disjointed and
coincidental. There is a Creator, a Guide, a Hand that plans
and directs. There is a scenario to history. The Jew has come
home for the third and last time. "But the third shall be left
therein" (Zechariah 13:8). "The first redemption was that from
Egypt; the second, the redemption of Ezra. The third will never
end" (Tanhuma, Shoftim 9).

We live in the era of the footsteps of the Messiah, the beginning of the final redemption. The rise of the State of Israel from
the ashes of Auschwitz marks the end of the night of black humiliation and agony, of *Hillul Hashem,* and the beginning of the
dawn of the final, total redemption, of *Kiddush Hashem,* sanc-
tification of G-d's name.

The State of Israel is not just one more Asian nation. It is
G-d's Land, raised high—*at last!*—to put an end to the humiliation of His name. "Therefore say unto the House of
Israel . . . I do this, not for your sake, O House of Israel, but
rather for My holy name which you desecrated through the na-

tions whither you came. And I will sanctify My great name that was desecrated amongst the nations . . . *and the nations shall know that I am the L-rd when I shall be sanctified through you before their eyes.* And I shall take you from among the nations and gather you out of all the countries and I will bring you into your own land" (Ezekiel 36:22–24).

The State of Israel is not a "political" creation. *It is a religious one.* No power could have prevented its birth and none can destroy it. It is the beginning of G-d's wrath, vengeance against the nations who ignored, disdained, and humiliated Him, who found Him irrelevant, who "knew Him not." But it is only the *beginning.* How the *final* redemption will come, and when, depends on the Jew.

"The exiles shall be ingathered only through faith" (Mechilta, Exodus). Faith! If we have it, if we truly believe in the existence of the Creator and Guider of history, the G-d of Israel, we can bring the final redemption *today.* "When will the Messiah come? *Today,* as it is said: 'Today, if you will hearken unto my voice' " (Psalms 95:7, Sanhedrin 98a).

But that faith is not a cheap thing, not mere words and lip service. It must be proved, tested in the fiery furnace of willingness to sacrifice. The readiness of the Jew to sacrifice and endanger himself in order to erase the worst of all sins—the desecration of G-d's name—is the true test.

The Arabs of Israel represent *Hillul Hashem* in its starkest form. Their rejection of Jewish sovereignty over the Land of Israel despite the covenant between the L-rd of Israel and the Jews constitutes a rejection of the sovereignty and kingship of the L-rd G-d of Israel. Their transfer from the Land of Israel thus becomes more than a political issue. *It is a religious issue, a religious obligation, a commandment to erase* Hillul Hashem. Far from fearing what the Gentile will do if we do such a thing, let the Jew tremble as he considers the anger of the Almighty *if we do not.*

Tragedy will be ours *if we do not* move the Arabs out. The great redemption can come immediately and magnificently if we do that which G-d demands. One of the great yardsticks of *real* Jewish faith in this time of momentous decision is our willingness to reject fear of man in favor of awe of G-d and remove the Arabs from Israel.

The world? The nations—united or otherwise? What do

they matter before the omnipotence of the Almighty!

"Why do the nations rage . . . the kings of the earth set themselves and the rulers take counsel together, against the L-rd and against His annointed. . . . He that sitteth in the heavens shall laugh, the L-rd shall mock them . . . " (Psalms 2:1–4). The Jewish people and state *cannot* be destroyed. Their weapon is their G-d. *That is reality.*

David understood "realism" and practicality" and "rationality." His last words before killing Goliath were: "And all this assembly shall know that not with the sword and spear does the L-rd save. *For the battle is the L-rd's and He will give you into our hands.*"

And then David removed Goliath's head from his shoulders and removed humiliation from Israel.

Let us remove the Arabs from Israel and bring the redemption.

THEY MUST GO.

Index

Temple Israel

Minneapolis, Minnesota

IN HONOR OF THE BAT MITZVAH OF
DAPHNE FRUCHTMAN
FROM
DEENA FRUCHTMAN